Born in 1947, Stephen Brook grew up in London. After studying literature and philosophy at Trinity College, Cambridge, he went to live for
seven years in the USA, where he worked for a variety of publishers. On
returning to England in 1976 he spent five years as an academic editor
before becoming a full-time writer. He edited *The Oxford Book of Dreams*
and is the author of *New York Days, New York Nights*, which is available
in Picador. He is now writing books about France and Canada.

Also by Stephen Brook in Picador

New York Days, New York Nights

Stephen Brook

HONKYTONK GELATO
Travels Through Texas

published by Pan Books

First published 1985 by Hamish Hamilton Ltd
This Picador edition published 1986 by Pan Books Ltd
Cavaye Place, London SW10 9PG
9 8 7 6 5 4 3 2 1
© Stephen Brook 1985
ISBN 0 330 29201 3

Printed and bound in Great Britain by
Richard Clay (The Chaucer Press) Ltd, Bungay, Suffolk

Contents

M. Verity

A

Hereford
Dimmitt

Amarillo

Hereford

Lubbock

NEW MEXICO

Midland

El Paso

T

Fort Stockton

0   100 Miles
0   150 Kilometers
——— Highway

Fort Davis

Alpine

Marfa

Langtry

Freer

Kingsville

Presidio

Laredo

Terlingua

Lajitas

Boquillas

Del Rio

Roma

Brac

Rio Grande
City

San Juan

MEXICO

B

Brownsville

OKLAHOMA

ARKANSAS

Wichita Falls

Greenville

Fort Worth

Dallas

Jefferson

Uncertain

Abilene

Longview

Tyler

Comanche

Brownwood

San Angelo

X   A   Waco   S

Calvert

Sonora

Taylor

Beaumont

Johnson City

Austin

Port Arthur

Fredericksburg

Stonewall

Orange

Luckenbach

New Braunfels

La Grange

HOUSTON

Leakey

Rio Frio

Pasadena

Castroville

Gonzales

Uvalde

ville

San Antonio

Galveston

Poteet

Helena

Panna Maria

Freer

See Inset A

See Inset B

To my father
and in memory of
my mother and grandmother

Acknowledgements

When Christopher Middleton casually suggested I write a book about Texas, he had no idea what he was letting himself in for. He and Ann Clark let me use their house as a launching pad, resting place, and warehouse for various times over three months, and their friendship and hospitality were invaluable. My warmest thanks to Alyce Faye Eichelberger, expatriate Texan, who put me in touch with many of the people who appear in this book.

I also wish to thank the following, who either offered me hospitality or went out of their way to help me and inform me: Gertrude Barnstone, Joe Bowden, Ray Brazzel, Robert Bruno, Chip and Rhonda Chenoweth, Hank Coleman, Sherron Cooper, Jonathan and Barbara Day, Dr James (Red) Duke, Don and Debbie Earney, Raymond and Martha Edgar, Gil Felts, Paul Foreman, Adalberto Garcia and Jo Ana Sanchez, Bill Hargis, Jim Humphreys, Don and Carole Jablonowski, Jerry and Susan Knight, Jane Koock, Nicholas Lemann and others on the staff of *Texas Monthly*, Meredith McClain, Sam and Carmen McCracken, Dolores Maxwell, David Murrah, Doug Nelson, Judge Tom Phillips, Regina Rogers, Jim Schutze, Kelly and Anne Shannon, Toni Street, Stephen Thayer, Sandra Washmon, and Walter Widrig. Finally, my thanks to Penelope Hoare and her colleagues at Hamish Hamilton for their support and editorial expertise.

S. B.

Think About It

'*Mamas, don't let your babies grow up to be cowboys* . . .' warned the voices singing in unison from the loudspeakers perched high in the corners, while in the booths below mothers shovelled burgers into the gaping, ketchup-stained mouths of wide-eyed children. As I was practising auto-dentistry in an effort to dislodge wedges of nachos from between my teeth, a waitress in scarlet came up carrying a burrito for me and a steak for Christopher. We ordered another round of margaritas, lime juice and tequila stratospherically cold in frosted glasses rimmed with salt.

'I'm not sure I'm going to like it,' I said.

'Oh, but you will,' Christopher assured me in his very English tones. 'Where we live it's like Provence.'

I looked round at the hunting trophies on the walls, the Confederate and Lone Star flags hanging limply from the rafters by the bar, and the pennants of favourite football teams, the Baylor Bears and the Dallas Cowboys. It was a confusion of emblems: bumper stickers publicising honkytonks in Houston, beer ads for Stroh's and Shiner, and stained posters announcing chili cookoffs of a decade before.

Christopher observed my anxious inspection. 'It's not all like this.' He spoke of the woods around his house and the birds that flew over at different seasons, of all-night parties and local festivals, of vast landscapes under glittering skies, of women as beautiful as the climate. Gradually he scoured away some of my scepticism. We stepped out of the raucous Texas Lone Star Saloon into the raucous London streets.

'Have a good trip back to Austin,' I said, shaking Christopher's hand.

'Think about it,' he urged. 'Next time you get tired of London, come to Texas.'

So I did.

American Bull

The flight to Austin, they announced, would be delayed. Two colour television sets lurching off wall brackets kept a passive bunch of weary passengers quiet, if not happy, as we waited in the departure lounge at Houston for news. Businessmen sat bucketed in plastic, their briefcases and raincoats sloped over adjacent seats while they flicked the pages of *Texas Business*, *Fortune*, and *Money*. Heavily-chinned women, bursting out of their blue jeans, had their noses into books with such titles as *Deafness* and *Shortness of Breath*. The men were making money; the women were reading about the health they so evidently neglected. And I was turning the pages of an especially minor Trollope novel, a small badge of Englishness I was carrying as a cultural St Christopher's medal on entering Texas.

Announcements from Southwest Airline officials kept us informed. Our plane was arriving via Dallas, but a norther had just struck that city. Northers are cold fronts that whoosh south across the great plains and hit the usually warm Texas air. The temperature can topple forty degrees in an hour or two, and if the cold norther hits a spongy humid tangle of warm Gulf air, all kinds of meteorological turbulence can result. It was just such a change in the weather that had grounded our plane in Dallas.

Two pretty flight attendants did their best to keep us cheerful. Eventually there was good news: 'Just thought you folks'd like to know, the weather in Austin is just *beau*tiful. And here's some more good news. We've been notified that the plane has just taken off from Dallas and is now airborne – somewhere or other.' Cheers.

Half an hour later. 'Ladies and gentlemen, this is a final update. We expect to start boarding at 8.55. To pass the time until then we're offering a free ticket on this flight to the first person who correctly guesses our combined ages.' We leapt from our seats and rushed to the counter, flinging numbers into the air.

'Fifty-two!' I yelled.

'Fifty-one!' roared the man next to me.

'Yay!' screamed the darker of the two women. 'Fifty-one is

correct. Or-*right*! Free ticket to Austin for the gentleman over here.'

It was a masterly stroke. Although only one of us had won the refund, our collective morale had been boosted by the sport devised for our distraction. At 8.55 precisely we filed onto the plane. Ten minutes after take-off we flew straight into a thunderstorm, which cuffed the plane all the way to Austin. Yet the landing was smooth and we spontaneously applauded as the plane taxied up the runway. The stewardesses beamed at us, then urged us to repeat our tribute while they opened the cockpit door so the flight crew could hear our appreciation. Once again we clapped our little hands off.

And so, though ground down by the now inescapable delays and frustrations of modern air travel, we all arrived in high spirits. The resolute sunniness of the Southwest team was contagious, and even after twenty-four hours continually on the move, I was all smiles when I emerged from the baggage reclaim to find Christopher, a volume of Trakl under his arm, leaning against a wall. By the time we reached his house in the hills west of Austin it was, by my watch, 6 a.m., which didn't deter Christopher from serving the *poulet aux herbes* and bottle of claret he'd provided for my dinner.

Provençal cooking in central Texas? Perhaps he was breaking me in gently, giving me a last taste of distant Europe. I happily ate it all, and went to bed listening to the rain slapping the fat leaves of the trees that brushed the windows of the secluded house.

*

At breakfast the next morning it was equally difficult to sniff Texas in the air. There was good English tea, baguettes and exotic honeys, and Vivaldi twittered on the radio. After almost twenty years in Texas, Christopher Middleton hadn't lost any of his Englishness, though it had been seasoned not so much by Texan influences as by his immersion in German literature, which he copiously translated and taught at the university.

Standing by his desk, he looked like a thoughtful mariner, with his bulky white sweater, his beard showing more signs of grizzle than his sleek hair, and sweet shaggy smoke from his pipe filling the air. On the desk reposed a typewriter, letters in neat piles, tobacco tins, and the notebooks in which he drafted

3

his poems. Books rose to the ceiling on all sides, books in many languages, and by the window were stacks of avant-garde periodicals containing his work. On the walls hung the witty, ingenious and often erotic collages he'd made a few years ago. There was little dust on the crowded shelves, just thin coatings of ash from two decades of pipe-smoking and the silky trails of spiders that treated much of the house as if it were a favourite spot for a vacation. It was a delightful room, warm and enclosing after dark, and by day soft and shady. It took discipline to remind myself that I had not come to Texas to rediscover Europe, and after more tea I slammed the screen door shut behind me and went into town.

On this first foray into Austin by daylight the state capital didn't present itself as recognisably Texan. The thunderclouds had vanished and the sun leaned on the pink granite of the Capitol dome. Along hilly Guadalupe Street, the main drag of the university campus, lean boys with notebooks under their arms compared schedules with fair-haired girls with fresh complexions and full figures that suggested they were striding out of childhoods fortified by orange juice, steak, and ice cream. Austin has the informality and vitality of any American university town. Bookshops, small cafés, boutiques, street stalls – it was little different from Berkeley or Ann Arbor. Ample parking bays were scarcely filled by the Toyotas and Volkswagens that had nosed into them. The intelligentsia here, as elsewhere in America, rejects the prevailing notion that big is beautiful – a rejection that flies in the face of the most celebrated of all Texan articles of faith.

'We seem to be a long way from the Gloucester Road,' I remarked to Christopher as we drove past the campus. 'Is this what people mean when they keep talking about the diversity of Texas?'

He frowned and paused for thought. 'It's not actually diversity. The truth is there's no such place as "Texas". People do talk about its immense diversity – it's an easy formula but I think it's wrong, because Texas is too amorphous.' He added more cryptically, 'In fact it's too amorphous even to be considered barbaric.'

I had decided not to linger in Austin, seductive though it was to sip chilled wine on the patios of small restaurants and browse in good bookshops. I spent a day or two accumulating supplies, rented a car, and filled the back seat with wine and fruit, a sleeping bag and tape recorder. I scattered maps and brochures over the front passenger seat, stacked my luggage in the rear, and then set off towards Dallas.

*

To avoid crossing downtown Austin I drove north on a new highway loop that slices through the limestone hills. Austin is now the fastest growing city in Texas, to the alarm of its settled residents who now fear that the qualities that make it so attractive will be whittled away. I drove past new 'townhouse' developments and condominiums curled around the slopes of the land like copulating insects; shrubs and meandering driveways made a stab at blending with the surrounding vegetation and the irregularity of the landscape. The American desire not to be where you are was reflected in the developments' names. Aspen Heights was typical. The curves of the highway revealed less harmonious structures, black glass boxes, finished but often unoccupied. Banners reading NOW LEASING were draped across them, and roadside signs identified the buildings as a BUSINESS PARK or CORPORATE OFFICE ENVIRONMENT.

Along Route 183, another loop that thrusts six lanes through North Austin, lies typical strip development, a band of shopping plazas, gas stations, discount cities, banks and savings associations, car-wash huts squatting on an acre of concrete, dentists' offices, Jack-in-the-Boxes and Arby's Roast Beef fast food restaurants. Single-storey shops and offices rub mansarded shoulders round three sides of the Grand Central Station plaza. The name is an absurdity, unrelated to anything on the landscape or in the history. Naming is unimportant; location and services provided, that's all that matters. There is nothing about these miles of interchangeable commercial developments that's peculiar to Austin or even to Texas. We're in Anywhere, USA.

Reaching the main interstate highway, I headed north, passing the Truxtop, its name an act of verbal economy unmatched by the lunar wastes of the parking lot around it. Gradually the pulverized landscape reasserted itself and grassy fields and occasional trees crept up to the edges of the road. I left the interstate on Route 79, which led through country that was dull and broad, with trees that shielded old frame farmhouses and newer bungalows. The excellent road, typical of rural Texas, was luxuriously laid out: only one lane in either direction, but each with a shoulder lane as wide as the road itself, and beyond the shoulder an ample grassy verge. I passed a nursery school. Behind a wire fence miniature people in dungarees chased each other with whoops and yells around a playground. A prettily lettered sign identified the nursery as the Early Lifehood Center, evidence that I was still within the orbit of a university town, with its booming sales of earth shoes, Jane Fonda exercise books, imported cheeses, and rare varieties of bean. These tots would doubtless be instructed in creative Lego, in respecting the rights of minorities, class action suits, getting in touch with their feelings, pollution control, and assertiveness training. Then they'd turn out much like the rest of us.

*

This part of central Texas was settled in the nineteenth century by Bohemians and Moravians and other mid-Europeans. In Taylor and the towns beyond it the Czech influence remains strong, and until recently a weekly newspaper kept the language and culture warm. Yet these ample fields are oddly characterless; the undemonstrative countryside and neat little towns are stolidly self-effacing. The names clomp heavily across mailboxes and shopfronts: Belicek, Kropp, Mikeska, Roznovak. Towards Rockdale the landscape became more undulating, and softened by grassy meadows and lovely trees. I was repeatedly passed by pickups adorned with bumper stickers, which combine the American love of slogans with a means of boosting a special interest. Bumper stickers invariably reflect the local culture. In New England it would be perfectly acceptable to plaster I BRAKE FOR ANIMALS AND SMALL CHILDREN on the back of your Volvo, just to tell the world what a nice caring person you are, but no right-thinking Texan would ever slap that particular sticker onto his fender. Texan bumper stickers enunciate Texan thoughts: HAPPINESS IS A WARM GUN.

The hot news in Rockdale was the forthcoming football game against Cameron High School. Empty shops had been daubed with mottoes urging on the local team. Signs outside the bank and the realtor's office spelt out in large plastic letters: GO TIGERS BEAT CAMERON. In Cameron the same issue was gripping

6

the populace, where GO BATS – or newts and mantises – BEAT
ROCKDALE was the prevailing view. Cameron was decent,
orderly, unpretentious, and deadly dull. Its commercial centre
consisted of the crossing of two modest highways. The streets,
as in countless other small Texan dorps, were lined with plain
brick buildings, some of which were topped by prettily decorated cornices or false fronts that gave the town a low-keyed
municipal dignity. The local nightspot, Saturday's, announced
as forthcoming attractions a Hollywood dance contest and a
pool tournament. I'd intended to lunch in Cameron but when
the establishment of my choice identified itself as a Restuarant,
the misspelling seemed a bad omen. If the food was as uncertain
as the spelling, I was in for an uncomfortable half hour. So I
drove on.

Beyond the Brazos River the countryside flattened out again.
Near Hearne a heron contemplated its reflection in a pond. I
entered a land of large grim farms. Without reducing speed, I
pulled over onto the shoulder to let a pickup race by. I'd swiftly
acquired this Texan polish to my highway manners, pulling over
to the right to allow faster vehicles to overtake. The pickup now
speeding ahead of me carried the heartfelt sticker CRIME
DOESN'T PAY . . . NEITHER DOES FARMING.

Stepping up the search for lunch, I spotted a place called
Diana's Café, besieged on all sides by dozens of pickups and
livestock trailers and battered station wagons. Deducing that
Diana was popular with the local farmers, I parked in the cool
shadow of some monstrous vehicle with tyres four feet high, and
entered. Behind the counter scurried a Mexican family,
assisted by a tall shapely black girl with an expressionless face.
At small tables sat groups of men in Stetsons; they looked more
like card players than diners. I seated myself at the counter.
The food on offer looked plentiful but not appetizing: boiled
beef in a heavy slick of gravy, mashed potatoes, exhausted
cabbage, predigested beans. Soft rolls, better used to stanch
shaving cuts than as food, lolled in plastic baskets next to
foil-covered tubs of 'whipped margarine'.

I glanced at the man next to me, praying he made no sudden
movement that might bring the rim of his hat into slashing
contact with my face. His belly rested on his lap like a sleeping
cat and he wielded his fork in his fist. Chewing beef, rather than
conversation, was preoccupying him, so while I consumed

some TexMex sludge I admired the decor. The dining area was plainly furnished, but behind the counter Diana and her kinfolk had luridly filled every inch of space with family portraits, photos of overweight children, Smurfs, and cheap coloured figurines made of plastic.

By the time I paid my bill, most of the customers had vanished, not through the front door but through swing doors that led to the back of the building. Pool hall? Strip joint? Barmitzvah party? I followed. To my surprise, for I was new in Texas, I found myself in the arena of a livestock auction. It was a regular Friday lunchtime event, beginning after the boiled beef and continuing, when there were a thousand lots as there were today, into the evening. In the front of the arena was a cattle pen with gates on either side, and above it the auctioneer's box. Bidders sat on the five rows of chairs that embraced the pen semicircularly, or in the bleachers behind the chairs. The auction had not yet begun, and bidders were slipping through to the stockyards behind the building where they could inspect potential additions to their herds.

It was a hot day and I was wearing a T-shirt, jeans, and sandals, unlike the bidders, who wore, almost to a man, loud-checked Western-style shirts, blue jeans, and boots. Few heads were bare, being covered either by Stetsons, summery straw hats, or gimme caps, those baseball hats of cheap plastic construction, with a large protruding eyeshade and a space over the forehead large enough to carry an advertising motto for Blue Seal Feeds or Sweetwater Tool & Dye. A reluctance to appear conspicuous, and a rapidly acquired practicality, soon forced changes in my wardrobe, and first to go were the sandals, which although cooling in warm weather, also offered no protection against snakes, ticks, midges, and chiggers.

The Calvert livestock auction was not the place, at least not that afternoon, to see Texas beef at its best. Cattle prices were depressed and many farmers and ranchers, unwilling to keep feeding their herds, were sending livestock to auction earlier than usual. Scrawny heifers were only fetching around thirty cents a pound, and I was tempted to buy one myself – a loping little Hereford with large eyes and no meat – and send it as a pet to Christopher.

The auctioneer carpeted the arena with the buckshot of his patter, pausing for breath only while a sold animal was being prodded out of the pen with poles and being replaced by the next. 'Dibbledidibble-dibble-di, wunnawunnawunna, *hey* twenny-two, dibble-di-dibble-di, hubblehubblehubble, *hey*, dibbledi-dibbledi, hey twenny-three *high*, all done now, are ya all done now, dibbledibbledibble, hey, cow number *six*!' Lot number and price were flashed onto a closed circuit TV screen at his elbow.

I wandered out to the back to look at the stockyards, noisy and malodorous on a busy day like this, and discovered another argument against wearing sandals in rural Texas. Making my way back to the car, I spotted a graceful bumper sticker that read EAT AMERICAN BEEF NOT FOREIGN BULL. I bumped my way over the rutted parking lot back onto the road, and passed one of the yellow triangular road signs to be found all over the state, occasionally colandered by bullet holes, DRIVE FRIENDLY.

No Smooching

It's hard to know why Dallas exists. Built on featureless prairie, it hugs a river, the Trinity, that's scarcely visible as it flows under highway interchanges and between warehouses. Its principal function is not navigational but to divide the city socially. Immediately south of the Trinity are slums indistinguishable from the shantytowns of other Southern cities, while to the north lies the booming downtown area, cheek by jowl with older parts of the city that have fallen into decay despite the commercial prosperity just a few blocks away. When people speak in hushed tones of Dallas, and conjure up images of country clubs, French restaurants, and spacious mansions set on shaven lawns, they're referring to North Dallas, a vast expanse of suburbia that sweeps twenty miles and more north from the centre. Dallas flourishes, as its proud residents will insist on telling you, not because, like Houston, it's a major port or industrial centre, but because of the resourcefulness and acumen of its citizenry.

The initial impression as one drives north into the city is of boastful commercial vitality but also of architectural confusion. Pride, and Dallas's rivalry with Houston, are changing this, and an aesthetic sense, which is alien to the soundest Dallas instincts, is slowly seeping through; chances are that some of its newer structures may even have some merit. Lost downtown, I asked a policeman to orient me. He said I'd find places to stay just off the North Central Expressway, so off I went, and promptly experienced Dallas's contribution to natural selection: rush hour on the Expressway.

It's one of only two highways linking downtown with some of the lushest suburbia in the Southwest. A relatively old highway, built before Dallas expanded endlessly northwards, the Expressway has only two lanes in each direction. I later met elderly Dallasites who attributed their longevity to their refusal to drive on it. Getting on the highway is the problem: the on-ramps are so short they can only accommodate three cars; it isn't possible to speed down them and merge imperceptibly with the main flow. Approaching the Expressway you must come to a complete halt, wait for a gap in the traffic, and then hurl forward and pray that you can accelerate quickly enough to prevent the car behind you from slamming into your rear. During the rush hour the wait can be a long one, and cars on the ramp behind you will rev their engines impatiently while you swiftly calculate whether the fifty-yard gap between cars on the inside lane is sufficient to permit a non-suicidal entry. And once you're on the Expressway you must maintain a good speed – peer pressure takes care of that – wondering every half mile at which a ramp appears whether the stationary vehicle poised upon it is about to make a kamikaze dash into your lane.

I lived. My car was untouched. I found a motel. I checked in.

*

I'd been warned to expect a warm welcome when I 'phoned Carmen and Sam in Dallas, even though I was no more than an acquaintance of an old friend of theirs. I wasn't disappointed. Carmen began by apologising that their guest suite was occupied, but when I returned to Dallas for a later visit I must be sure to stay with them. (I did.) They couldn't ask me to dinner this evening as they had to act as chaperones at the Homecoming Dance of the Episcopalian School which their daughters attended. Perhaps I'd like to join them there? Well, why not? It would be a change to play the watchdog rather than the wolf. I drove into deepest North Dallas and made my way to the lavish school. The main hall was darkened and beribboned for the occasion. On the far side strutted a band, very loud and very bad. Boys and girls were divided evenly with about twenty yards of shyness between them. There was no dancing. Sam and Carmen had somehow spotted the Englishman and were advancing in my direction.

'Well hi!' said Carmen in her throaty and very Texan tones. 'Welcome! This is Sam.'

I stared up at a large man whose face expressed a bafflement in sharp contrast to the eager smiles of his wife. Perhaps he was trying to remember who I was, what I was doing there, what *he* was doing there. I extended a hand.

'And this is our daughter Mary Elizabeth.' I turned to greet a ripe girl with dark eyes, her satiny complexion set off by a puffy-sleeved low-cut evening dress. Carmen was beautiful too, in a way I came to recognise as peculiar to Dallas. She had height, an elegant figure, shapely bones; these gifts had been strengthened by the artifice of unguents, varnishes, lacquers, shadows and highlights; and by beautiful clothes, including a scarlet jacket with sleeves that billowed over her shoulders as if her arms were snakes that had eaten a rabbit or two; and by as much jewellery as a woman can wear without toppling over. Gold earrings protruded from the waves of perfectly coiffed blondish hair, enough thin gold bracelets for a game of quoits jangled on her wrists, four heavy rings coiled round her fingers, and two rows of pearls lapped her neck. She looked good. No, she looked better than good. The word, grown rusty in a world of denim, is glamorous. Pretty is too slight, lovely too soft, beautiful only tells part of the story. She was glamorous, just like thousands of other young and not so young Dallas matrons, asserting their status, their wealth, and above all their confidence in the social order they decorate. Large-eyed Mary Elizabeth, pushing sixteen, was already climbing her way onto the ledge of glamour, though I later caught her slipping back whenever she wore her bunny rabbit slippers.

'It's too noisy here,' yelled Carmen, and clutching my arm she steered me into the headmaster's office. 'We can talk better in here.' We exchanged biographical notes. Sam joined us, but was too deeply preoccupied with his role as watchdog to linger and soon left to patrol the pathways.

'Sam's mad this evening,' explained Carmen. 'Mary Elizabeth came downstairs in that lovely new dress and Sam thought it was too low-cut. We call him Archie Bunker at home.' Sam's troubles weren't over. When he returned he told Carmen with throttled anxiety that no one was guarding the doors out into the grounds. Kids might be sneaking out to commit smoking or touching. With a fine sense of duty Sam returned to the hall to maintain his solitary vigil by the doors.

Carmen was keen for me to appreciate that Texas consisted of more than cattle and oil wells. 'People hear our accent, our slow way of talking, and they think we're hicks or something. They don't realise we're pretty sophisticated. You know, I wish you'd been in town a couple of days ago. I do fund-raising for the public TV station in Dallas, and we gave a party for Julia Child when she was here last week. Too bad you weren't around. You'd have found it interesting.'

Various teachers and parents trooped in and out of the headmaster's office. Not one escaped without an introduction.

'This is our new friend from England. I thought he should see what a Homecoming Dance is like as he's doing a story about Texas.'

'Truly that will add to it,' commented one matron, with some asperity but with diction so archaic that I warmed to her at once.

On the headmaster's desk I saw a folder entitled Master Plan. Naturally I opened it and began to read. It was divided into three sections: Concept, Need, Master Plan. I closed it again, unsurprised. Middle Management is, I was reminded, the principal dialect of Middle America. Despite the Master Plan, his pupils didn't know how to dance. I returned to the hall, where a few brave teenagers confirmed Sam's worst terrors by locking into close smooches on the dance floor. No place for me here, so I took my leave, abandoning Sam and Carmen, who as chaperones had to stick it out to the bitter end, guarding maidenheads and sniffing for liquorous aromas on minty breaths.

Back at the motel I climbed into bed and struggled through another dreary chapter of *John Caldigate*. I'd learned to co-exist, albeit reluctantly, with frisky northern cockroaches, but I'll never be able to welcome to the peaceable kingdom the giant Southern cockroach, the Mexican cucaracha, or the huge black water bug. Out of the corner of my eye I discerned motion. Something the size of a baby's shoe was crossing the floor. I leapt from my bed and pounded the beast with an adult's shoe, then punted the carcass into a far corner. Back to bed. Lights out. Realised the fan was still on, switched on light, and spotted disconsolate mate of liquidated roach trotting mournfully across carpet. The shoe missed this time, and the beast, all two inches of it, scuttled away. Roaches and bugs, I knew, shun the light (not that these two had batted an antenna when I dazzled them with wattage), so I turned on all the lights, switched on the air conditioner, and under these promising conditions slipped into a fretful sleep.

*

'Ours is the colonial with a circular driveway,' Carmen had said as she invited me to lunch. I found an imposing but not overwhelming little mansion in a section of North Dallas just beyond the ultra-fashionable Park Cities. When Sam opened the door I pressed into his hands a small gift: two tins of good English tea. Acting as if I'd handed him a grenade, he muttered something about giving it to Carmen to deal with. She courageously unwrapped the gift, which she inspected from all sides.

'It's tea,' I explained, recalling that to Americans tea is a powder that grows inside a small white pouch. Carmen had had a change of rings as well as clothes since the previous night. She was wearing a dark brown cotton dress tightly belted at the waist, 'fifties-style, and a black silk choker above the collar. She'd had no time to cook, she apologised unnecessarily, and said we were going instead to Sam's country club. We set off in the Mercedes. Sam was wearing a shirt on which the club badge was embroidered.

'Tell us about the article you're writing.'

'It's a book actually.'

Carmen stared at me with renewed interest, her arm across the front seat, her chin on her arm. 'A book! Did you hear that, Sam? Sam hasn't read a book in two years. Isn't that right, Sam? That book I gave you about Churchill – he's interested in Churchill – the Christmas before last – you haven't read it yet, have you?'

Grunt.

'If you're writing a book you'll want to know all about this part of Dallas.' Minutes later I knew how much their house cost, how much the one across the road cost, how much more expensive the houses were a few blocks south in the Park Cities. I also learnt how much it cost them to send their daughters to private school. Driving east, we passed a new development of townhouses called Glen Lakes. Formerly a country club, the land became so valuable that it was bought by eager developers. Ringed by a high fence, Glen Lakes is entered through two guarded gates. Many suburban dwellers prefer to live in planned communities rather than individual houses, and this one was equipped with a pool and jacuzzi, and circling the estate was a jogging track made safe after dark by regularly spaced lamps. Glen Lakes resembled a luxurious prison farm.

The country club looked fine to me – large comfortable clubhouse, with large comfortable rooms, a choice of dining areas, and oak-studded golf course – but Carmen was apologetic. There were, she told me, three other country clubs in

Dallas that were more fashionable, but Sam had joined this one because it had the best course and because the waiting list didn't stretch into the next century.

After lunch Carmen thought I'd like a tour of Southern Methodist University, her *alma mater*. Not a single structure was left unidentified. It's a pleasant campus, with lawns and drives separating the faintly neo-Georgian buildings. 'Around here – drive more slowly, Sam, how can I show Stephen – around here we have more sorority houses – this one's Delta Delta Delta – and over here, that one near the trees – why they don't pick up the trash in the yard I'll never understand it – and here on the left . . .' She told Sam to stop outside her former sorority house, and startled girls in curlers, T-shirts and striped jeans stood back as Carmen swept through with me in her wake. There was an awful smell in the place, caused by the sisters' latest investment: a commercial popcorn popper. 'Y'know in the late 'sixties, early 'seventies, kids didn't want to join fraternity houses and sororities. You remember all that, everybody wanting to do things independently. All that individualism. But now,' she said with satisfaction, 'there's been a return to sorority values. Mary Elizabeth, she thought of applying to Stanford until she heard they didn't have sororities there, so she changed her mind.'

Sam was getting edgy. The Cowboys game began at three, and he'd had the tour before. 'Sometimes,' Carmen told me, 'Sam has tickets for the game, and it's a real shame he doesn't have any for this one. He'd have loved to take you.' He would? 'When I was dating him he had a season ticket to all the Cowboys games, but he had to give it up when we got married – he couldn't afford both.'

Seated side by side in deep armchairs, Sam and I watched the game on TV. After an hour Sam, exhausted after having had to define at my request such essential terms as rushes, incompleted passes, and third down, fell asleep.

*

In the Automobile Hall, dozens of new models stood gleaming on their stands, their doors wide open as though, at the same instant, a hundred drivers had leapt from their cars and fled. Inquisitive men peered in to inspect dashboards, digital instruments, ashtrays, price stickers. Ford was running a competition that day: fill out a card for the draw that afternoon and you could win a special gift. I filled out the card, then asked a pert Fordette what the gift was.

'A wristwatch,' she said, showing me a nasty black plastic object on her arm, 'just like this.'

'Are you serious?'

She nodded, then added sympathetically as I tore up the card, 'I know.'

I was passing a day at the Texas State Fair, held each October in Dallas's Fair Park. Sam had particularly recommended the vast Automobile Hall, but there was more to admire elswhere, for the Fair is the showcase of Texas, at which its arts and crafts and crops and beasts are proudly displayed. The Park buildings, rows of white limestone halls divided by pools and statuary, will appeal to anyone with a taste for Art Deco at its most bombastic. The grandest of the structures is the Hall of State, built, as was most of the rest of the park, to celebrate the Texas Centennial in 1936. A hundred years earlier Texas had fought free of Mexico and become a Republic, a less brazen act than it sounds, since independent Texas was always intended as a temporary condition between its domination by Mexico and its eventual incorporation into the United States. Yet Texans remain proud of those years when the Lone Star flag alone flew over the State, and the Hall of State memorialises Texan heroes and contains murals that depict great moments in the history of the Republic. Very grand and very cold.

These lifeless Art Deco structures formed a ponderous backdrop to the activities on the paths that wound between them. Stalls and counters offered a full range of fast food, including the local speciality, the corny dog, which is as disgusting as it sounds. You can hire strollers for flagging infants, and while your family is queuing for the Portakabin, you can have your silhouette drawn by a winsome artist. After wading through piles of discarded corn husks and candied apple cores, you reach the Midway, a fairground enlivened by the piquant screams of small children trying not to throw up as they hurtle through the air on terrifying wheels and wagons. (Two days later a wagon whirled loose and free, and a youth had taken his final ride.) T-shirted teenage girls with their home towns – DENISON, TEXAS – stencilled over their shy breasts strolled excitedly about, affecting embarrassment whenever swaggering boys whistled at them.

In the Women's Hall I marvelled at the advances our age has made for the benefit of the fair sex: fibreglass garden furniture, Snoopy telephones, and kitchen cabinet resurfacing systems. In the Tower Hall I participated in the Pepsi Challenge, an invitation to blind-taste Pepsi and Coke and vote for the more palatable. To get the taste out of my mouth, I crossed the hall and downed an Owen's Sausage 'N Biscuit, and to get that taste out of my mouth I gulped coffee at a dime a cup, the sole bargain of the fair.

The Embarcadero was full of delights. Under the sign WE BRONZE MEMORIES a stallkeeper demonstrated how, for a modest sum, you could preserve forever your most precious souvenirs by bronzing items dear to your heart, such as baby shoes, dog collars, pipes, and hats. If bronze didn't match your domestic decor, an alternative service was available: Porcelainize your treasured artefacts! Elsewhere you could buy photomugs and photoplates, personalised sunglasses, and for the kids, Mike Stone's Amazing Dip-er-do Stunt Plane, and for the mantelpiece, ornaments, such as owls and frogs, made out of shells. The John Birch Society distributed bumf from a stand and nearby a badge manufactory had available in six colours a button reading RUSSIA SUCKS.

Native produce was celebrated in the Food Hall: nuts, shrimps, Hell-on-the-Red Picante Sauce, Blue Bell ice cream, wine. The Creative Arts Hall showed what Texans could do with their hands. There were quilts and dolls, pieces of embroidery, handmade baby clothes, and photographs of old men and old cows leaning against fences. Trestle tables creaked under the weight of delectable pecan pies, each to a different recipe. I was engaged in close inspection of the hundred or so rich brown confections, until a white-smocked lady tapped me on the shoulder and asked if I were a judge for the imminent pecan pie cookoff.

'As good as any,' I replied, and she firmly steered me away from the roped-off stand.

This is all for the tourists. The serious business takes place in evil-smelling halls in a far corner of the park. Animals. There were hundreds of rabbits, so floppy and furry that they no longer resembled bunnies at all, and a variety of rodents and chicks and goats and sheep. Miniature horses, so small I could step over them without brushing their heads, snuffled hay in miniature pens. A large livestock pavilion housed immense steers – Brahmans and Beefmasters and Charolais – bred to a bulk that immobilized them into an apotheosis of beef.

A succession of activities are devised for the entertainment of those wearied by exhibits. Football at the Cotton Bowl stadium, fireworks, the Junior Broiler show, a free circus, fashion shows, country music on tap, the Coors Laser show, and rodeo most evenings. On the small plaza in front of the Hall of State I was privileged to see the North Texas Square Dancers, who had been specially released from the geriatric ward for the occasion. Little octogenarian women, their wrinkled sinewy legs emerging from short flared skirts, linked arms with equally elderly gentlemen in red shirts.

On came the taped music, a screeching of violins and accordions, and the dancers hopped to it while a voice boomed steadily over the loudspeaker system: 'Waltz away, twinkle, twinkle, deep centre, two point turning waltzes, now whirl by threes, manoeuvre, manoeuvre, balance left and right, twinkle, twinkle, close to butterfly, left turning box.' Eventually some-one led this lunatic away and the dancers staggered off for their mollusc-juice injections and heart massage. Some must have died during the recuperation period, for when the dancers returned they were a few reelers short and volunteers from the crowd stepped forward to take their places. By the end of the day not a single member of the original troupe was still alive. So noble was the manner of their passing that we all felt a deep reverence for this Texan approach to euthanasia, so spirited, so colourful, so complete. Twinkle, twinkle.

Queen Jane

I had pressing business in Tyler. Dallas would have to keep. Negotiating the highway interchanges over downtown Dallas was no easier than tracing a little blue wire through micro-circuitry, but somehow I made it onto Interstate 30, which led me through the uninviting suburbs of Mesquite and Garland, past countless condominium developments so new the turf had not yet been laid. In a landscape without feature or personality – other than a fingery lake near Rockwall – developers have had to root around for names that will lend either romance or cachet to properties that possess neither. The highway passed between Lake Bluff Condominiums, Faulkner Creek, Spyglass Hill, and the brazen Chateau Magnifique. New homeowners, driven to despair by hidden costs and fittings that don't fit, can take their troubled spirits to the Church on the Rock at the Ridge Road intersection. To help you find it, a huge billboard shortly before the exit proclaims: PASTOR LARRY LEA PRESENTS . . . JESUS. It's a great show, should run and run.

Continuing east on Route 66, I came to the grim thorp of Fate (pop. 286). After a simple twist the road took me past the Independent Baptist Church, which bore the following motto on its plain white features: FUNDAMENTAL MISSIONARY PREMILENNIAL. I'm unable to untangle all the theological distinctions between the many varieties of Southern Baptism, but I recognised this as hardcore stuff. The Baptists, unlike the Catholics or Episcopalians, have no hierarchical structure. It has always been perfectly acceptable for new communities to establish their own churches under the umbrella of Baptism, and to administer them according to the wishes of the local community. Consequently, sectarianism is rife. Almost all would subscribe to the tenets that could be identified as fundamentalist, puritanical, and socially as well as religiously conservative, but all over Texas and the Deep South individual churches will assert their independence just as the little church in Fate did.

Greenville was the first town of any size that I came to. Although hardly a spot to attract tourists, it was, to my eyes, accustomed to the orderliness and economy of the English countryside, faintly shocking to see how profligate Texans are with their land. On the edges of Greenville, which trickled out into the fields for miles, were depots, warehouses, funeral homes, factories, all flung onto immense lots, all constructed without the slightest concern for their aesthetic interrelation. If you own the land, you can build on it. What you build, how you build – that's your own business. The great resource of Texas, long before oil was discovered, has been land. Any settler in the first half of the nineteenth century could claim hundreds of acres if he and his family were prepared to work the land. Because Texans can afford to spread themselves, they have usually built horizontally; there's been no reason to conserve space by building up into the sky. So commercial buildings seep and slink out from the edges of the towns, gathering services as they go. A new factory attracts garages and a Dairy Queen, perhaps a bar or two and some workshops, and after a few years a Royal Oak Bluffs housing estate. These little towns spread themselves with as much decorum as a broken egg.

North of Cumby the landscape took on a fluffier, less austere aspect. I passed through a shabby farming village misnamed Peerless, and a twin a few miles further on by the name of Birthright, illustrating the sad principle that the more spectacular the name the harder it is to live up to it. At Mount Vernon I turned south and encountered for the first time some of the great pine woods of East Texas. Outsiders conceive of Texan landscape as expanses of ranchland punctuated by cows, windmills, and oil derricks, but to the east lies an immense band, about a hundred miles wide, of forests that stretch from the Louisiana border until they fade into the farmlands of Central Texas. And from north to south the woods extend for about two hundred miles to the very edges of Houston and Beaumont. The forest is patchy, often broken by farms and lakes, but the dominant vegetation is tall pine wood, beautiful and forbidding. By late afternoon I was nearing Tyler and checked into a motel on the outskirts of town.

Downtown Tyler is typical of small Texan towns founded in the last century. Like LaGrange and countless other settlements in East and Central Texas, its commercial centre is ranged around a plaza which is likely to contain a war memorial, some benches, trees, and a historical marker giving information about the community. If the town is a county seat, there'll be an oversized courthouse along one side of the square, flanked by a bank or two, drugstores, an insurance office, and a few deserted shops displaying clothes last fashionable in 1955. Most of the population and industry and shops will have moved out of the centre, leaving the downtown area mildly depressed and shabby. Tyler, a town of 70,000 inhabitants that calls itself the Rose Capital of America, was no exception. Route 69 runs from north to south through the town, and most of the commercial activity – garages, restaurants, banks, shopping malls, motels – lines the highway for ten relentlessly ugly miles.

The next day I made my way through comfortable suburbs to the 22-acre Tyler Rose Garden, a showcase for 500 varieties. They take roses seriously in Tyler, as well they should, since the area grows half the commercial crop in the United States. Each year the Tyler Rose Festival, a few days of local pageantry, culminates in the coronation of the Rose Queen, one of the most lavish of the two thousand beauty pageants that take place each year in Texas. It's good for tourism, good for business, and it gives the debutantes something to do. The Festival is run by a local association, whose president selects the Queen for that year. This is not a beauty contest – just as well. This year's president, Jim Deakins, a lean banker with a handsome weathered face, had selected a girl called Jane Hartley, who came, I was told, from 'a prominent local family'. They always do.

Arriving early for the formal opening of the Festival, I inadvertently drove into the wrong entrance to the gardens. A tall youth flagged me down: 'We're gonna need have you reroute and drive around the other way,' he said in that fractured Southern American English that flourishes in a verbal no man's land between error and dialect. I had time for a stroll past the 38,000 rose bushes within the walls of the Garden. Large bunches of roses were for sale, still dewy and wet, their glorious colour and aroma somehow surviving their displacement into cheap aluminium vases. Sipping coffee, I sat out on a small terrace and teased the Tyler Rose Cat, a stubby-tailed tortoiseshell. Cats look out of place in Texas – it's dog country – but here in genteel Tyler it wasn't too much out of keeping.

As the great moment of the ribbon-cutting approached, I rejoined the hundred or more people gathering in front of the

Garden Center building. It was very much a local occasion; everyone knew everyone else. The crowd was entirely white and there wasn't a Stetson or a Western shirt in sight. This could have been Alabama or Arkansas. When integration came to the South in the late 1960s and 1970s, it was somehow forgotten that East Texas was, culturally and politically, scarcely distinguishable from its neighbours to the east.

Before the Civil War, East Texas, like Mississippi and Louisiana, had been plantation country. Theirs was a slave-owning culture, rooted in a practice hardly known, let alone encouraged, further west on the frontier beyond Fort Worth and San Antonio, where the land was more harsh, the climate more parched, the Indian presence more hostile. The expanses of the west were better suited to ranching than to farming, and the cotton plantations, and their patrician ways, never spread west from the eastern parts of the state. The rugged individualism of the frontier had little in common with the Augustan gentility of the Deep South, and this aspect of Texas, still noticeable in towns such as Tyler, has been overwhelmed; the image of the state is the Stetson more than the parasol. Happily ignored by the rest of the nation, East Texas was slower to change its ways after the passage of civil rights legislation than many far more notorious parts of the South. Driving through the Piney Woods I would see villages where blacks still lived in paintless shacks on the far side of the tracks, remote from the modest but spruce white sections of town. It looked no different from the backward, overtly racist counties of Mississippi I'd visited twenty years before.

While much of West Texas was still only precariously inhabited by intrepid frontiersmen and women who battled against the aridity of the climate and the ferocity of the Comanches, the east was already well settled. When people in Tyler spoke of 'old families' they could do so legitimately within the context of American history, whereas the oldest family in Lubbock, Texas, a town twice Tyler's size, couldn't have arrived before 1890. Tyler, then, was rooted in a culture that could just about get away with boasting of its 'society' and 'debutantes'.

Two men came threading by with boxes full of buttonholes. We helped ourselves and soon resembled the crowd at a wedding. Two infant train-bearers arrived with their mamas –

again, as at a wedding – to a chorus of 'Ain't they purty!' and 'They're so darlin'!' Someone called for hush and an official began a long speech in which he thanked every single person who'd contributed to the Festival.

'And now,' said the official, 'I'm gonna call on His Honour the Mayor to say a few words –'

'He ain't here, Bill!'

'Is that so?' The official looked around, and a spasm of annoyance brushed over his face. 'He makes baby christenings. I can't believe he didn't make it here.' The local state senator and representative were also absent, and the official lightly rebuked them for their lèse majesté. Then he spoke about Jane, and told us 'Her Most Gracious Majesty Queen Jane Hartley' was studying business at 'the greatest university in the southern hemisphere' – Southern Methodist, of course. Jane, a puffy-cheeked girl, the folds of her chin billowing more than is desirable among youthful royalty, stood alongside, smiling steadfastly, sealed into her white suit. Opposite her stood her mother, Billie, unreticent in scarlet, and a forbidding anticipation of how Jane would look twenty years hence in the full summer of matronhood. Next to Jane stood a wimp called Alton, who had red lips, a weak face, and an air of unsullied dimness.

Jane stepped forward and snipped the rose-chain ribbon and declared the Festival open. Was it ineptitude or risqué wit that led to the choice of 'Secondhand Rose' as the music that poured through loudspeakers as the ribbon fell? In any event, we all trudged indoors to look at the Rose Show, an exhibit of lavish costumes worn by queens long deposed, against a background of rose-covered trellises; in other rooms were well-arranged displays of intensely beautiful prize blooms.

I returned to my car. The cops on duty were bored. There wasn't much public disorder to attend to at the discreet ceremony. So they were amusing themselves by constructing a slalom from orange cones and were trying to steer their motorbikes between them without knocking them over. This is part of an excellent scheme sponsored by the town to keep motorcycle cops off the street.

Jane's big moment was still to come. After the Ladies' Luncheon and the Queen's Tea she would prepare for her coronation that evening in a downtown auditorium; and two days later she would star in the Rose Parade as its fifteen floats rumbled slowly through the streets. The actual coronation was preceded by a long show honouring the festival and its fifty-year history. No expense had been spared. After the band had swung its way through an overture, a voice boomed 'Let the memory begin!' and a wobble-voiced crooner in a tuxedo strolled on and sang 'Memories'. The golden curtain swished up to reveal a tableau of a ballroom with white and purple draperies. One by one the Duchesses appeared. Are you still with me? These are ace debs – we're talking aristocrats here, as the MC reminded us by introducing each duchess in the following manner: 'Duchess Jennifer Jane of the House of Smith'. One at a time each duchess would totter downstage and make a low curtsey before staggering back to her assigned position on the many-tiered set.

A duchess, indeed the whole damn court, is chosen, it's important to remember, not because of her grace and beauty, but because Papa is a local banker or controls the Coca Cola concession in his neck of the woods. Aristocracy manifested itself in the form of ungainly posture and a tendency towards embonpoint and ruddiness of cheek. The peeresses did not carry themselves well, and were further hampered by their heavy costumes. It was the curtsey that prompted the greatest terror. Spasms of alarm crossed their faces as they sank mightily onto their haunches, biting their lower lips as they flapped their arms in the effort to keep their balance. It was a close thing – and once their well-wrapped pudenda had made it to two inches above the floor, a fresh wave of anxiety crashed onto their features as they wondered whether they'd ever make it up again.

The Duchess of Florida did a thirty-second cancan, the Duchess of University Park appeared as Eliza Doolittle, while others did sartorial impersonations of Halley's Comet, the Spirit of Theatre, Anna from *The King and I*, an Eskimo, and a bluebonnet (the state flower of Texas). The seemingly endless parade of lovelies, bedecked in their multi-coloured fantastical dresses and capes of crêpe and feathers and glitter, was interrupted by entr'actes provided by close-harmony songsters, and a couple who jitterbugged. Then more duchesses. On came The Freshness of Rain, the Yellow Rose of Texas, 'the unsurpassed beauty of an enchanted garden', and a butterfly. At long last, it was over. Back came the MC: 'And so an error has come gracefully to a close.'

But it wasn't so. True, all the duchesses had made their curtseys, but we hadn't yet met the ladies in waiting. This part of the proceedings took a further forty minutes, as identically clad bumblebelles trooped on one by one, shadowed loyally by their escorts, who wore tails and had names like Travis Heard Beall III. The curtain fell and the two diminutive trainbearers ('They're so darlin'!') tottered onto the stage. A drumroll, and then the curtain whooshed up again to reveal Her Gracious Majesty in a gold dress with an Emanuel train. Gasps and applause. Jim Deakins, more upright than ever, strode in wearing tails, and ushered ahead of him an infant sceptre bearer, who handed Jim the implement with which he dubbed the new Rose Queen of Tyler. Her Majesty moved to centre stage, the band played 'Land of Hope and Glory' (why?), and as she paraded regally about, her loyal court swarmed onto the stage. Once again they tumbled onto their haunches to honour her. Wild cheers. Curtain.

*

'Aw honey, you're real nice to me, you always are. Why are you so nice to me? You're real good to me. I must be a pain in the butt sometimes. I love you.' Then he lurched forward in an attempt to sling his thick arm round the slender middle of the waitress. She stepped out of reach but smiled and shrugged.

'Now you finish your dinner, Turner, and I'll be back in a whiles to bring you some coffee.'

'You'll do that? Isn't she a honey? I love you.'

The couple sharing the booth with Turner smiled wanly. These drunken ineffectual yearnings – and every waitress that passed within ten yards was summoned over for a cuddle and a declaration of love – had been going on for the best part of an hour, and we were growing bored. Turner was a regular, and here in Longview, about twenty miles further east from Tyler, everyone knew everyone else, and you did your best to be nice. Longview isn't far from Louisiana, and the cooking at Johnny Cace's Seafood Restaurant was essentially creole. While I listened to Turner's outpourings and watched his gropings, I forked into excellent fish *en papillote* with a generous garnish of tiny shrimps and crabmeat; parked on my table was a battery of breads and spreads and pickles.

Turner, fiftyish, heavy-set, had lumbered over to the cash register. He'd already paid, but he was pretending he hadn't. 'Gosh durn bill. I ain't gonna pay that durn bill.' He took a fancy to the phrase, and repeated it endlessly as he took up a position by the register from which he could survey the waitresses and laugh at his own jokes.

I paid my own durn bill and moved on to the Reo Palm Isle, a large shed set in an even larger parking lot. It's the oldest country dance hall in Texas, they say, but that evening the two-beer (one in each hand) was more in evidence than the two-step. No place for a foreigner in a plain shirt and shoes, so after a longneck (Texan for beer bottle) I returned to the motel. I drove through the neon night past Whispering Pines, Bertha's Motel, Bluebonnet Inn, Lakeview Motor Lodge. Now, which one was I staying at?

*

The road northeast to Jefferson took me through woods and clearings. A few neat bungalows commanded low mounds, but most of the housing here consisted of caravans and shacks. In front of the shacks cars and pickups slouched on the grass or, more often, on reddish mud where the grass had been squelched down by the tyres. Everywhere there was junk. Since the climate is conducive to life outdoors, the front yard functions as an extension of the interior, and is usually strewn with chairs and benches, torn-out back seats of discarded Plymouths, a basketball hoop and backboard, a set of swings. Towards the rear might be a clothes-line, old gas tanks, beer coolers, tree stumps that couldn't be budged, and a supply of firewood for colder nights. It was a messiness that perversely asserted a curious pride in one's property. Whereas a European, intent on privacy and anxious to make the best use of a small amount of land, will draw everything within, so that only the disposition of a garden or the colour of external paintwork will give any clues to the personalities living within, here in Texas, where property is sacrosanct, an indiscriminate dispersal of possessions over one's half acre registers a declaration that this is mine, and I'll do whatever I goddam please with it.

26

Jefferson, except for a few blocks near the river where the blacks live, is neat and orderly. It used to be the greatest inland port of the Southwest, but when the railway came to East Texas Jefferson thought it could survive quite happily without it. So the Texas & Pacific laid its lines some thirty miles away, and from that moment on Jefferson languished. From a prosperous port, with large frame mansions housing the merchants whose offices filled the fine brick commercial buildings on the main streets, it became a backwater, and so it remains, its population of 3000 a tenth of what it used to be. If a town stays a backwater long enough, it unknowingly transforms itself into an object of antiquarian curiosity, and Jefferson has become a favourite tourist haunt in this remote backwoods area. One can still stay at the Excelsior Hotel, founded in the 1850s and the oldest in Texas. There are good restaurants and a dozen bakeries and ice cream parlours, all run by white-haired ladies in blouses and floppy bows, suggesting a clientele of Elks' wives. Even the more modest old buildings are labelled and dated: the Alley-Carlson Cottage proclaims that it's been lived in by the same family since 1861. After admiring the Victorian furnishings and sepia photographs of military heroes, visitors can trot back to Austin Street to look at Jay Gould's railway carriage. Gleaming and luxurious, this example of Victorian opulence has been donated to Jefferson and deposited opposite the Excelsior as a cruel reminder of what might have been had the town accepted Gould's offer to let the railway pass through. Then, before leaving for home, there's time for another pastry or dish of ice cream.

I left town by the bridge that crosses Big Cypress Bayou. Before the Louisiana border I turned off and got lost among the lanes of Uncertain, Texas. Nosing down badly paved roads, I came once more to a bayou, an expanse of thick sluggish water. Tall reeds nodded over riverbanks; large cypresses were bearded with Spanish moss. The air was heavy and sultry, broken only by the erratic swoops and buzzes of aerial livestock. Everything about the place was eerie. In just such a swamp, surely, Southern Gothic had begun its rich orchidaceous growth. If I waited long enough I'd be sure to see a long-haired barefoot girl in a torn smock come fleeing down the path pursued by her whiskered uncle, the preacher, who had seduced her by syphoning juleps down her white throat and was now desperate to prevent her hysterical denunciation of his depravity. Sech goin's on down in the bayou!

*

The thirty-mile strip of forest a hundred miles south is coloured green on the map and labelled Sabine National Forest, giving the impression that the entire area is government land. Not so. Private individuals are the largest landowners, followed by timber companies, and then the federal government in the form of the Forest Service. It would be more accurate to splash the map lightly with green dots. The forest village of Hemphill adjoins a 13,000-acre area that was the subject of a fierce political row. Congressman John Bryant of Dallas had proposed legislation to set aside a total of 65,000 acres of Texas's four national forests as wilderness areas, primarily as a conservation and recreational measure. This was modest enough, since 65,000 acres constitutes only 10% of the national forest in the state, and a mere 0.5% of all Texas timberlands. Vociferous opposition had been voiced by the congressman from nearby Lufkin, Charles Wilson, who is so closely involved with the timber interests that he's known locally as Timber Charlie. Wilson acts as though convinced that God's sole purpose in creating trees was to give men something to cut down. In his eyes conservationists are 'fern fondlers and orchid sniffers'. Wilson's rival bill would have only set aside a derisory 9000 acres, but intensive lobbying was gradually forcing him to compromise.

It had been light, in a feeble way, for some time when I skidded the car up the muddy track that leads from the main road to the log house in the woods. Raymond had built the house himself, and lived there with his wife and daughter. Dogs yapped round my feet as I stepped onto the porch and pulled open the screen door. There was a welcome whiff of coffee. It was seven o'clock and the household had been up for hours. Raymond told me he is usually out of bed by five, but that was the only suspect thing about him. Passing me a mug of coffee, he said 'Let's go!' and moments later we were bouncing down the drive in his pickup while the coffee slurped all over my jeans. The air outside was moist and misty, and surprisingly tepid given the ungodly hour. Raymond drove a few miles along blacktopped road before turning onto a lumber road that lurched through the forest towards Indian Mounds. We parked in a clearing.

Through the undergrowth we thwacked our way into woodland, winding between pine, holly, oak, magnolia, hornbeam and other less familiar models. Names of trees are deceptive in Texas. The holly there bears little resemblance to the European species, and there are over a dozen varieties of oak. Raymond – lean, taciturn, clean-jawed, with reddish hair and pale blue eyes – cleared a path ahead of us, and after about fifteen minutes we came to a beech grove of rare beauty. The tall trees were well spaced, and because of their age the uppermost branches had formed a canopy that kept the forest floor below shaded and cool.

'That canopy prevents the undergrowth from spreading. See how clear the ground is. Nothing but leaves and the tall trees. This is what we're trying to preserve. If they cut this wood down, they'd replant it with pine and in a few years it would be as dense as that undergrowth back there. Sometimes, when Martha's away, I'll come out with my bedroll and sleep out here. I'll wake at dawn and just look around me at those beeches. Then I get up and go to work . . . I want to show you something else.' He led me to a tree on the other wide of a hollow, and pointed to a primitive carving that resembled a gingerbread man with an animal by his feet. 'We think it's probably an Indian carving but can't be sure.'

'Can't you date the tree and the depth of the carving?'

'No, the tree's hollow.'

Ray felt the chances of getting the forest designated as wilderness were about fifty-fifty. 'The timber people come out here and they say that this forest is dead. They mean it isn't very productive in terms of lumber, and that's true because of the way the trees are spaced. But that's also what makes the forest beautiful.'

Driving back along another lumber road, we passed a hunter with two dogs. He waved at Raymond, who waved back. It was the mayor, squirrel hunting. Looking down on him and on us from the branch of a tall pine was a burly barn owl.

'Nature's out in force this morning,' I remarked.

'Not around this corner,' replied Raymond, turning into a clearing. A loud snarling sound was rasping against the noise of the pickup engine, and I soon saw what was producing it. Before us was a site on which acres of trees had recently been felled. What remained were brambles and thickets and saplings – all mature trees had been taken out some days previously. In the middle of the clearing an immense Caterpillar 8 growled and roared as its huge claws, snapping like a demented lobster's, sliced and wrenched any vegetation in its path. We stared in silence at the final hours in the life of a wood.

'Soon they'll have cleared this area completely, and then they'll be back to replant. Don't get me wrong. We're not opposed to taking timber out of the forest, even from the National Forest. Some federal land is often leased to timber companies on the basis of competitive bidding, and that's OK. What worries us is that they're logging too much, and the way they do it bothers us too. Most of this forest is a mixture of hardwood and pine. But in come the timber people, as you can see right here, and they clear-cut it, and then they replace what they've cut with machine-planted monoculture pine. Pine grows fast, it's a good commercial wood. But the system is destroying the kind of forest that has always existed here. Now even the Forest Service is clear-cutting. This is just a small patch of woodland. Out on the Pineland road they've just clear-cut a thousand acres. Usually the timber company leaves a thin line of pine along the roadside as a screen, but not this time. They've cut up to the roadside itself.'

Later, when Raymond was at work, I went to see for myself. He was right. The sight was painful and grotesque, like photographs of First World War battlefields a week after the guns have stopped firing.

Over dinner Raymond and Martha talked about the Sabine Forest.

'It's pretty depressed,' said Raymond. 'Always has been.'

'But it's changing. A lot of professional people, doctors and such, have moved in and bought up land as tax shelters. And Midwesterners retire down here for the fishing and the climate.'

'The climate?' I said, feeling my shirt sticking, as it had done all day, to my back.

'It's wet,' nodded Raymond, 'but it's warm.'

'Wet!' exclaimed Martha. 'Sometimes it rains for days, sheets of it that go on for hours and hours.'

Sabine County is deeply conservative, yet staunchly Democratic. The county was one of the few in Texas to have voted for Carter – again showing cultural and political affinity with the South. And inevitably these remote counties of East Texas are Baptist too.

'But it's not as bad as it sounds,' said Martha. 'We're not church people, but we find the Baptists fairly tolerant. People here have their foibles just like anywhere else, and the Baptists don't try to interfere. They're some drunks in town – the Baptists don't approve, but they don't ostracize them.' I thought of Turner and how he had been gently indulged. 'We even have a couple of weirdos around here. Raymond, remember that guy in the beard who used to stand on the lawn of his aunts' house, twirling a baton all day?'

'Uh huh. But we figured it was just an act to get his aunts to send him to Europe so he could escape from Sabine County.'

Nuke the Frogs

I found the woods oppressive, those tall dark ungiving pines, but although I pressed doggedly south it would be a while before they would be behind me. I passed through Woodville, a town that still looked and felt segregated even if it wasn't, and on towards Kountze (pronounced Coonts) where, for the first time since leaving Longview, I began to see liquor stores in some profusion.

Out of 254 counties in Texas 84 are still dry, selling no liquor at all; about 35 are wet, and anything goes; the remainder have a variety of restrictions, some selling only beer, others permitting bars but not liquor stores. What they call 'local option' decides the matter, and some counties have both wet and dry areas, according to the will of the people. Fashionable North Dallas, for instance, is, astonishingly, still dry. I gratefully stopped in wet Kountze for a beer when I filled up the car. It is a God-given right in wet Texas to be able to buy booze at gas stations.

From Kountze I plunged into the Big Thicket. Nobody can quite agree where the Big Thicket is. It's obvious enough when you're in the midst of this most remarkable of Texan forests, but its edges are ill defined. Originally about 3.5 million acres in extent, its size has been severely reduced to 85,000 acres by logging and clearing. The Thicket and adjoining forest stretch from Polk County to the outskirts of industrial Beaumont to the southeast. It is less its size than its variety of flora and fauna that draws naturalists to the Big Thicket. Plants quite alien to swampy East Texas flourish here – cactus and yucca, for instance. More species of wild flowers lurk in these woods than in any other comparable area in the United States; rare orchids perfume barely penetrable corners of the forest. Bears were common earlier in the century; wild hogs and panthers are said to dwell deep in the Thicket. I saw the edges of these woods from my car, but that was meaningless. To experience the Thicket, as opposed to glimpsing it merely, I would have had to hole up in Saratoga for a few days and do some serious hiking or canoeing with guides. No thank you. Long live the weeds and the wilderness yet, but, equally, let the panther leap on some other tourist. I headed on to Beaumont.

*

But where was Beaumont? Driving down Route 69 I came to the expected neon city: mile upon mile of motels, Pizza Huts, shopping malls, pawn shops. It was dark and I had no sense of the landscape. I was dazzled by the noise of the high-way and the colour show in the sky. Surrendering to the confusion, I managed to loop around Beaumont on I–10 without ever finding it, so I gave up and checked into a motel. Then I made another attempt and did succeed in driving into downtown Beaumont, which was, naturally, dark and deserted.

Only the next morning did it dawn on me that I hadn't wanted to be in Beaumont anyway. I actually wanted to be in Port Arthur some twenty miles further south. Not that it made much difference. What's twenty miles down the interstate? The two cities, with Orange to the east, form what's known locally as the Golden Triangle. The oil industry, especially refining, has brought wealth to this corner of Texas, but not beauty. It still felt seedy, and the dull drive into Port Arthur intensified that impression. Climate has much to do with it: it's moist and humid here, in summer unbearably so, though even now in October it was eighty and sticky.

Instinct took me downtown. This is a foolishness of which long experience of American cities should have cured me. Yet on entering an unfamiliar city my first impulse is invariably to find its centre, gauge its character, and then fan out to explore its flanks. In most American cities, however, downtown means decay; though in a few cities it remains the business centre and in others attempts are made to pump new life into architectur-ally distinguished streets, in most cases downtown is a mess. This was certainly so in Port Arthur, where the tallest down-town building is an abandoned hotel and the few shopfronts that haven't been boarded up display wigs, shampoo bottles, exhortations to prayer, and invitations to enter the Sportsman's Lounge behind heavy barred doors. Broad boulevards lead out into the residential districts, and palm trees flap over modest bungalows and more spacious houses that lazily spread along the streets that run parallel to the Gulf shore. The Queen of

Vietnam Church – an allusion to a little-known Asian appearance by the Virgin Mary? – reminded me of the large Vietnamese community in this area. I could see why they chose to live here: the bungalows and the almost tropical climate must give Port Arthur as close a resemblance to Saigon as the Occident can provide. Not only is there peace here, but prosperity, in the form of the world's largest petrochemical and refining complex, and a passion for takeaway food.

Carmen had tried hard to talk me out of going to Port Arthur. She couldn't think of a single reason for visiting the place. I had just one: to attend the Cavoilcade, an annual fiesta in praise of the oil industry. The Princess had been chosen the night before, and the day after there would be the parade, various sporting contests, and a firehose fight. There'd be lavish floats, barbecue on the streets, pot-bellied refinery workers and roustabouts pissed out of their minds on Stroh or Lone Star – I decided to leave. I had alternative plans that attracted me more. Even if I hadn't, I couldn't wait to get out of Port Arthur. I now understood why Janis Joplin, a native of the city, had been so anxious to acquire a Mercedes Benz.

Even my modest Toyota was good enough for my getaway, out to the west on Route 90. I flattened some airborne inhabitants of nearby marshes, and the obliterated insects left blobs of Colman's mustard over the windscreen, blurring my view of the slow-moving station wagon in front of me carrying the bumper sticker LUV YA JESUS. Other dead creatures had been kicked onto the shoulders of the road, notably a good crop of armadillos (pronounced 'amadiller' or, more affectionately, 'diller'), their ribbed grey casing muddied and bruised and their silly feet and belly sticking up into the air. Texans have a deep fondness for these creatures, adopting them as mascots and emblems, modelling them into keyrings and stencilling their form onto T-shirts. They're only slightly more attractive when alive.

Approaching Cleveland, I felt my stomach twitter with hunger. Time for lunch. I liked the look of a shack called Millie's, and so, it appeared from the cars lined up outside, did the sheriff. That must be a good sign: no haute cuisine within, I dare say, but portions of meat and beans and greens large enough to fill the most noble of pot-bellies. And indeed my hamburger was weighty and meaty, and the french fries plentiful and hot. The sheriff, grand in grey and with a small armoury on his hip and dark glasses on his nose, munched with bovine satisfaction at the table opposite. On a rack behind him I admired a whole gallery of *objets* that Millie had for sale: dolls, mugs, ceramics of powerful hideousness, mermaid tankards, and plastic ketchup and mustard bottle sets in a specially designed wooden rack.

I kept pushing west and came to Cut 'N Shoot, its picturesque name supposedly a reference to the volatility of its inhabitants. It's little more than a two-mile strip of shabby dwellings and motels along a wooded road. Texas, like many other states settled by earnest or rowdy pioneers, has its share of memorable place names. My wheels had already taken me through the dim dorps of Peerless and Birthright, but a true love of the boondocks could lead one to Dime Box, Wizard Wells, Dimple, Noodle, and Baby Head. The enterprising National Lampoon Company has produced a bogus map of the United States, and peppered it with such absurdities – that may exist for all I know – as Heat Rash, Free Lunch, Kneejerk, Sixpack, Cheesedip and Doubleknit. Nice, but not a patch on Dimple and Noodle.

Turning north I passed through Huntsville and Centerville, past small farms and spreads such as the La De Da Ranch. I expect Doo Da Day Ranch was on the other side of the tracks. Small copses of oak, sycamore, pine and cedar broke up the fields into irregular shapes. It was rural in a way too picturesque to be entirely convincing, and a chat later in the day with a real estate broker in a bar confirmed the hunch. Much of the land here has been bought up by city people, either for investment or for retirement homes. It's mostly grazing land for herd cattle, beautiful, tranquil, and increasingly populated by gentleman farmers playing at cattle raising. A successful Texan increases his status by buying land, rather than yachts or jewels. As they prospered, politicians from modest backgrounds, such as Lyndon Johnson and John Connally, bought large spreads near to their place of birth. There was, and is, no more sure way of saying to the community, 'Look, I've made it', than to buy 10,000 acres of the county where you grew up. That the idyll was under threat around here was suggested by this sign on a hillock: LEON COUNTY CITIZENS ARE OPPOSED TO THE DEPOSIT OF NUCLEAR WASTE AT THIS SITE.

By late afternoon I was in Waco. Do not irritate the natives of this pleasant university town by calling it Whacko. The Thrift Motel, where I unloaded for the night, certainly lived up to its name. The single light had a fifty-watt bulb, the orange carpet had been discoloured by decades of coffee spills and bodily fluids, there was nowhere to hang my clothes (better to keep them locked in a case where the bugs can't get at them), and a ventilation system embedded in the wall noisily impersonated the refilling of a water tank. The room smelt like a hospital.

I dined at what can only be described as a family steakhouse, Jess Radle's. Defiantly charmless, it concentrated its efforts on feeding about three hundred people at a time. Most tables were occupied by family parties – courting couples and solo travellers were thin on the ground. Pre-prepared salads curled crisply in plastic bowls in a refrigerator; each table supported six sauce bottles. Steaks were basic, properly cooked, and cheap. The place suited my mood: the waitresses smiled at me, the beer was cold, and it only took five saws of the knife to sever the steak.

'What's the house dressing?'

'Ranch dressin'. Kinda Italian with berdermilk. It's real guwerd.'

Near me sat two families. The men talked among themselves about football, while the women sat in silence, occasionally attending to a dribbling baby in a high chair. One of the men growled, 'Them stinkin' Bears', an allusion to the forthcoming Baylor football game, and on leaving he assured his friends: 'If Ah don't get shart in the fayerce, Ah'll see y'all at the party.'

*

The drama of the day to come revolved around the bitter struggle between the Bears and the Frogs: it was to be the leitmotif of the weekend. 'Them stinkin' Bears' had been a brave utterance, since Waco's Baylor University football team, the Bears, were about to confront the heavies of the Texas Christian University Horned Frogs. Sentiment in Waco was flowing thick as honey in support of the local boys. This was no ordinary football game. It was Homecoming Weekend, and 23,000 alumni were descending on the Baylor campus, where an immense bonfire had been lit on the college lawns to fête them – and possibly to help them find their way back to the dorms after they'd drunk themselves to the edge of catatonia. Before the game there would be a parade, and Baylor, it's acknowledged, stages the largest Homecoming Parade of any American college. Come the morning they'd be jamming the streets with twenty-four floats, plus a hundred other 'units' such as marching bands and clowns.

When the parade began it took over two hours for all the floats to pass through the downtown streets on their way to the campus. From a sorority float, bedecked like a Crivelli altar-piece, lovelies with smiles as broad as their hair was long threw candies at children jumping up and down on the pavements. Innumerable princesses – runners up for the post of Homecoming Queen – trundled by, together with judges and professors and other worthies of Waco. High-stepping drill teams were followed by marching bands, cheerleaders trooped by screaming 'Go Bears!', a truck creaked past carrying a live black bear (very popular with the crowd), and bands of clowns, wearing Groucho specs and moustaches, created maximum havoc; most successfully disruptive was a character dressed up as Darth Vader and zipping about on roller skates.

Ah, but those cheerleaders and drill teams! How do they get away with it? Even the most tired flesh could scarcely fail to respond to those expanses of thigh, those supple teenage bodies, the determinedly radiant smiles, and the unflagging energy that enables them to jump high in the air time and time again with only the faintest flush on their peachy faces to betray the exertion. Dressed uniformly in their silly uniforms, short skirts and frilly knickers and ornament glittering on their costumes, they are too much of a oneness to provide a clear target for the erotic marksman. I would spot an especially pretty girl in the team, glance away for a moment, and then be unable to re-identify the object of my attention. The regularity of the drill neutralises the sexuality of young women hurling their bodies around the unremarkable streets of Middle America – but only to a limited extent. That the girls were interchangeable alarmingly increased desire by constituting an emblem of excess that, by overwhelming, simultaneously depressed it.

As the flashing thighs disappeared around the corner at the end of Main Street, the attention of the crowd was distracted by the approach of the Governor of Texas, the amiable Mark White, smiling and waving, and his wife, waving and smiling.

'Hey! It's the Governor!' realised a surprised black pater-familias next to me.

'So? Ain't done nothin' for me,' countered his wife.

A larger car came by stuffed with elderly alumni, and then in a white antique convertible I spotted the burly figure of the controversial Attorney General, Jim Mattox, a politician in the populist mould, but whose private dealings have led to a spate of accusations and writs. Mattox was a political brawler, and Texans appreciate that. Nor do they mind a fair amount of roguery from their politicians, so long as those same politicians do not neglect the people's interest while attending to their own. The masonic love of silly clothes was displayed by the Shriners of the Karem Temple. Wearing purple fezes, these good charitable souls squeezed their hips into go-karts and whizzed round the street doing choreographed figures of eight. Soon after came teams of swirling cyclists holding balloons in the Baylor colours, green and yellow. After such japery it was a relief to applaud half-naked beauty in the form of Miss Waco (our very own Tammy Pope) and a campus sylph called Jaynellen Prude. Most of the floats alluded to the impending battle. A black coffin with the letters TCU rumbled by; a bear-bearing float wore the witty inscription POOH ON THE FROGS; even more hilarious was the bear by the lavatory bowl under the banner FLUSH THE FROGS. Not to mention STICK 'EM BEARS, the oil derrick float (DRILL THE FROGS), and the highly amusing NUKE THE FROGS.

By the time the big game began at Baylor Stadium, excitement was at a high pitch. I bought myself a ticket for the endzone and went for a piss. A tiny blonde boy tinkled brightly into the adjacent urinal.

'Hi!' he piped. 'Who you for?'

'I'm from out of town, so I'm not really for either team. You for the Bears?'

'I guess. Don't think they gonna make it though.'

I treated him to a lecture on supporting your side through thick and thin, come rain come shine, teaching him to be a good little Texan. He thanked me.

Inside the stadium banners persisted with the theme of the day: DISECT (sic) THE FROGS and PUT THE FROGS IN SOVIET AIRSPACE. I found a sunny seat in a corner, and brushed away the peanut shells and shooed off the granddaddy spiders quivering among themselves. It was 1.30 and the teams were doing physical jerks. At the Baylor end, a man in a bear suit encouraged the athletes as they practised their plays and did their push-ups. Drums in the distance announced the arrival of the Golden Wave Marching Band, all three hundred of them striding down the ramp and out into the sunlit stadium. Before and after came baton-twirling nymphs in swimsuits, flagwavers, and somersaulting gymnasts. Above buzzed a small plane bravely trailing a Frogs banner. The carnival from the streets seemed to have spilled into the stadium. After the invocation the band played 'The Star Spangled Banner' and most of the spectators placed hands on hearts and faced the Stars and Stripes that fluttered over the endzone. Now that God had been enlisted onto the side of Baylor, it was time for the band to give a fine display of strutting and pattern formation. The cheerleaders roused the rabble with their yells, and with the Baylor song, and then with a strange cheer that began with a Nazi salute with shaking wrists and a note that builds into a great roar before the arm is lowered.

On the stroke of two the electronic scoreboard went ape and the momentous words KICK OFF did a psychedelic dance across its surface. The crowd roared throatily as it welcomed the centrepiece of the Texan weekend. There's high school football on Friday nights, pro football on Sunday afternoons, and Saturday afternoon is dedicated to college football. Which leaves Saturday morning for the supermarket and Sunday morning for church.

The Bears won.

Supremely Blest

The hot sun was slapping down on the relaxed gum-chewing crowd as they clustered around stalls offering TexMex snacks and so-called arts and crafts. A band pounded in the distance, teenage girls in shorts touted raffle tickets, expensive cameras whirred and clicked, but behind the throng rose high stern walls, watchtowers glowering in the corners. We were converging on the celebrated Texas Prison Rodeo, held each October Sunday in Huntsville, site of one of the largest jails in the state. Over the last fifty years this rodeo has become, like its sponsor, an institution. It takes place in an arena adjoining the jail that was built by inmates using prison-made bricks. All the participants in the rodeo are convicts, and five hundred of them have competed for fifty coveted positions as Convict Cowboys. Winning a bareback riding or calf-tieing contest can bring a convict not only brief celebrity but will put some welcome money in his pocket too.

In a box to the side sat the convicts, like animated stick candy in their black and white stripes, while some of the contestants were making the acquaintance of some restless bulls stomping in their stalls. High up in a box, also encased in thick wire mesh, the Inmate Showband was playing noisily and well, accompanying the ceremonies that preceded the rodeo itself: The Posting of the Colours by two riders galloping dustily around the arena, the Grand Entry with riders and flags, the National Anthem, and 'Texas Our Texas':

'Texas our Texas! All hail the mighty state!
Texas our Texas! So wonderful – so great!
Largest and grandest, withstanding ev'ry test;
O Empire wide and glorious, you stand supremely blest.'

Action! First came the Mad Scramble, a simple contest in which ten mounted Brahman bulls erupt from the chutes; all the cowboys astride them have to do is stay on board for about twenty seconds and cross the arena. Cowboys who toppled off were dragged out of danger by jabbering rodeo clowns, who while appearing to be getting in everybody's way also played the important role of being on the spot in case a cowboy ran into difficulties, or into a rampaging bull.

'All down, all OK,' said the MC. 'They're gonna get some of that Freeworld money.' Not much: about forty dollars.

After some bareback bronc riding – the cowboys were roundly applauded if they managed to remain on the horse for a mere eight seconds – on came the Redshirts for the wild cow milking. The Redshirts are also convicts, but not riders; they perform in other events that require guts and bravado but not the ability to remain astride two thousand pounds of irritable livestock.

'Would you believe it?' began the MC. 'We have a thief in this prison. Yes, we do, and they've stole our milk pails. So instead, our Redshirts are gonna have to milk these cows into a Coke bottle. And to make it jest a bit harder, we've provided the meanest mama cows you ever seen.'

The Wild Horse Race that followed involved teamwork: six horses spring from the chutes, the cowboys attempt to saddle them and ride them across the arena. It was hard enough to catch the horse, let alone tie a saddle around it. Only two teams made it.

During the interval a pickup truck drove into the arena and deposited the singer Sylvia in the middle. She tried to win our attention but without success. Who wants to listen to a country singer from Indiana? Instead people queued up for Cokes and waved at the convicts down in their large wire pen. Quite a few of the spectators were clearly relatives of the convicts and took advantage of the occasion to exchange messages.

After her act Sylvia made a quick round of honour in the pickup, while the MC plugged: 'Thank you, Sylvia. Wasn't she great folks? She'll be riding around now in that beautiful new 1984 Dodge Ram Pickup Truck.'

The art of rodeo is not simply to stay astride a beast that doesn't want you there, but to do so with style and finesse. Judges award points for spurring and body action and form. A successful rodeo rider needs technique as well as persistence: a bad fall can lead to a severe trampling or dragging by the stirrups. In the Saddle Bronc Riding event, one cowboy did fall and lay motionless in the dirt. He was carried off and white-coated doctors hurried to the ringside. Two stretcher bearers removed the injured man. Murmured the MC: 'Guess that cowboy's shook up a little more than we thought.' Probably dead.

The bull riding events are always great fun, especially after a cowboy's been thrown and has had to run for his life pursued by three bulls. Without the aid of the clowns, who distract and confuse the charging bulls, some of those cowboys might have ended up as shish kebab.

Cow-milking is kindergarten stuff compared to the Redshirts' main event: Hard Money, an act unique to the Prison Rodeo. All you have to do is remove a bag full of money from the horns of a Brahman bull. Brahmans come in three sizes: big, monstrous, and terrifying. Red, you will recall, is a colour of which bulls usually take some notice, so forty convicts in scarlet shirts offer an *embarras de richesse* to the beast. The minimum prize, donated by the prison authorities, is a hundred dollars, but the sum often reaches four figures, since local businessmen are encouraged to 'sponsor' the event. A thousand dollars will buy a lot of dope, so the Redshirts are thoroughly motivated and quite willing to risk a skewering in pursuit of loot. They did well that afternoon: only one stretcher case, and eventually a brave soul did manage to sneak up on a ton of Brahman and snatch the bag.

Some of us had rented cushions from the stewards at fifty cents each to lessen the ache of sitting on hard bleachers for hours, and after the rodeo was over and we began to disperse, the MC urged us to leave them behind on the seats: 'If you try to leave here with one of them cushions, we'll have you here next week selling 'em.'

*

Local heroes have rarely played as admirable or momentous a part in history as their legends would have us believe. Sam Houston, though, does seem to have been a man of epic stature, and here in Huntsville he lived out his old age. Born in Virginia, he became governor of Tennessee. His burgeoning political career was ruined by marital scandal when his wife left him for reasons never specified, and he moved to Texas. For a man with a taste for adventure, his timing was admirable.

Texas was not at this time part of the Union. This huge territory, larger than any European country, had belonged, since 1821, to Mexico, and for three hundred years before that was part of the Spanish Empire. It only changed hands in 1821 because Mexico won its independence from Spain, and Texas, consequently, became part of the new country, though the Anglo-Saxon Protestant gringos of Texas far outnumbered Mexican settlers. Independent Mexico was not the most orderly of regimes. Its leader, General Santa Anna, settling into a pattern that was to become as traditional as tortillas, began his political life as a liberal and ended it by assuming dictatorial powers. Mexican politics were inevitably influenced by reactionary Spanish models, and the white settlers of Texas, who had come to this still undeveloped territory from other parts of America, had little intention of being pushed around by high-handed Mexicans. The two cultures were entirely out of sympathy: language, religion, ideology, they were all opposed. Mexicans regarded Texans as unruly colonials, while Texan settlers looked upon Mexicans as an alien presence. Conflict was inevitable.

The Texan Revolution occurred as much by accident as design. It began as an act of resistance more than as a planned quest for independence. Nor was the revolt conspicuously successful. Sam Houston was appointed military commander of Texas in November 1835, but his troops were scattered and divided. After the Battle of the Alamo, when Santa Anna's superior forces exterminated the recklessly gallant Texan defenders besieged within the old mission at San Antonio, Houston found himself very much on the defensive, and ordered a general retreat. Finally, on April 21, 1836, his troops were drawn up in the marshes of San Jacinto, near present-day Houston. Once again the Texans were faced by superior Mexican troops under Santa Anna's command. A combination of guile and scarcely credible luck came to the aid of Houston and his men, who, while the Mexicans were enjoying their siesta, marched unobserved across the marshes in broad daylight and attacked the dozing enemy. Crying 'Remember the Alamo!' they charged the Mexican positions, captured Santa Anna, and routed his army, inflicting enormous casualties while suffering hardly any of their own. The war was over.

Sam Houston was now the unchallenged leader of the newly independent Republic of Texas, and was overwhelmingly elected president. There was nothing vainglorious about Houston's desire to lead the new nation, since he and almost every other Texan with a vote had expressed a wish to seek annexation to the United States. (The vote was 3277 to 91, and wags insist it was Texas that annexed the United States, not the other way round.) Houston was a nationalist rather than a regionalist, and so he remained. His contempt for any vision of Texas that smacked of parochialism eventually led to his political decline, since he left the people of Texas in no doubt that he opposed the Confederate cause in the Civil War of the 1860s. In 1836 he had fought to wrench Texas free from Mexico and join the Union, and it dismayed him to see his adopted countrymen joining the forces of secession. There were others in Texas who didn't support the Confederacy. German settlers in the west were particularly unenthusiastic. Their indifference to the merits of a society based on slavery and the plantation system was, however, matched by the identification of East Texans with the Confederate cause so passionately espoused by the neighbouring Deep South. Indeed most Texans, like plants that have straggled into an adjoining garden, had their origins in Southern states. Their allegiance was unequivocal.

To Houston, however, an overriding principle was at stake, and he would not bend despite the cost to his popularity and reputation. In 1860, an old man, he spoke at a Unionist rally shortly before Lincoln was elected President. 'I ask not for the defeat of sectionalism by sectionalism, but by nationality,' he proclaimed. He poured scorn on the Confederacy: 'Here is a constitutional party that intends to violate the constitution because a man is constitutionally elected president.' They were brave words, but the mood of Texas was against him, and they had little impact. When Texas joined the Confederacy, Houston was still governor. He refused to renounce his allegiance to the overriding principle of Union and would not take the oath to the Confederacy. Removed from office, he retired to Huntsville, where he died at the age of 74, while the Civil War was still raging, in 1863. Later that year the Confederate legislature, which he had defied, passed a resolution honouring Houston and urging that he 'be held in perpetual remembrance by the people of this state.' That his bitter opponents could pay such tribute is the best evidence of the man's stature.

Nor have Texans forgotten Sam Houston, though he is revered more as the architect of Santa Anna's defeat than as an embattled Unionist. A park in Huntsville, with flowering shrubs beneath tall pines, and geese and swans gliding over ponds, is named after him, and the house in the park is crammed with Houston memorabilia. And not far from the centre of town is Oakwood Cemetery, wooded and still. Here are the graves of many celebrated Texans, including the splendidly named historian Henderson Yoakum, but it's the tombstone of Sam Houston that draws knots of pilgrims. I joined them.

*

The look of the land was beginning to change. I'd been driving steadily west and now, beyond Waco, the hills billowed more spaciously, the vistas expanded. Trees were gathered in groups too small to be called copses, and lines of oaks made irregular strides up the farm roads. Near Gatesville, farmland gave way to rolling low mesa which supported more scrub than crops. I passed Pancake, then Hamilton, a small tree-filled town with attractive creamy limestone buildings. There were more of them in Comanche, including the old square jailhouse, which is still in use. The name of the town keeps one in mind of the fiercest Indians any settlers along the Western frontier had to contend with. With their mastery of horsemanship, the Comanches could sweep down across the plains from the north in plundering parties that could traverse a thousand miles. The Comanches could always find a way to get to you, and once they did find you the custom of the tribe often demanded a slow barbecue of captives. When, days later, Comanche camps were found with the horribly mutilated corpses of captives whose writhings under impalement had entertained the warriors for a few days, the sight and consequent reports only further inflamed the fear and hostility between settler and Indian.

The Comanches, swift and mobile, penetrated far beyond present-day Comanche. A hundred miles to the east I had passed Fort Parker near Groesbeck. Here in the 1830s the Parker family had settled and built a stockade. In May 1836 the Comanches raided: they killed, scalped, castrated, raped. They also took captives, including nine-year-old Cynthia Ann. Adopted by the Comanches, she later married the chief of the Noconi Band. Twenty-four years later she was recaptured by white settlers in a skirmish and was identified as the Parker girl. To the dismay of her family, her sole desire was to return to her

Comanche home. Repeatedly thwarted, she starved herself to death.

There were many other instances, equally tragic, of captives uncertainly caught between two cultures, white Protestant settler and peripatetic Indian, that seemed to touch at no point. Their value systems, their sense of territoriality – held with equal conviction on either side – were incompatible, and there was no way the two peoples could ever co-exist. Indian tribes to the east were less warlike, and some lived peaceably with their white neighbours. But the ferocity of the Comanche came to be regarded as the norm, and even mighty Sam Houston, who knew it was possible to live in harmony with such tribes as the Cherokee, was unable to persuade the new Republic of Texas to curtail its perpetual state of war against the Indians. It was, too, unrealistic to expect the tough determined settlers on the western frontiers of Texas to regard the Comanches as anything other than the most dangerous of enemies. In too many places they had left their visiting cards – hot coals in eye sockets, dismembered genitalia, the impaled bodies of raped old women.

Conflict between white settler and native Indian continued for most of the century. Although the last white Texan to perish at the hands of Indians died in 1881, the Indian menace, as it was perceived, was effectively eradicated six years earlier. A last Comanche uprising took place in 1874 and a year later their forces surrendered. Texas initially agreed to set aside 3 million acres as an Indian reservation for the remaining Apaches and Comanches, but the offer was pared down and the Indians had to settle for a mere 160 acres per person. The Comanches, whose mastery of horsemanship had at one time given them control of an ocean of plain and prairie, were reduced to the existence of small-time farmers. By the time the last Comanche chief, Quanah Parker, died in 1911, the Indian population of Texas was no more than 1000. The revival of Indian claims and culture that has occurred in other states in recent years has not been echoed in Texas, where the Indian presence today is scarcely discernible.

The country around Comanche looks tame today. Poor chalky scrub sometimes giving way to grazing land; and oak and mesquite growing along the edges of dry creeks. Roadside stores sell watermelons, peaches, pecans. At Rising Star, some thirty miles northwest, a church notice-board spelt out the following apothegm: IF LIFE HANDS YOU A LEMON MAKE LEMONADE. As I pressed on to Cross Plains, the landscape was noticeably drying out. A few head of cattle stumbled about on rocky, mesquite-infested scrub land. Fat green bunches of prickly pear cactus hugged the fences.

I'd arrived, it seemed, in West Texas. It's hard to speak of West Texas, since it's an idea as much as a place, a repository of identity, part reality, part myth: the frontier spirit, the vast ranchlands, the big skies, the desert. It would be easiest to say that West Texas appears on the horizon some miles west of Austin and Fort Worth. At this point the farmlands of central Texas give way to the limestone Hill Country and the even more arid treeless landscapes of the Panhandle, and even further west to parched deserts and mesa. These landscapes differ; what they share is a climate that brings no more than twenty inches of rainfall each year. In the Trans-Pecos region, far to the west, the average is closer to twelve inches. This overwhelming fact dominates both the landscape and the occupations of those who inhabit it. It is not enough to own land in West Texas; without access to water that land is useless.

I was approaching Abilene, an uninspiring town of 100,000 inhabitants. It was founded in 1881 as a railway town, but the deity had greater plans for Abilene, which now has no fewer than three Christian colleges. On the outskirts are other indications of what makes Abilene's economy tick: numerous seed and feed stores, farm and ranch supply establishments, a few light manufacturing plants. Suburbia has sprung up even here, and a huge sign advertises a new condominium development: Canterbury Trales, with its motto IT'S A GREAT PLACE TO HANG YOUR HAT. An admirable pun, but I'm not sure I want to live in one.

It was late afternoon when I arrived and I was keen to buy a book before the shops closed. There are plenty of bookshops in Abilene, but they only sell Bibles and revivalist sermons on cassette. A telephone directory revealed a chain bookstore in a remote shopping mall, and I asked an old man how to get there.

'Well,' began a dotard – old-time resident? knows Abilene like the back of his spotted hand? – 'go down this street, then turn down Willis –'

'Which way?'

'Make a right.'

'OK.'

'Mebbe Mockingbird would be better. Then head along North Tenth.'

'Right. North Tenth.'

'Perhaps South First. It'll be the same thing.'

'Which would you recommend?'

'South First, I guess.'

'OK.'

'Keep driving a whiles and you'll come to it.'

'Drive which way?'

'Out. West.'

'Got it. Many thanks.'

'You bet.'

I sped to the next corner and asked someone else.

An hour later I bought my book and then found a motel for the night. It was not unlike the Thrift Motel in far Waco, only smaller. All surfaces were stained rather than dirty, the bathroom was green, the bedroom a cream that was rapidly turning brown. The walls were speckled with the remains of squashed mosquitoes and cockroach cocktail. Coloured photographs of Mount St Helens hung crookedly on the walls, and next to the door was a printed homily: 'Because this Motel is a human institution to serve people and not solely a money-making organization, we hope that God will grant you peace and rest while you are under our roof. May this room and motel be your "second" home . . . Even though we may not get to know you, we hope that you will be as comfortable and happy as if you were in your own home.'

I turned on the TV, which was screwed to its swivelling wall bracket, and watched a programme that was scissored by an ad for 'real homogenized milk', as if homogenization were a quaint old country custom preserved for an abused nation of consumers by a beneficent milk processor. The ad narrowly failed to kill my appetite and shortly after I left the human institution and drove to a seedy part of town – even more seedy, that is – where I found Joe Allen's Pit Bar-B-Q. A shack of course – no money to waste on fancy decor – with a non-functioning fan in the centre of the ceiling, from which oversized dummies of Coors bottles were suspended. On the walls hung yellowing framed cartoons, neon beer signs, and photographs of local sporting contests and eminent steers. To order a steak here you tell the waitress how thick a piece you'd like; she then tells the cook to slice it, weighs it, and you are charged by the ounce. I ordered a modest ¾-inch slab, apologising to the waitress: 'I'm afraid I don't have a West Texas appetite.'

'Don't have a West Texas accent either,' she replied. That was a cue too rich in possibility to pass up, and by the time I left Joe Allen's Sheri had given me the names of her relatives in the Panhandle, insisting I visit them. The steak was good: cooked rare over a mesquite fire, and beautifully seasoned. The french fries were made from potatoes rather than from frozen coagulate revivified by the miracle of microwave. On a stainless steel buffet unit were arranged the 'fixings': cole slaw, beans, potatoes, cornbread, white bread – as much as you wanted. As I munched, I was joined at my table variously by Sheri and the other waitress, the cook, a black waiter. Later Joe himself stumbled out of the kitchen carrying his own supper. He nodded to me before sitting down at a booth by himself. Separated by a foot of steak and a yard of floor, *le patron* and I chewed contentedly.

Steaked Plains

'So what do you think of the Chenin Blanc?'

'Good. Very fresh, lots of fruit, plenty of zip, not too sweet. It's the '82?'

'No, the '83.'

Kim McPherson took a clean glass and marched over to another large stainless steel tank and turned the tap. 'This is the Sauvignon Blanc. What do you think?'

So I told him. There was nothing unusual about this conversation between winemaker and tippler except that it was taking place in Lubbock, Texas, out on Farm Road 1585 at the Llano Estacado winery. Texas's international reputation for fine wine is slight, and having sampled the products from half a dozen other wineries – there are fifteen or so scattered across the state – I knew why. But Kim had studied in California and his wine was several notches above the local average. He can't sell his product in Lubbock itself, which is dry – or more accurately, in German oenological parlance, *halbtrocken*, since immediately beyond the city limits is a strip of excellent liquor stores.

Llano Estacado means Staked Plain, and that was the name given to the expanses around Lubbock by the Spanish tourist Coronado over four hundred years ago. They form the southernmost portion of the Great Plains that stretch down from Canada. The land around Lubbock is entirely flat, although the plateau is 3200 feet high. Other parts of the Panhandle rise to a height of 4500 feet, yet these shifts of contour are barely perceptible. The plains slope very gently across hundreds of miles. From the south and the east, though, the ascent to the South Plains is marked indeed. Driving northwest from Abilene, I passed Snyder and saw before me the great escarpment known as the Caprock. Near Crosbyton, to the east of Lubbock, the Caprock is even more dramatic – a sheer cliff gouged by canyons.

Heavily agricultural, the South Plains and the more northerly plains around Amarillo present a landscape not immediately recognisable as Texan. The grain elevators, the cotton gins, the immense fields stretching hedgeless across the treeless prairie – they could have been a southern extension of the slabs

50

of Kansas or Nebraska. Yet the Llano Estacado is as truly Texan as any region of the vast state. Many of the great ranches that gave rise to a national mythology of cowboys and chuck wagons and cattle drives were, and still are, situated here in the Panhandle. The plains were once Comanche territory, and long after the so-called Wild West had been settled, this whole area was still perilous frontier country. Lubbock, a sprawling city of 200,000 inhabitants, was a sea of grass a century ago; in terms of settlement, the Panhandle is as new as any place in the United States. The presence of 24,000 students at Texas Tech University has had a civilising influence on the town, which otherwise would have retained the Bible Belt severity of Abilene or Amarillo.

So although Lubbock is unprepossessing – ungainly pylons marching around the city, mile after mile of service road linking warehouses and plants devoted to agribusiness, and the pervasive smell of piss emanating from cottonseed processing plants – for all that, Lubbock has a certain panache. Not style, that would be going too far, but a vivacity, an integrity that give it a character recognisably different from the other farming cities of West Texas. There's even a hint of dottiness in the name of its newspaper: the *Lubbock Avalanche Courier*. Avalanche? In Lubbock?

The panache stops at the city limits. The small farming communities scattered across the South Plains seem closed and grim. There isn't much to do after dark in Muleshoe, Earth, Happy, New Deal, or Idalou. A woman who used to live in a town south of Lubbock had told me that the only entertainment for her teenage daughter had been the single cinema, and even that closed down each winter, during which the sole alternative diversion was seeing how fast you could drive round the town square. I met this daughter, and the experience had evidently scarred her: a more surly, resentful young woman I have rarely encountered. Another Lubbockite confessed: 'A friend who also grew up around here once said there were two things to do. Play ball or throw each other to the ground.'

*

Near to the downtown Civic Center stands a statue to Lubbock's most famous son. I refer, of course, to Buddy Holly. He's buried here too, and pilgrims amble about the cemetery looking for his simple grave. Joe Ely, Waylon Jennings, John Denver, and many other musicians of lesser repute bought their first guitar in Lubbock, Texas. The city fathers, after decades of ignoring the sole cultural contribution their city has made, have at last begun to take some pride in it. Fuchsia Akins, who works at the Texas Tech Museum, is helping to assemble a section devoted to local music.

'The music around here's strange,' she told me. 'It's not pure hillbilly. Combine Country & Western, black music, and Mexican rhythms, and you'll be getting close. The lyrics, they often deal with things that happened locally, like the tornado of 1970 that flattened most of downtown. All these great musicians started out in Lubbock, but the sad thing is they never stay. There's no future for them here, they go off to Austin or Nashville. The town's changing, of course, though it still feels like a town more than a city, which is nice, and we still have a losing football team.'

'Is your name really Fuchsia?'

'I had an aunt whose name was Wanda May. When she was eighteen she went to New York to try to get into musical theatre. Somehow she thought Wanda May wasn't the right name for a chorus girl. So she changed it to Fuchsia, and it's become a family name now.'

'It's been pleasant talking to you, but there's no fuchsia in it.'
She smiled wanly. She'd heard it before.

*

'Now in Lubbock Texas the other night, drinkin' beer and about half tight, me and Paul and Jim and a guy named Al – we were drawing pictures and writing songs, sitting there talkin' – before too long Paul said we ought to move this party over to Stubb's. The smoke was hanging low and thick . . . and Joe Ely was in the back room shooting pool. Now we all went back there to check it out . . . Pretty soon we're shootin' pool and jest raisin' hell . . . Joe and me kinda drew a crowd; the place got drunk and the place got loud, and Joe reached over to a sack and pulled out a big ole onion. He placed that onion on the felt, said 'Here's where you're gonna need some help. We're gonna use that hamburger helper for a cue ball! . . . We battled back and forth all night, the tears were streaming from our eyes' – and Tom T. Hall won the famous event commemorated in his song 'The Great East Broadway Onion Championship of 1978'.

You can still trek out to East Broadway, crossing the tracks from downtown Lubbock into this dilapidated section of town, and you'll soon come to Stubb's. The pool room is still in the back, and Stubb is still in the kitchen cooking his famous barbecue. I went there one night with Doug Nelson, the driving force behind what will eventually be Lubbock's museum of music. Doug works as a bartender, but this was his evening off and he was showing me round nocturnal Lubbock. The restaurant was empty, and Stubb was able to emerge from the kitchen and join us at a table while we had a few beers. He drank milk.

His full name is C. B. Stubblefield. A very tall, well-built black with a slightly mournful air, he seems reluctant to smile, but quite happy to talk. He's a legend in this part of Texas, and beyond, not just because of his cooking (he'd once had to airfreight 200 servings to a party in New York), but because his shack has been the haunt of musicians for many years. He can seat about seventy-five at the formica-topped tables, more when a band's playing. The walls are plastered with old posters and record sleeves and portraits of musicians. Along one wall is a podium for performers. Linda Ronstadt, George Thorogood, Muddy Waters are among those who've played and sung here.

Although he clearly relished his status as one of the godfathers of Texas music, respect and affection hadn't brought Stubb wealth. 'I'm almost broke. You know that? Lotta people have asked me to move my place up to Nashville, offered me a lotta money to go there, but I don't want to leave. May have to, though. The truth is Lubbock don't deserve me.'

'That's right,' nodded Doug.

'The place is empty. Why?' I asked, abandoning tact. 'You serve the best barbecue for miles, you're a famous man. How come there's hardly a soul in here?'

'Colour.'

'Seriously? Here in West Texas?'

'Uh huh. There's no violence, nothing like that around here, but the colour thing is still there.' He told his version of a familiar story. 'One day three white ladies comes in here and says to me, "You serve white folks here?" And I says, "No, ma'm, I can't cut 'em up small enough to fit on a plate." They stayed and ate here. 'Nother time this Meskin guy comes in, asks if I serve Meskins. "No," I says, "I don't serve Meskins, peckerwoods, or niggers." So he starts walkin' to the door. I raise my voice and says, "But I do serve the best barbecue in Texas," and he came back. And one time I was in the kitchen and this man and woman walks in and wants to know if I'm real. That's the truth. They said, "Stubb, we was wondering whether you was real."'

He must be in his early fifties, though he won't admit to his age. Despite his self-proclaimed woes, Stubb looks youthful, carries himself with a dignity flecked by a beguiling roguishness. He rose and went to the counter to fetch more beers, and came back with a bulging photo album. Slowly leafing through it, he showed me pictures of himself standing beside innumerable country music stars. Then I turned a page and found myself staring at the order of service for Muddy Waters' funeral.

'One night I was in the kitchen. Heard the phone ring. It was George Thorogood in New York. "Stubb," he said, "there's been a death in the family," and then he told me Muddy Waters was dead. George flew me to Chicago for the funeral, and I didn't spend more than fifty cents all the time I was there. I never seen anythin' like the flowers in that church. The casket was in the front and they had flowers all the way round. Wreaths like crosses and angels and guitars.'

I turned another page. A sombre Stubb was shown standing beside Johnny Cash.

'Uh huh. That was the best moment of my life, when Tom T. Hall introduced me to Johnny Cash.'

Snaps showing him during the Korean War induced a more philosophical mood. He was perplexed by the hostility between nations; a world scarred by wars and killing distressed him. 'One thing's for sure. We're all gonna die.'

'I'd like a little more time first.'

'Yeh.' He grinned. 'Y'know something. I love life. I love people. Though I've had a sorrowful side in my life . . .'

*

Doug drove me over to Cold Water Country, an immense barn down on the loop that circles the town. One of the best honkytonks in Texas, it's less commercial than, say, Gilley's in

Pasadena near Houston. The nine pool tables were all in use and beyond the large dancing area a live band played rather ancient country music in front of three flags: US, Lone Star, Confederate.

'It's Stubb's birthday next week,' said Doug. 'Every year people – musicians, friends – come to Cold Water from all over to eat barbecue and celebrate. Too bad you'll be gone. It's a great occasion, if you can get in.'

We moved on to Fat Dawgs, the bar where Doug works. It's a jazz spot mostly, catering to the university students and their informed musical tastes. But Doug hadn't brought me here to listen to the music. He took me into a back room.

'I want you to have some of this.' He handed me a small package of what looked like a strip of hide. 'This is the purest beef jerky you can get. Really good stuff. Keith Richards wanted to import it into England, but the customs people wouldn't allow it.'

Some days later when I found myself stranded in an oilfield at lunchtime I ate the jerky, which was full of hot intense spicy flavours. I wish I'd kept it; I'd be a rich man. Eight ounces of Texas jerky sells at Harrods for twenty pounds.

*

Robert Bruno's house in Lubbock is, from the outside, utterly conventional, a two-storey colonial with white columns, a smaller sister of Sam and Carmen's house in Dallas, a standard design that can be found in every state of the Union. The living room too held few surprises: comfortable furniture and a scattering of art books. And then I looked at the furniture more carefully and realised how exquisitely made it was: tables and desks crafted from exotic African woods, with forms as sinuous and inventive as Art Nouveau, but without the preciosity and whimsicality.

'Did you make all these?' I asked suspiciously.

He nodded. 'They're all made specially for the new house.'

Bruno is a tall, calm, well-rounded man, about forty, meticulous, patient, authoritative, confident as a monsignor. On the outskirts of Lubbock he's building single-handed a large house that, even in its incomplete state, has attracted worldwide curiosity. I'd seen it perched on a cliffside over Lake Ransom canyon after I'd visited the winery. It had intrigued me so much that I'd got in touch with Bruno, who'd offered to take me out there. I left my car at his house and we set off in his pickup. The elevation of the cab gave me a clear view of the fields outside town. Lubbock is so flat that I could double my range of vision just by leaping into the air. From the cab I could plainly see that much of the land was under water.

Climatically the South Plains is designated a semi-arid area. The week before, however, seven inches of rain had fallen in two days. Bruno pointed at the acres of empty warehousing rubbing up against the town. 'All these warehouses belong to the farmers' co-operatives. They're supposed to be full. In a normal year, they'd be packed to the roof, and the fields all around would be stacked with bales of cotton. Usually we produce about 20 per cent of the country's cotton. But last week the rains destroyed most of the crop. That's why the warehouses are almost empty.'

It surprised me that there were farmers' co-operatives in so conservative an area as West Texas. Bruno explained that the farmer produces his own crop and takes it to the gins for separation. Then it's compressed into bales and stored. The co-operatives only take care of storage and selling, and have nothing to do with production, which is left to the individual farmers.

Bruno, who grew up in California and Mexico, came to Lubbock many years ago to teach at Texas Tech. Like so many academics in the American system, he failed to get tenure. The end of his academic career may have put financial strains on his family, but it also liberated him to complete the project that has absorbed him since 1974: the construction of his steel house at Lake Ransom, which he hopes to finish before the decade is out. It seemed odd that he should have chosen so remote and unlovely a spot on which to realise his ambitious architectural fantasy. Although I was developing some affection for Lubbock myself, I never even toyed with the notion that one could choose to live there. The landscape was dreary, the climate equally brutal in summer and winter, and the city and its environs were starkly unbeautiful, proudly mundane and practical. Good barbecue, lively honkytonks, and a few decent restaurants did not add up to an irresistible environment. I asked Bruno if he liked living here.

'Yes. I used to live in southern California. The climate was beautiful, but some days I'd go for a drive and I'd pass this attractive little town with expensive houses and a golf course, and then there'd be a wooded area, and then I'd come to another little town with expensive houses and a golf course – and on it went. And I wondered what all these people did. They were well off, but there was no work for sixty miles – no factories, no farms.

'Here in Lubbock I can sense the productivity all around, and I can see that people labour for their living. They don't just work nine to five for insurance companies. Look over there. See that small yellow house? It only costs a few thousand dollars to buy a little house like that in the middle of a field, but that farm equipment in back of it is probably worth a hundred thousand, and the house is surrounded by hundreds of acres which the farmer and maybe his two sons work together. There are links between the land and the people who live on it. That's what I like about Lubbock. The land and the people depend on each other. But there's nothing romantic about it. Many small farmers here are going broke, not just because of the weather but because of the high costs of irrigating this land.'

Lake Ransom sits at the base of a small escarpment. As it's one of the few cracks in the tabletop plateau on which Lubbock sits, it was inevitable that developers should have seized on the land. Now the lakeside and the winding roads on top of the escarpment are flanked by tidy houses on tidy lots. Bruno's lot dips steeply down a cliffside at the edge of the road, and jutting forth over the cliff is an immense rusting steel sculpture that rests on four tapering stilts and is linked to the road only by a small bridge. It's like an armour-plated beast, irregular, lumpish, and swaggering. From the very top of the house projects a crane Bruno has built so that he can swing round the outside of the structure – there's a fifty-foot drop to the lakeside if he miscalculates or leans too far – and weld and shape the weathered steel skin.

'Unfortunately I have a poor head for heights. Seating myself in the bucket at the end of the arm of the crane and working on a tricky corner calls for one part skill and two parts adrenalin.'

The entire carapace is made of welded steel plate, but what makes the house remarkable structurally is that both external and interior surfaces are of the same material. The rusted skin folds in on itself and is equally visible from the inside, though

Bruno will counter the austerity of an interior made entirely of steel by applying white plastic mouldings modelled on the human form over certain surfaces. Hardwood floors and some stained glass will also moderate the severity.

When the house is completed, a drive will lead down to one of the stilts. From the car one will walk into a lift that will fill one of the stilts. The sides of the lift will be of stained glass, and will fit snugly into the leg; but since the stilt is tapered, so as the lift rises the steel will seem to peel away as you ascend to the luminous centre of the house. The other stilts will contain a library and a wine cellar, and will give access to the heating and cooling systems.

The Bruno house is on three floors. If there's a straight line anywhere other than along the floors, I didn't spot it. All the windows, and there are many, are irregular ovals, and because of the curvaceous forms of all the surfaces, all spaces, including windows, alter as you move about. Curved steel walls partition the house and divide the space; every part of the house offers glimpses of other parts, and of the outside. There are no boxy spaces; everything is linked by vault, arch, aperture, vista. From the immense top-floor study there are no fewer than nine openings that frame views onto the canyon; certain windows are positioned, as in the breakfast room, to allow the sun to fall on the right spot at the appropriate time of day.

Despite the irregularity of the structure, the last thing Bruno wants is discomfort. His plump features suggest a fondness for good living, and his exquisite furniture was ample evidence of refinement. He showed me the main staircase of the house, a lazy spiral. Each step, I pointed out, was of a different height – sculpturally intriguing, but surely a damn nuisance when you're walking up and down.

'Ah,' said Bruno, 'what you don't see is that each step will be covered with walnut boards, and those boards will also be of different heights so as to even out the steps. What I'll have is two irregular elements that will combine to form an entirely regular whole.'

The house began conceptually after Bruno had built a large sculpture on stilts. Standing underneath it one day, he thought to himself that it would be thrilling to live inside such a sculpture. Soon afterwards he began to convert the design into one for a habitable sculpture. 'I'm still designing it as I go along. The conception is quite clear to me, but I have no hard and fast blueprint in my mind. New ideas come to me as I work. Remember, when you look at this house, that I have no architectural training. Academics are always telling students to master technique before they attempt to produce original work. But for me it's more important to have a conception, and once that's clear to me, I'll find a way to realise it, bring it to life.

'I do want this to be a comfortable house, but I also want it to reflect the environment. The South Plains is a primitive place, the weather is primitive, nothing ever happens here by halves, and the house, I hope, derives its power from that. But I also want it to be delicate and human.'

Two Ranches: Pitchfork and Cadillac

Water, water, everywhere . . . but in the Panhandle, a third of the annual rainfall in two days is a cruel joke. The cotton fields were under water, and yields, it was estimated, would be down about forty per cent for the second year in succession. The government assists the cotton farms by a payment-in-kind programme, which gives the farmers surplus cotton to sell in exchange for an undertaking to reduce the acreage under cultivation. This scheme cuts down the surplus and keeps prices up. In other words, Mickey Mouse economics, and still the price of cotton has scarcely risen in over thirty years.

Cattle ranching is less vulnerable to the batterings of the climate than cotton farming. On the other hand, the rancher has to fight for every nutritious blade of grass that pierces the arid surface of the rolling prairies. The ubiquitous mesquite tree, which, it sometimes seems, would sink roots into your feet if you stood still for long enough, not only provides scant nourishment for cattle, but inhibits the growth of other more wholesome grasses. Water, the *sine qua non*, is present deep under the surface, but must be coaxed out of the ground with windmills.

An eager woman called Maisie at the Ranching Heritage Center in Lubbock told me what it was like growing up in a spot without access to underground water. 'Rainwater was the only source we had for drinking and for washing clothes. The cattle drank from a creek but it wasn't good for people. Creek water makes you sick at your stomach. This wasn't that long ago – I'm fixin' to be forty-two.'

Because of the poverty of the land, the acreage required for each head of cattle was astonishingly high, anything from twelve to thirty depending on the location. That meant there was no such thing as a small ranch; it is almost impossible to raise cattle on fewer than 1000 acres. Old-style family farms and ranches are no longer practicable, and corporate farming is on the increase here as elsewhere in the United States.

A hundred years ago, in the heyday of ranching, the largest spreads covered up to three million acres. Those were the legendary times of the great cattle drives north to Kansas and beyond, where the cattle were fattened and slaughtered. The development of the railways at the turn of the century made the long drives obsolete. But it was still necessary to move the livestock to the loading stations, and until recently cattle were still being shipped out of Texas to California for fattening. Then in the late 1950s Texan ranchers realised it was stupid to ship cattle and then grain to far-away places, when they could fatten their livestock closer to home. Large-scale feed lots were set up, allowing Texas cattle to be fattened into succulence and profit before being dispatched. Feed lots in turn encouraged the cultivation of cattle corn, which has led to the increasing diversification of Texas farming; far more grain is being grown here than ever before.

The Ranching Heritage Center has collected old structures – farms and chuckhouses and outbuildings – that have been transported intact from their original location, reconstructed, and then restocked, when possible, with their contents. Maisie showed me a dirt-floor cottonwood cabin from the Matador Ranch that her uncle had occupied in the 1930s when he was a cowboy; he'd burnt his name into one of the logs and it was still there. I saw schoolhouses that had been moved from place to place across the prairies on a sled, according to local need. But ranching as a way of life is not extinct. Although the vast Panhandle ranches – Matador, XIT, Spur – were broken up long ago, ranching is still big business. Farmers usually live on their property; ranchers rarely do. The Matador, like some others in the Panhandle, was owned for decades by a syndicate of Scottish businessmen. Most ranches are still controlled by syndicates or corporations, and their daily operations are supervised by a resident manager rather than by the owners.

Pitchfork Ranch is no exception. Founded in 1883, it's the last of the great nineteenth century ranches to survive in this area. While other ranches were selling off parts of their estates, Pitchfork was slowly expanding, not just in Texas, but into Wyoming and Kansas, where the different climates and grazing conditions made it possible to control the growth of livestock more economically. Pitchfork's total acreage is approximately 200,000. Owned by a group of St Louis businessmen, it is managed by Jim Humphreys, who has been there since 1948 and is only the fourth manager in a century.

Early one morning I drove east from Lubbock through the

sodden cotton fields. So flat is the landscape that any sign of verticality is dramatic: a clump of trees around a farmhouse seems defiantly pushy in an environment where the local crop rises only a few inches above the dark surface of the land. Telephone poles that would be unnoticed elsewhere march boldly across the temporary lakes of ruined cotton and up the endless straight roads. The outlines of the simple frame houses have an exactitude of definition, so precisely can their form be measured against the immensity of the skies. And then after about forty miles there's a tension in the landscape: its relentless unfolding ahead no longer seems predictable and secure. It all remains flat as glass, but the horizon is tentative. Suddenly it all becomes clear. The regular fields give way to a spasm of scrub and cactus, and then the road swiftly dips down and a vast panorama hits the eye. It's the Caprock, of course, and here near Crosbyton at one of the most spectacular edges of the escarpment, the plateau drops hundreds of feet into a jumble of hillock and canyon and creek. The South Plains were behind me, and I was back in the scruffy rolling prairie of North Central Texas.

*

Turning right under the tall spindly arch lintelled with the sign PITCHFORK RANCH, I drove up to a small compound containing a few houses, the ranch offices, the chuckhouse, various outbuildings, and some welcome trees. Pitchfork is spread over large tracts of Dickens and King counties. King is about thirty miles square, but has only five hundred inhabitants, most of whom live in Guthrie. A few other people live on the ranches, but the numbers are astonishingly small: no more than twenty-five workers and their families live on the 165,000 acres of Pitchfork's holdings in Texas. Such towns as there are have lost population. Jim Humphreys would tell me: 'Used to be on Saturday nights you wouldn't find a place to park in Spur, but now the younger people have mostly gone. Now they're left with mostly widders.'

Jim's a heavy white-haired man in his sixties, a paunch slipping down over his cowhide belt. Wearing clothes that didn't match and a battered straw hat, he looked dishevelled, not quite at ease in his position of authority. People in Lubbock had spoken warmly to me of this slow-moving, slow-speaking, somewhat ponderous man. Ranching is steady, stable work, not an occupation for those who like variety and kicks. The turnover rate on these large ranches is low, with the exception of single men who do move from spread to spread.

Jim ushered me into his 'rig', a large battered car, and we drove off to the north-east section of the ranch. The land we were traversing, bumpily, along dirt roads, was among the best on the ranch, and it was here that the farming, as opposed to ranching, operations took place: wheat, cane, sorghum, are all grown here. The enemy is not so much the miserable soil or lack of water – Pitchfork is littered with windmills and cisterns – as the mesquite trees that hunch over the prairie. Some of the trees were dead, others lay uprooted on their sides, others were thriving, with their wispy leaves and tenacious roots.

'We sprayed the mesquite some time ago,' rumbled Jim, 'and after two years we went in with Caterpillars and anchor chains to tear the stuff out. But you can't eradicate it easily. Those taproots, they can spread for thirty feet. Cut it off at the ground, it'll come right back. Cut a single stem, it'll come back multistem.'

By the verges of the road grew a rough profusion of plants: sage, beargrass, careless weed, cockleburs. 'Cockleburs won't grow on real sorry soil – their being here is a sign of good land. But they're sort of a nuisance. They stick to your clothes and to the horses' tails.'

Pitchfork, which is about twenty-five by sixteen miles square, raises about 7500 head of cattle and a thousand pigs. The ranch has its own grain elevator and feed mill, but they can't fatten all their livestock on feed lots. 'That's why we bought that good grassland up in Kansas and Wyoming. Grass gains are often a lot cheaper than grain, especially the way grain prices are these days.' Cattle bound for Wyoming are no longer transported by rail. 'We used to drive our cattle north through the Swensen land to a railroad shipping point, but it closed down in the 'sixties. Very few railroads will haul livestock any more. They can make more money shipping coal or something heavier and less messy. We can truck 'em to Wyoming in eighteen hours, but it sure is expensive.'

On our way to check a windmill, we spotted a coyote darting across the road ahead of us; it paused and cheekily cocked its head at us until we'd driven by. Nimble as foxes, sleek and arrogant, coyotes have an aggressive beauty – and a taste for sheep which makes them especially unpopular with sheep-raising ranchers. Pitchfork has 118 windmills scattered over its lands, and employs two men solely to maintain them. No water, no ranch. The shallowest well, close to the creek, is 28 feet deep, but elsewhere the water is drawn up from a depth of 500 feet. 'Two hundred's about average. The water don't have a good taste, but for livestock it's OK. Cattle'll go for rainwater if they can get it, and I don't blame 'em.'

Ranch hands and cowboys work long hours. They'll breakfast at 6.30 and return for dinner at noon and then for supper at 6 – sometimes later, depending on the work to be done. Cattle drives, even short ones, are a thing of the past, and although the fundamental needs of cattle haven't altered over the years, major changes have come to the ranching business. Some days later I was talking to the quarter-horse breeder and novelist Jack Walker and was surprised to learn that he'd grown up on a Panhandle ranch north of Amarillo and had worked with Pitchfork and Four Sixes cattle.

'We used to dread unloading any of Pitchfork's livestock when it was being shipped up here. Don't know why, but they had the wildest cattle I ever seen. Ranching's different now, and I'll tell you why. It's the horse trailer that's revolutionized it. In my day a cowboy would have to ride two, three hours just to get to the section for his day's work. Now they put their horse in the trailer and take the pickup out to the section. Saves hours each day.'

Sure enough, when Jim and I returned to the compound shortly before noon I saw drawn up by the chuckhouse half a dozen horse trailers. There are other innovations too. Like many other large spreads, Pitchfork leases a helicopter. 'Still,' said Jim, 'the guy who flies it needs to be a cowboy as well as a pilot.'

A lean, angular man in boots, jeans, and a pale blue shirt came up to us; his hard features were shaded by a fawn-coloured hat, as meticulously creased as his face.

'Are you Jim Humphreys?'

Jim grunted.

'Then you're the man I'm looking for. DeWayne Wilkins is the name. I'm lookin' for ranch work, had plenty of experience.'

'Well, I don't have anything I can offer right now,' said Jim gruffly but not unkindly. 'Get yourself some dinner at the chuckhouse and we'll talk later.'

At the end of the chuckhouse a counter divided the room from the kitchen beyond; it was stacked with plates and jugs of tea and water. A swing door led onto a porch that ran the length of the room, and as I entered the chuckhouse I saw the cowboys moving onto the porch from the grassy area where they'd parked their trailers. They hung up their hats before coming through the swing doors. Nobody sat down until a bell rang, and then they moved swiftly to their places at the long refectory table and helped themselves energetically from large platters heaped with T-bone steaks, french fries, a salad speckled with cheese and tacos, and the unavoidable beans. While some were loading their plates, others strode to the counter and filled their mugs with the beverage of their choice. Nobody spoke. There was the clink of ice in mugs, and the slurp of sauces being coaxed out of bottles.

How fast they ate! And as soon as they'd finished they bore their plates and mugs to the kitchen sink and rinsed them. No Campari while waiting for the dinner bell, no lingering over petits fours and coffee. I tried to chat to the cowboy next to me; he did respond monosyllabically but was more intent on devouring his pound of flesh. I couldn't blame him: he'd probably been up since 5 and had last eaten at 6.30. Opposite me sat a young cowboy with a moustache and flamboyant yellow bandana. He eyed me suspiciously. 'Where you say you from?'

'England.'

'Uh huh.' Ominous pause while he gathered his aggression. 'How come you folks aren't supportin' us in Grenada?'

It was a few days after the heroic American conquest of Grenada and reports of the British government's reservations had trickled back even to the Panhandle. The last thing I wanted was a political row with a belligerent cowboy, so I murmured uncertainly: 'I'm not sure, but I suspect it had something to do with the fact that Grenada is a Commonwealth country.'

He nodded, holding about a quarter-pound of charred steak impaled on his uplifted fork, then said: 'In that case, they oughta have gone in, done it themselves.'

Although no more than ten minutes had passed since the summoning by bells, the room was almost empty, and apart from the murmur of Jim's interview with DeWayne and the rattle of crockery being rinsed and stacked, the only sound, but one that resonated across a culture, was the swishing of leather chaps and the jangling of spurs. There were no courtesies here. Routine, decorum, yes, but a total absence of conviviality. A visitor such as myself had no place on the ranch and the cowboys were not disposed to make room for me. Their meal over, they sauntered out and leaned against a fence, smoking cigarettes or sliding some Skoal tobacco behind their gums. They'd been taciturn over their meal, but were chatting among themselves now. I didn't join them. My failure to belong was too conspicuous, the gap between us too great for either side to attempt to bridge it in the middle of a working day. I said goodbye to affable Jim Humphreys and drove out through the gates in my inappropriate Toyota, and turned back towards Lubbock. I passed a field full of fluffy wild turkeys, and twenty minutes later I climbed the Caprock and found myself back on the treeless plains.

*

North of Lubbock the outlook over the plains is, if possible, of an even more excruciating dullness. Huge flashy sunsets and the accidental geometry of the spacial relation between the few objects on the horizon do provide some slight diversion, but the unrelieved hedgeless tedium of duplicated areas of wheat and potatoes seems the perfect landscape in which to go mad.

Aching for contrast, I turned off the main road at Canyon and drove twelve miles or so to the Palo Duro Canyon State Park. It is, of course, the Caprock again, here performing a spectacular feat of expressionist landscaping, but with the help of the Prairie Dog Town Fork of the Red River, which has carved canyons up to 800 feet deep out of the escarpment. Some of the sedimentary rock layers have proved more resistant to erosion than others, with the result that pillars of mudstone and sandstone, quaintly dubbed the Lighthouse or Sad Monkey, stand unsteadily on the canyon floor. The shelter beneath the cliffs and the access to watercourses are congenial to rare shrubs and grasses, which in turn attract up to 200 species of birds. Above the Caprock, to the west, Nature is synonymous with crop – if you can't pick it for profit, it shouldn't, and probably doesn't, exist. The theatrical maw of Palo Duro is more hospitable, and it's not only birds that enjoy the grubs and the shelter.

Indian tribes frequented the canyon, and in 1874 the famed Indian fighter Colonel Ranald Mackenzie more or less eradicated the Comanche threat to the Panhandle by sending his troops down the cliffs and into the heart of the Indian encampment. Most of the Indians and their squaws were able to escape out of Palo Duro. This didn't trouble Mackenzie at all. He destroyed their supplies and fourteen hundred horses, and that was sufficient to bring these most ferocious and volatile of Indian warriors to a literal standstill. Horseless, the Comanche couldn't hunt, and certainly couldn't raid and kill. Mackenzie's brilliantly executed onslaught emasculated the Comanches and provided the security that made possible the first settlement of the Panhandle. Two years later Charles Goodnight set up one of the first Panhandle ranches here in the canyon.

The sun was dipping low and the warm colours of the sunset were hotting up, so I pressed on to Amarillo to the northwest, as I was anxious to find a suitably horrible motel before dark. I succeeded. I've nothing against boring towns – I'd taken quite a fancy to Lubbock – but at first glimpse Amarillo struck me as a hole, and by the time I departed I hadn't changed my opinion one jot. Of course Amarillo isn't in the charm or tourist business. The city isn't even a hundred years old, and its efforts have gone into the exploitation of the three commodities that have brought it wealth: agricultural produce, livestock, and helium. The stockyards here are authentic and functioning. Each year 500,000 head of cattle are sold, making Amarillo the largest cattle auction centre in the world. The *Amarillo Livestock Reporter* gives weekly details of rainfall, steer trends, hot carcass prices, contrasting reports on feeder cattle and slaughter cattle, and monitors political and legislative changes that will affect the industry. Acres of wooden pens and feed lots spread out behind and around the auction ring, and the sound and smell of thousands of snorting cattle are inescapable.

On a hillock in the northwest corner of town is its monument to helium, for beneath the dreary acres that surround Amarillo lie a large proportion of the world's helium resources. Neat steel gas tanks and pipelines demurely clutter fields the size of Liechtenstein, giving little indication of the riches which those helium deposits have brought to farmers and entrepreneurs in the region. Helium isn't much to look at, but Amarillo's other distinguishing features are more open to inspection.

Old Amarillo, such as it is, survives in the form of substantial mansions on Polk Street, erected by magnates at the end of the last century, and I would also draw the visitor's attention to the Ramada Inn, which could be a stage set for the Borneo National Opera production of *Lucia di Lammermoor*. Additional whimsy twitters coyly from streets named after twelve-year-old girls: Lynette, Linda, Janet. Amarillo may be dowdy, but it has its share of tycoons, such as the resplendently named T. Boone Pickens, Jr, who owns Mesa Petroleum, and the helium magnate Stanley Marsh III. Marsh, whose assets are inert and invisible, has found other ways to leave his mark on Amarillo. He is known in Texas as an eccentric and an enthusiast for the avant-garde – much the same thing in Texas. His most celebrated act of patronage is Cadillac Ranch (not to be confused with his home Toad Hall). About ten miles out of town on legendary Route 66, ten vintage Cadillacs have been lined up in a row and buried nose down in the middle of a field. Only the bonnets are underground; the rest of the cars rise from the earth to form a collective ten-fin salute. So well known has Cadillac Ranch become that when the Hard Rock Café in Los Angeles pinched the idea and thrust a 1959 Cadillac into their roof, the three artists who devised the Ranch promptly sued for a million dollars on the grounds of 'image appropriation'.

The image is indeed extraordinarily potent. Perhaps it was achieved with more luck than calculation, but Cadillac Ranch resonates as sonorously as abbey bells. Frivolous it may be, but the frivolity is literally rooted in the soil. Cadillacs were, and among pimps and Texans still are, status symbols, yet here their existence is shown to be as transitory as our own: all things must come to rust. And then the display of Cadillacs that date from 1949 to 1963 provides a far from uninteresting commentary on the history of American design. Cars, notorious examples of planned obsolescence, here both embody their disposability and their resilience in the face of it. Neatly junked, they've become immortal. Cadillac Ranch also illustrates the character of the Panhandle. Put anything in the middle of a field that stretches as far as the eye can peer, and chances are you'll improve the landscape. No one complains that Cadillac Ranch has messed up the scenery or wrecked the view.

A decade of visitors has added a splendour of graffiti to the original conception. Fiona from England has signed her name with a spray can, someone else has daubed KISSING UNDER THE CADDIES, and I also spotted the flowing black-painted scrawl ANGEL AYALA, which I take to be a learned and witty reference to Trollope's little-read novel *Ayala's Angel*. Graffiti usually detract, they deface and belittle; asserting the presence of even the most crass individual corrupts the dignity of, say, the Duomo in Florence. Here, though, graffiti seemed an appropriate, even necessary contribution. Themselves the objects of nostalgia, the Cadillacs were serving as a magnet to inscriptions whose primary purpose, other than self-advertisement, was as an investment in nostalgia. An Italian cathedral will last for as long as acid rain permits, but Cadillac Ranch is certain to disintegrate gradually, as rust and rot eat away at it. Let it take its own commentary with it.

Further north is another alteration to the landscape, more grandiose than Cadillac Ranch but less successful. About ten miles up a side road a few mesas rise from the land, and the artist Andrew Leicester constructed a sky-coloured strip that is wound round the mesa some fifty feet or so below the top. The effect is to give the impression that the upper part of the mesa is floating unsupported in the air. Lovely idea, pointless and flamboyant, only the sky tiresomely changes colour, even in the Panhandle, and doesn't always match the artificial strip.

It wasn't easy to eat in Amarillo. There's good barbecue available, but most BBQ places are closed by eight, which is just the time that my appetite leaps up. Dinner at 6.30 followed by an entire evening either watching television or counting the trucks on Interstate 40 was not an inviting prospect. I was quite tempted by the Big Texan Steak Ranch, where you can order a 4½-pound steak and won't get charged for it if you can finish it in under an hour. (A patron in 1977 wolfed it down in eleven minutes, still the record.) Conceptually amusing, but did I really want to observe, let alone participate in, such exercises in Brobdingnagian appetite? I ended up at a roomy place just down the highway called Texas Tumbleweed. With a name like that you can be certain that it's a chain restaurant, and even if it's not, the food will undoubtedly resemble, even aspire to, the cuisine of a franchised operation. Which is not to say it would be bad – only predictable. I was drawn to this particular steakhouse by its proximity, the live music, and the cheap special. The pretty waitress did her best to conceal the existence of the catfish special, but I wasn't put off. As she walked off towards the kitchen with my order, I was reminded, as I was every time a waitress came by, of the writer Richard West's remark about someone who wore jeans so tight you could read the date on the quarter in her back pocket. Yes, indeed.

The folksy Western style was all-encompassing: menu, waitresses, live but mediocre music from the band, and planks on the walls painted with such chortle-making slogans as NO HAT STEALIN'!, REMEMBER THE DUKE, and PRIVATE SIGN: DO NOT READ! Back came Wanda with my salad and soft rolls (blandnesses required by law to be served before steak dinners anywhere in the United States). Her big milky smile creased as she trotted out one of the ten sentences she'd been taught during waitress training: 'Is everything all right? Anything else I can get you?'

'The wine?' She'd forgotten it.

'All righty!'

Back she came. 'Hope you're enjoying your meal!'

'Thank you.'

'You're welcome.'

The trouble with this ultra-friendly repartee is not so much its insincerity – 'How are you tonight?' she'd greeted me, as if I were a regular who suffered from uncertain health – as its inhibition of any real response. Give an honest answer to those formulaic questions, and the result would be embarrassment. Not that Wanda couldn't have coped. She hadn't been through waitress training for nothing.

When, after I'd spun out my meal to the limits of my tolerance for dim country music, Wanda returned with my change, she mouthed: 'Come back and see us again real soon.' I nodded, and picked up the receipt. Across the back she'd scrawled: 'Happy Trails, Wanda.'

*

The trail down which me and my little ole Toyota cantered at sunrise the next day was called Interstate 27, and I was making tracks for Hereford. It was foggy and cool, appropriate weather for Halloween. A local radio station was advertising haunted houses – three in Amarillo alone – where kids could go for a good scare, and running a competition in which women were invited to 'phone up and scream as loudly and horribly as possible down the airwaves.

Hereford is named not after the county town in England but after the cow. Texas, after all, is the only state with more cattle than people. The beast was well represented throughout the fringes of town, which seemed to consist of little other than vast feed lots, some of which can fill the bellies of up to 100,000 head. The smell was a treat. Hereford, indeed the whole of Deaf Smith County, of which it is the seat, is resolutely, uncompromisingly agricultural. If you want to talk here, you talk onions and heifers. Travellers unfortunate enough to pass through this thriving but noisome town can escape from the aroma of cowshit by taking refuge in the National Cowgirl Hall of Fame. Alternatively, they can follow my example, and flee.

Driving south I came to Dimmitt, the seat of Castro County and a major producer of grain sorghum, corn, and vegetables. Despite the semi-arid climate, the land, irrigated by water drawn from the subterranean Ogallala Formation – true fact – is rich and fertile. Dimmitt, like many other High Plains communities, is visible from far away, thanks to the grain elevators that rise like white castles from the horizontal land. These palaces of grain, linked concrete canisters lined up like cigar tubes, have a sculptural quality that can be quite beautiful. As the only structures of any real size on the plains, they have a monumental presence, gathering into their cool concrete recesses the produce of the surrounding expanses.

I took out the map Sheri had drawn for me in Abilene, and following her directions came to the elevator owned by her family. Her father and uncle didn't seem too surprised by my appearance and were happy to show me round. From the walkways along the tops of the bins, the view was impressive. The absence of contours between Dimmitt and the horizon added to the sense of height, and my perch of 130 feet, while high enough, seemed immensely lofty as I looked down on the minuscule houses and out over the implacable fields. The grain rattles along belted trays and up the sides of the elevator and is poured into the bins from near the top; another system of belts allows grain to be transferred from bin to bin. Some contain enormous fans that cool and dry so as to prevent spoilage, and from time to time the grain must be aired or turned to keep it in good condition. This particular complex, with a capacity of about 3 million bushels, is slightly larger than average, but the place is run with the help of no more than a manager and two unskilled workers. Grain elevator operators are middlemen; they may occasionally buy grain from a local farmer, but more usually they earn their living by collecting storage fees from farmers or government agencies that use their facilities.

The view from the top induced mild agoraphobia, and riding up and down the bins in a tiny noisy lift almost brought on a fit of claustrophobia, so I was relieved to find myself on terra firma again. I also found myself covered with dust, but a special blower near the exit blasted away every speck by the time I re-emerged into the yard. Back at the office I gave Sheri's relatives a fairly full report on her welfare – fulsomely couched but with a distinct absence of detail, since I hardly knew her – and then I vanished into the South Plains, where I counted the telegraph poles and prayed for hills.

The Greatest Guy in the Whole World

Back in Austin I'd attempted to open a bank account. No problem, except that it wouldn't be possible to cash a cheque at any other place apart from that specific bank. The reason for this absurdity is that branch banking in Texas is against state law. A few of the more powerful banks have formed holding companies, which allows them to purchase other banks, but even when two banks in separate cities are owned by the same company, those banks may not share services. I thought I'd ask Don Earney to sort out what was going on. Earney is a man with the rare distinction of having owned seven banks and lost them all in a matter of days. On my way back through Abilene I went to see him.

A small dapper man with a neat moustache, the kind of man who never carries his own luggage, Earney welcomed me into his small suite of offices a few blocks away from the only tall building in town, which happens to be Abilene National Bank, of which he'd been president until the previous year. A smoker, Earney automatically slid a large ashtray over his large desk towards me. It rattled. Four bullets skidded about inside it. On the walls were Western prints, and in a corner sat a shoe-cleaning machine such as one occasionally sees in what used to be British Rail hotel corridors.

Earney declared himself sternly opposed to branch banking. The inconvenience to would-be users such as myself was, to him, a lesser consideration than the fact that it removed decision making from local areas to the big cities. Directors of bank holding companies in Dallas or Houston could never have the intimate knowledge of a local economy that an independent banker in a smaller town could. Moreover, powerful bankers in the cities had little interest in the needs of more far-flung corners of the state. 'They've got some big company in Dallas that's after tens of millions of dollars for some development, and next to that a little ole million-dollar loan out in Abilene isn't going to look that important.'

It was the slump in the oil market that did Earney in, just as it ruined so many other men who had profited from the boom of the early 1980s. Abilene, like Midland further west, had prospered mightily while oil prices were high. Those good times were over. With prices falling, exploration and drilling and pumping had involved greater risks for smaller rewards – and many middle-level entrepreneurs were in serious trouble. It wasn't only the men in the field that had been burnt by the slump; investors and bankers had suffered too. Over six years Earney had doubled and redoubled the assets of Abilene National and turned it into the third largest independent bank in Texas. He'd made money, lots of it, but he also loaned a great deal. As the oil business boomed, the loans grew larger and, some said, less judicious. Oilmen became over-ambitious; huge loans were made that would never have been extended in times that were more economically tranquil, and when the prices slumped many of those loans were uncollectable. A combination of false rumours, inaccurate press stories, and, according to Earney, sinister pressure from some federal agencies, shook the foundations of the bank, as they were intended to do. Days later Abilene National was taken over by Mercantile of Dallas. 'One day I owned seven banks and a week later I wasn't worth shit – though I've still got my home and my lovely family.'

Was it easy to acquire seven banks? Or just one?

'It's a lot easier than it used to be. For many years it was a totally political decision, but about five years ago that changed. All you do is you document a need for a new bank, you put a group of investors together, you find your site, and you put in your application. It's not a difficult process.' He smiled. 'It's not as difficult as writing a book.'

And how do the investors raise the capital for their venture? Why, they go to another bank and ask for a loan.

Earney's easy expansiveness struck me as very Western as well as very Texan. Did he feel he had much in common with a Texan from, say, Port Arthur?

'Of course. First you're a Texan and secondly you're a Cowboys fan. There's a lot of things Texans are very proud of, they're right to be. Here in Texas it still seems the American dream is alive. You can come here with nothing in your pocket, no family tradition or anything else, and you can still make a lot of money. If you're good at what you do, you can do very well. A lot of outsiders have come to Abilene, and they're nearly all staying.'

In Dallas I'd seen a van with the bumper sticker KEEP

TEXAS BEAUTIFUL. PUT A YANKEE ON A BUS. Didn't Texans resent outsiders? Was there no hostility towards Easterners in particular?

'None whatsoever. The only rivalry that exists is between football teams.'

*

Don invited me to stay the night and later that day I drove over to his house.

'It's too bad you weren't here on Saturday,' said Don, welcoming me. 'We'd have taken you along to a great costume party.'

'But it's Halloween tonight.'

'Yeh, but we don't have any parties tonight. They had them over the weekend, mostly. We love Halloween. Especially dressing up, the whole shooting match. Let's go find Debbie.'

Debbie is Don's second wife, very blonde and soft and gentle. Her sphere of influence was over the upstairs rooms, with their pastel colours, immense beds floating on deep pile carpets, fluffy cushions and framed photographs; while downstairs Don's spirit ruled over the pool table and gun racks. As in so many Texan houses, the main reception rooms are ceremonial. The dining-room sported a large candelabrum, but the formal room was clearly only used on occasions of state. A pool table filled another room, a green tarn of baize under soft lights. We ate in the kitchen and the rest of the evening was spent either outdoors or in the den. Colour the den brown, with low leatherette couches and armchairs, enough brass knick-knacks on coffee tables and sideboards to fill a flea market stall, a television and video recorder, a telescope on a stand, a gun in a holster strapped to the wall, two ornate wooden cabinets filled with rifles, a harpoon and a clutch of tankards, framed maps.

It was a Monday night, and throughout America that means football – yet again. Don was nervous. He had a $200 bet on the outcome of the game to be televised that night, and he was having doubts. 'I've put my money on a seven-point spread and I don't think that was so smart. Tell you what. Pour yourself a drink while I call Darrell. Did you go and see Darrell?'

I had indeed. Darrell was a businessman I'd looked up in Lubbock, but I hadn't found him much help. My attempts to draw him out had failed.

Don got through. 'Hey Darrell! How ya doin'? Is that right? Guess who's here, right here right now. Steve. Remember Steve? English guy who came to see you last week? Sure you remember . He'd like to talk to you.'

I did? Don thrust the receiver into my hand.

'Darrell? How are you?'

'Arrgh, frrarrgh, urrr.'

'Sorry, Darrell, didn't quite catch that.'

More growls and grunts and cackles. I gestured desperately to Don, trying to convey that there was a lack of communication.

'Don't mind Darrell,' said Don soothingly, stroking his moustache, 'he's had a drop.'

'Arrgh, waugh, frrargh.'

'Darrell, could you speak a bit more slowly? I'm having a little trouble understanding you.'

'Y'ah? Way-ell, goddam murtherfurker – canya ernerstan' me nah?'

'Loud and clear. Well, it's been great talking to you, Darrell, but I think Don wants to have a word with you about the game tonight, so I'm going to pass the 'phone back to him. Good night.'

'Heh heh, goddam murther –'

'He's had a few. Stroke of five and the bottle's open,' said Don, taking the receiver from me and proceeding to consult Darrell about the game.

'You know,' he told me after Darrell had given his considered advice, 'Darrell's the greatest guy in the whole world –'

'He really is,' chimed in Debbie, sloshing the ice around her Diet Tab.

'Only he does like his drink. Fact he likes to get roaring drunk most nights. He'll be hootin' and hollerin' for hours.'

'He's making good progress tonight.'

'We're not. Let me freshen your drink and I'll show you round.'

We stepped out from the den into the back yard, which was lit both by lamps in the trees and by logs blazing in a large square pit.

'Is this for barbecue?'

'No, no. The barbecue's already started over there by the pool.' The aromatic logs in the pit were just decorative, though the warmth they gave out was welcome, since the soft autumn evening was being lightly touched by a chill in the air. Don led me over to the bar by the pool and reached into the refrigerator for more ice. Unemphatic music dribbled from the extension loudspeaker nearby. The whole yard was, in fact, an additional room. There was hardly any grass, but the fences were lined by about a hundred potted plants. In the far corner Don had built a large playhouse for his daughter, and to the side a two-storey guest cottage.

The doorbell rang and we hurried indoors and down the hallway to the front. A dozen tots in improvised costumes were shuffling on the doorstep under the smiling eyes of a tall young woman.

'Trick or treat!' warbled the tots. This ancient Halloween custom has been piously maintained as a means of ensuring that vicious old people have at least one opportunity each year to hand their obnoxious little neighbours candy bars stuffed with broken glass.

'Over here, Stephen, you can help me with this.' And I followed Don into the adjoining living room where on the floor stood two buckets filled with sweets. 'Grab a handful.' I did so, and he and I lined the trembling palms of four-year-olds with sugary goodies. Twittering their thanks, they stumbled back down the long path, the sheets of their costumes trailing behind them.

'The candles!' Don cried. 'We forgot the candles!'

The path was sentried with paper sacks that had been weighted with sand, and inside each was an unlit candle. We brought them to life with cigarette lighters and soon the front lawn glowed with flickering yellow light. Down the street we could see the next troupe of infants on their way to terrorize us.

'Quick,' said Don. 'Take those buckets and fill 'em with hot water!'

I obeyed and on returning to the hall found Don hacking dry ice and flinging it into buckets, which I carried out onto the porch steps. White clouds cottoned forth and hung low over the lawn. Just in time, as we soon heard the squeals of sheeted children coming up the path to bewitch us. Again we handed them fistfuls of sweets, and Don invited the whole lot of them in to admire the big black spider suspended on elastic from the lights, and the white ghost hanging from the top of a dresser in the dining room, and the pumpkin heads in the windows. We saw the burbling children off down the path, and walked back into the house. WELCOME – DON EARNEY, it said on the mat.

I went into the kitchen to help Debbie.

'Don's kids will be round later,' she told me. 'They're from his first marriage.' She looked at me with her round eyes, and went on: 'We'd like to have a baby too. In fact I've just come off the pill and we tried last night. Don called me from the office this morning to ask me whether anything was kicking.'

It is intrinsic to Texan hospitality that you tell visitors all about yourself. That's why Lyndon Johnson used to display his post-operative scars to visitors. Hell, it's only neighbourly to make strangers feel at home.

As we sank our teeth into wodges of bun and burger, and coated our lips with mustard and ketchup, Don told me how he'd started out as a paperboy and worked his way up until he owned five small newspapers, some of them weeklies. 'But I wasn't happy doing that. Newspaper owners have a lot of power, especially in a small community, but I wasn't interested in power. I was interested in making money.'

The doorbell rang again, and Debbie went to see who was there. She returned followed by a young woman whose clothing on this last night in October consisted solely of a black swimsuit and a black cloak.

'Well hi there, honey,' said Don, clearly pleased to see this vision from the black lagoon. 'Chuck with you?'

'Sure. He's in the car. He can't get out.'

Why not? Tied up? Tied down? Don took me by the arm and propelled me out of the kitchen door, followed by Esther Williams and Debbie. 'I want you to meet Chuck. He's my son. A good kid.'

Walking down the path towards the car I could discern a ghostly white figure in the passenger seat. Peering in, I saw a body swathed from head to toe in white bandages. One eye was left exposed, as was the mouth, enabling the creature within to suck juice through a straw.

Ebullient Don greeted his son, then gestured towards me. 'I want you to meet our English friend who's staying with us tonight.'

I reached through the car window and shook some bandages. Chuck's girlfriend flung her cloak on the back seat and clambered into the driver's seat. She waved. We waved. Chuck laboriously tried to raise his arm as they drove away to the country club hoping to win the prize for the best Halloween costume. They deserved to win on grounds of discomfort alone.

The football game had begun and Don was in his lair, crouching forward, elbow on knees, to follow the plays. He groaned as some padded oaf fumbled the ball.

'See that? That guy's ass is in trouble. So's mine. No way there's gonna be a seven-point spread if they play like that.'

His team collapsed. Don lost two hundred dollars, and shrugged.

*

I couldn't, Don insisted, claim any serious acquaintance with Texas until I'd done time on a drilling rig. I agreed, and the next morning Don led me into the industrial suburbs of Abilene to visit Ray Brazzel, who owns the Bandera Drilling Company. Oil companies can't function without the services provided by a host of small companies: drilling contractors, refiners, pipeline contractors, engineers. It had been these dependent firms, rather than the larger operators and distributors, who had been hurt during the slump. The boom had made it possible for Ray to expand his outfit to nine rigs, but it was proving a struggle to keep them all fully operational.

'He's been having a difficult time,' said Don. 'We've all been having a difficult time, of course, but I'm telling you this now because Ray probably won't tell you himself.'

'Why not?'

'We just get tired of saying that business is bad, so even when it's terrible we tend to say things are just fine.' (Texan boys don't cry.)

Don strode into Ray's office and introduced me. 'I don't think this fella's got much money, but maybe you can help him.'

'Think he's got friends with money?' said Ray, playing along.

Don looked me over. 'I doubt it very much.' We all laughed. 'But you can have some fun with him. Talk to him, lie a little bit, and send him out to one of your rigs.' And with that Don shook my hand and went back to town.

Ray, a lean man in his early forties, had first worked on an oil rig during school holidays, and after college he'd returned to the oilfield until he managed to buy a secondhand rig for $80,000 and set up his own company. Like any drilling company, Bandera is dependent on the operators for work. It's the operator who selects the drilling site and then hires a contractor to sink the well. In these hard times, though, it was becoming more common for operators and wildcatters, uneasy about the risk as well as the cost of drilling and extraction, to enter into partnership with rig contractors, requiring them to subsidize the drilling costs in exchange for a percentage of the profits – if any.

In the Abilene area the wells tend to be shallow, between 3000 and 4000 feet. It's rapid work to drill to 3000 – it can be done in four days with rigs working round the clock. After 4000 feet the drilling has to be done much more slowly, and it's then that the costs rise. In the far west of Texas, and on many offshore sites, oil lies at much greater depths, and the cost of exploratory drilling can run into millions, whereas the price tag on a 3000-foot well is a mere $200,000. There had been a slow but distinct improvement in the health of the industry over the past year. About 10% more rigs were in operation than there had been a year before. Ray foresaw an even steeper increase in activity over the next year.

'Do other people in the oil business agree with that?'

'I don't know if they agree, but if they don't, they'd be wrong.'

On the intercom Ray summoned Charles, the tool pusher – a kind of oilfield foreman – on Bandera No. 5 and told him I'd be going out to the site with him shortly. Charles was a big toe of a man, who seemed both dependable and unapproachable.

'Roughnecks are independent-minded,' said Ray. 'Like most Texans. If someone ever tried to unionize on the oilfields, it would be the roughnecks as much as the operators who'd throw them off. The roughnecks like to control their own destiny. It's a tough life, but that's what they enjoy. They earn enough to drive a beat-up old car out to the rig and to drink a few beers in the afternoon. Often they're members of the same family – they like to work with people they trust. My brothers were roughnecks like me.'

'Has the work changed since you were on the rigs yourself?'

'There's been some technical changes, but the job is essentially the same as I used to do.'

Charles put his head round the door. He was ready to go, and I followed him in my car. We drove east about sixteen miles into Shackelford County, 900 square miles of dry sandy hills. I trailed Charles's pickup onto a dirt road. My Toyota wasn't built for high speeds on rough roads, and the pickup ahead of me soon disappeared from view. Although there were forks in the road, it was easy for me to find the way simply by following the clouds of dust kicked up by the wheels ahead of me. I eventually spotted, lancing the sky from behind a hillock, the unmistakable Meccano-like outline of a drilling rig, a hundred feet tall and stylishly painted in Bandera's blue and yellow colours. Descending the last crest I saw below me the rig platform and the small parking area hacked from the mesquite-dotted hills. I parked, donned the hard hat Ray had given me, and climbed the two steep flights onto the platform itself. Charles tried to answer some questions I put, but the noise was deafening and I caught little of what he was saying. On the far side of the rig were pits filled with muddy water to provide the fluid essential for drilling. In dry country such as this, water has to be hauled in by truck after the pits have been dug. The primary function of the water is to bring the earth and rock loosened by the drilling bit to the surface; pumps regulate the flow of fluid in and out of the hole.

Roughnecking is repetitive work. Pressing down on the bit are lengths of thirty-foot pipe. This well was relatively shallow and so the thirty feet of pipe had pressed into the hole after only twenty minutes. The principal task of the roughnecks is to detach the bushing that spins the pipe and attach to it a new length. New pipe, which is kept in vertical stacks on the platform, is screwed on with chains, then the bushing is replaced and slotted into the platform. Then drilling continues until it's time to attach the next section of pipe. The work is routine, but dangerous too. Miscalculate for an instant and your fingers could be tutti-fruttied between rapidly spinning chain. Words, whether of instruction or warning, are useless on the platform – the noise is volcanic – and communication flickers from the eyes or hands. To add to the clamour, the platform would suddenly start to shake and rattle and roll as the bit, that had been drilling through shale, hit harder rock.

While new pipe was being tripped in, I kept out of the crew's way and waited in the doghouse on the side of the platform.

Here the men keep their clothes, lunch boxes and other possessions; here too are the charts and instruments that monitor the progress of the drilling. After the new pipe had been attached, James Irwin came in and made some notations on a chart. He certainly looked like a roughneck: he was an immense man of about twenty-five with reddish hair and a florid weathered face. His overalls were smeared with grease and oil, and sweat ran down his gammony neck. Despite his ferocious appearance, he was more willing to chat than Charles. I asked him how long he'd been at this work.

'I've been doing it right out of high school. If you live in a small town around here like I do, it's the only way to make some decent money.'

He denied that the work was dangerous, except when something unexpected happened, such as a chain breaking. But to judge from a log of injuries posted in the cabin, serious injuries were not uncommon. Minor damage, such as a fractured finger, resulted in no days lost, but a hernia had put someone out of commission for sixty days, and an eight-inch cut on a knee had sent another man off the platform for ninety-six days. I was seeing the rig operating under ideal conditions on a sunny morning. The rigs drill round the clock with four men on each of three tours (pronounced towers) and in all weather conditions. At 3 a.m. on a February morning the picture might look very different. And if it's snowing?

'It don't make no difference,' said James.

James was a local man, but Tom from Gary, Indiana, was typical of another group of oilfield workers. He'd moved south to make a new start after his divorce. There were few jobs in the north, but here in the Sunbelt Tom had both found a job and hung on to it. He didn't find it too arduous, though the work on deep wells, where the drilling proceeds more slowly, could be tedious. Slender, well-built, he sported a pale moustache and long hair that was ragged with sweat. His white T-shirt had also grown a darker shade of pale as a result of his morning's exertions.

He'd come into the doghouse to munch on a sandwich, and seeing him eat made me hungry too. I'd brought no food with me. Then I remembered I still had the jerky Doug had given me, and I went back to the car to find it. Seated by the open door of a station wagon next to my car was the mud engineer.

I'd seen John earlier, a small bespectacled man, not dressed for rough work. He'd been checking the charts with James and crouching near the water pits. His job was to regulate the injection and extraction of fluids into and from the well. The process varies according to the stage of the drilling and the kinds of formations the bit is encountering two thousand feet or more below the surface. Sometimes the water must be treated with chemicals, and it's the mud engineer who decides what's required and when the fluid needs to be changed. He intimated that his skilled profession is not held in high regard by his comrades in the industry.

As he talked I chewed on my jerky, and the hot spicy flavours climbed up and down my throat. Wonderful stuff, but it made me as parched as a dry hole. James spotted me making for the tap. 'That's awful cold water,' he warned. 'Got some over here that ain't near so cold.' I let the tap run for a moment to ensure it wasn't flaked with mud or some of John's noxious chemicals, then slaked my considerable thirst. The noise was getting to me by now, and my temples felt as tender as a dartboard. The crew were too busy to talk much and their work scarcely varied. Charles had driven off without a word, so I said goodbye to James, and then headed off down the dirt road. At various forks I had to trust to my instincts, since I had no Charles to follow. As I paused to inspect a small yellow plant I hadn't seen before I could still hear, from two miles away, the regular thumping of the rig.

Paisano Pete

It was rather foolish to make a three-hundred mile detour to Dallas, but a friend from New York had casually mentioned that she would be in that city in early November to give a recital, and I'd unthinkingly said I'd do my best to meet up with her. So I pounded east across the blank countryside, Waylon Jennings on the radio ('I've always been crazy, but it's kept me from going insane') and an occasional bumper sticker to divert me: THREE THINGS THAT SET US FREE: GUNS, GOD, GUTS. Presumably in that order. A billboard advertised Lone Star, 'The National Beer of Texas', a joke that bows to a sense of cultural and even political identity that is not entirely illusory.

I drove straight into downtown Dallas to change some money. This transaction had been arranged in advance by a representative of my London bank, and I'd been assured that the whole operation would take no more than ten minutes. I bought half an hour on a parking meter, but forty minutes later I was still cooling my heels outside the office of some senior paperpusher. I dashed out to feed the meter. Tripping down the steps from the bank to the street, I had a clear view of the cop who was adorning my car with a ticket. Traffic moves slowly in sedate Dallas, so I had no difficulty zigzagging my way through stately processions of limousines and presenting myself before the cop with my account of how I'd been detained by obstructive bank officials.

'You've got yourself a ticket, mister,' he said, implacable. 'You should have been back here fifteen minutes ago.'

'I would, officer, if it had been possible. But you know what it's like –'

'And what's more, you're in line for a second ticket.'

'Why?'

'I saw you cross the street just now. Don't you know that you're only supposed to cross when the Walk sign is on? Sure you do.'

'You're right, of course, but I was eager to reach you before you slapped that ticket on me.'

'Too late. Fact, I'm considering whether to write you a third ticket. The temporary registration on this car expired two weeks ago.'

'Scribble away, officer, it's not my car. By the way, now you've ticketed me, do I still have to feed this meter?'

'No, you can stay here the rest of the afternoon if you want.'

'A bargain! Thank you, officer.' But I was not overjoyed at having been dealt my first Texan parking ticket, and as the cop walked off I tore the ticket from behind the wipers and carried it into the bank. By now I was allowed to have my money. I gratefully pocketed my dollars and demanded to see the indolent apparatchik who'd been responsible for the costly delay. I was granted an immediate interview. With eloquence that surprised even its practitioner I held the bank exclusively responsible for the parking ticket and demanded compensation. To my astonishment the gifted and perspicacious vice president of one of Dallas's great banks offered to waive commission, an offer I instantly accepted, since the ten-dollar charge would exactly pay my fine. It was a just world after all, and I was beaming with satisfaction as I once again tripped lightly down the steps to the street. Once again I glanced over to where my car was parked.

And once again a cop was writing me a ticket. I had removed the original ticket as evidence against the bank, but in so doing had stripped my Toyota of the talisman that would guard against further punishment. Two tickets in twenty minutes is an enviable achievement, and with some pride I presented myself ten minutes later at the division of the police department where motoring offences are dealt with. At the inquiry desk I informed the young lady that I was willing to pay the first fine but not the second, which was for the same offence. She was interested by my case, but said I would have to go to a court upstairs and plead with the bailiff or judge or some such official. It then occurred to me that my car was now on another meter and by the time I'd negotiated, with who knew what outcome, with the gauleiters upstairs I'd have almost certainly acquired another parking ticket, and would be obliged to spend the rest of my time in Texas incurring and discharging penalties for parking offences. So I returned to the inquiry desk and the helpful young lady. I put the issue to her. She was sympathetic but noncommittal.

My face brightened. 'I have another idea. I'm a foreigner

driving a rented car. I could, could I not, faced with the intractability of the situation, simply tear up both tickets?'

'You could . . .'

*

Dallas's most famous department store, Neiman-Marcus, presents each year a fortnight devoted to the promotion of a national style; the store is then filled with goods from one particular country, as well as entertainers and travel agents plugging the country in question. Not to be outdone, Neiman's rival Sanger Harris was mounting a Japanese festival, and it was as a contributor to these commercial festivities that my friend Sachiyo had come from New York to demonstrate her art, Kabuki dancing, on a bandstand near the shoe department. When it was over she seemed clearly relieved to see my familiar face in strange Dallas, and accepted my invitation to dinner. I took her back to her sumptuous hotel so she could change and while she was doing so I waited in the lobby and watched businessmen ordering large drinks for women of questionable virtue. Strange people, probably Canadians, arrived in limos and queued patiently at the registration desk. Bell boys lounged against the marble walls waiting for the Baron de Charlus.

Forty minutes later the lift doors slid apart and a diminutive figure in a dazzling kimono came shuffling out. Sachiyo's eyebrows had been raised by the artifice of pencil, her cheeks shone creamily, and her ebony hair was ornately gathered and secured by long pins. Her legs were constricted by the tight length of her ravishing silk kimono, but her small feet worked busily in their traditional slippers as she approached.

This Oriental jewel leaned lightly on my arm as we headed for the street. I tried to match a slow stride to her rapid shuffle. To confuse Dallas further we decided to go to a good Mexican restaurant, where we enjoyed the sheer incongruity of our presence. As we entered Chiquita's stares crossed our path like tripwires. Texas has a taste for the bizarre but not for the exotic.

*

I left the city the next day. Halfway to Abilene I found myself crossing Hog Creek and entering Desdemona, where I asked the postmistress about the origin of the name. She didn't know.

Some people maintain the village was named after an Indian maid, but no one was sure. Further on, near Alvarado, I passed a Baptist church that exhibited a fine specimen of sloganeering: A GOING CHURCH FOR A COMING LORD. Cute.

I was soon back in Comanche. Its familiarity was reassuring. The limestone buildings, the trees – in two weeks nothing had changed; it hadn't been a stage set after all. Just out of town a large sign announced that this was the day of the Dudley Brothers Annual Bull Sale. A large tent had been pitched in a field in front of a makeshift stockyard. Cars and trailers were parked nearby. What persuaded me to join them was not just the prospect of watching 204 Hereford bulls coming under the hammer, but the tables of food lined up near the entrance to the tent.

I commend to Sotheby's the admirable practice of feeding the customers an hour before a sale, as was the custom at this and other Texas livestock auctions. The Dudley bulls were far superior meat to the Calvert cattle, and a great deal of money would be exchanged before the afternoon was out. I made straight for the long trestle tables laden with brisket – carve your own – and sausages and salad. I perched uncomfortably on a fence top and balanced the paper plate on my lap while I ate. I ambled into the yellow and white tent just in time. The place was packed with men and women filling the raised benches. Well-pressed jeans, expensive boots with multi-coloured stitching and sleek felt Stetsons with ornate feathered hatbands told of the presence of prosperous ranchers as well as working farmers.

The auctioneers, Bert and Ruben, settled into their booth and four men charged with spotting the bidders stationed themselves around the pen into which the bulls would be driven lot by lot. First we were introduced to the family: Clinton and Eltos and Claude and Cameron. And then to their wives. We applauded. There was a hush as the auction began: buying bulls is a serious business, not just because you could expect to part with at least two thousand dollars but because the quality of the bull could affect the sex life of your heifers and hence the development of your herd. This was no ordinary steak: we were bidding for the offspring of Lucky Domino, Tex Husker Dom, Big Arthur, and other bulls of potency and pedigree. One by one the huge beasts, white-headed, brown-bodied, thickly humped behind the horns and with an anthology of sexual parts scraping the dirt floor, were hustled into the small pen.

'Sixteen hundred going-up-going-up-going-up sixteen hundred do Ah hear a half a half a half pullapullapullapullapulla –'

'Yay!' An unearthly shriek leapt from the throat of one of the four men who'd spotted a significant dip of the hat from a rancher in the third row. While pausing for breath the auctioneer rapped his gavel to cover any hint of uncertain silence.

'Seventeen, seventeen hundred going-up-going-up anna half anna half do Ah hear it –'

'YAY!'

*

I arrived in Brownwood just in time for the afternoon tour. This county seat boasts a Southern Baptist college, Howard Payne University, to which is appended the Douglas MacArthur Academy of Freedom. According to one of a pile of brochures thrust into my hand, the Academy 'is a fully accredited college program preparing informed and active teachers, diplomats, politicians and churchmen for the fight to strengthen our American heritage'. I pulled into the driveway and parked behind a car that had a bumper sticker informing me: GOD SAID IT AND THAT SETTLES IT. So much for inquiring minds. I hurried into the lobby and approached a girl sitting behind a desk.

'Am I too late for the tour?'

'No sir, Ah'm jest fixin' to start.' And two minutes later she beckoned me and two elderly couples and we dutifully trooped after her into the first of the Academy's five great halls, the Hall of Christian Civilization, 'where the walls are ablaze from the Wall of Light with one of the largest murals in Texas, a pictorial representation of man's relationship to God.' This monstrosity fills 2877 square feet of wall, and was executed by what a detailed explanatory booklet calls 'the individualistic' painter Charles Sweitzer. The booklet points out that the university authorities do not see eye to eye with self-taught Mr Sweitzer's symbolic interpretation of Christianity. The student showing us round steered clear of theological controversy but did point to various motifs Sweitzer had employed, such as a green serpent.

'What this means,' she explained patiently, 'is that even in the most beautiful things of the world are launched things of evil, that are not what they seem. Over on the right wall you'll see a picture of Christ with his hands outstretched. Wherever you stand in the hall, you'll find his hands are reaching out to you.'

Without the generous hands of onion magnate Dr Othal Brand signing cheques made out to the Academy, this vast painting would never have seen the light of day; nor would Sweitzer have been plucked from the obscurity of being principal muralist of the Municipal Airport at Charlotte, North Carolina, to undertake what all Howard Payne alumni agree is his masterpiece.

Next the guide led us into the Magna Carta Hall, a weird stone structure with side chapels under arches, replicas of armour along the walls. A mural depicts King John and the nobles at Runnymede, and standing among them is none other than Howard Payne University's president Dr Guy D. Newmann in his academic robes; he carries the Golden Book of Knowledge, which symbolises mail-order encyclopedias. The artist has also portrayed a Madonna-like Mother America in a bonnet, and a gormless straw-hatted Boy Texas carrying a dove, which symbolises birds. A representation of Mother Earth carries on her head a flat basket containing an onion, which symbolises the bounty of Dr Othal Brand. In the Mediterranean Hall we were shown a model of the Parthenon and replicas of the Rosetta Stone and an Egyptian temple. Finally, in a room dedicated to the college librarian Betty Ann Fudge, we were left to linger over the display cases filled with MacArthur memorabilia, including a large series of spectacularly dull letters to and from Howard Payne officials.

*

I drove southwest to Brady. There were few farms around here, and the soil was sandy and sparse; low mesquite and oak pimpled the land. Brady calls itself the Heart of Texas, and geographically that is more or less so. Brady may be at the heart of the state, but it struck me as a bloodless spot. Beyond it I crossed a hundred miles of undulating emptiness, until at the end of the day I arrived at the dull town of Sonora. I was six months too late (or too early) for the Goat Barbecue Cookoff. The only other attraction is subterranean: the Caverns of Sonora, which apparently contain some of the finest limestone formations in the world. In the morning I tried to visit them, but a brochure I'd picked up gave the wrong times for tours, and I had too far to drive that day to be able to risk spending the whole morning underground. So I drove off again, cursing the local Chamber of Commerce for misinforming tourists.

After Ozona the boring plateau country gave way to more dramatic mesa, and the Interstate sliced boldly through the hills, exposing walls of sandy-coloured rock. It was 167 miles from Sonora to Fort Stockton and I arrived at lunchtime. This town of 10,000 inhabitants is a busy place, perched over the huge triangle of land that reaches down from here to the Mexican border. As the name suggests, it was an old military post and some vestiges of the old fort and a handful of modest but charming nineteenth century structures can still be visited. There's the Old Grey Mule Saloon, and opposite it the Annie Riggs Museum, built of adobe bricks. Fort Stockton's best-known artefact is the eleven-foot-high statue of Paisano Pete the Roadrunner (not to be confused with the ten-foot jackrabbit statue in Odessa and the even larger shrimp statue in Aransas Pass). The roadrunner is a large scatty bird, long-tailed and scruffy-headed, related to the cuckoo; it prefers to run at high speed across the plateau rather than flap its wings and fly. Some bird.

I lunched at Railsback's Café on the main drag. I was the only stranger there but Mrs Railsback made me welcome. A popular *patronne*, she was greeted by all her customers as they entered. Stetsoned men sauntered from table to table, shaking hands with their friends and nodding at me as they passed. The greetings were standard.

'How ya doin'?' 'Fahn, jes' fahn.'

Conversation focused on three topics: catfishing, dog-catching, and giving up smoking. When Mrs Railsback came over with the bill, I saw printed at the top the words: SMILE. GOD LOVES YOU.

After lunch I headed south towards Big Bend, an immense expanse of mountain and desert; at its southernmost tip is the 1100-square-mile Big Bend National Park. I still had 150 miles to drive before I reached the park. On either side I could see mesa and mountain, perhaps thirty miles distant. To the left I noticed a sign: PRIVATE ROAD. DRIVE AT YOUR OWN RISK. I turned up it for a hundred yards, then stopped and walked into the desert. It was the silence that struck me as most awesome: no birdsong, no sounds of distant traffic, only the buzzing and creaking of insects hovering around splashes of orange flowers and a small purple bloom that crept along the desert floor. Cactus gesticulated all round, not just prickly pear but varieties unique to the Chihuahuan Desert, such as tall spiky lechuguilla. But it was space rather than detail that overwhelmed: mountain ranges so far off that they sat like tumorous shadows on the horizon.

South of Marathon the mountains began to loom more ominously: thunderclouds were gathering and squatting over some of the ranges. The land became more undulating as I passed the Pena Blanca Mountains and headed round Persimmon Gap; this territory appeared quite empty, yet it was all fenced. This was desert but not wilderness. Like almost every other inch of the state that wasn't parkland, this was private property. In Texas it's safe to assume that however remote the spot in which you find yourself, if you walk off the road for more than fifty yards, you're trespassing. Only inside the park did the fences vanish.

There'd been some rain that afternoon. Here in Brewster County, the largest in Texas, annual rainfall is a pityful fifteen inches, and the dessicated earth responded rapturously to the gift from the clouds. Through the open windows of the car a light breeze thrust a bouquet of herbal aromas. About thirty miles into the park I came to Panther Junction and took the fork to the west, skirting the sheer walls of the beautiful Chisos Mountains that rise to a height of 7800 feet. I drove another twenty-five miles and by five o'clock had arrived where I wanted to be: just outside the park at the ghost town of Terlingua.

*

'Are you the guy who's looking for Gil?'
    'Yes.'
    'He's just got back to the office.'
    'Thanks.' I walked back towards the small building that housed the offices of the Big Bend Trailer Park. You can pitch a tent in the National Park at specified campgrounds, and there are a very few RV (recreational vehicle) hookups, but most tourists who haul their accommodation round with them stay

just outside in one of the trailer parks. The federally managed National Park is impeccably organised; structures and signs and parking places are discreetly placed so as to minimize their intrusion on the primitive landscape. Leaving the Park and re-entering the realm of private property, one is returned to the grubby disorder of unregulated building. Big Bend Trailer Park was better than most such developments, and was attractively sited in a hollow near a creek shaded by tall cottonwood trees. Behind the offices was the usual detritus: old fridges, tyres, piping, gas canisters, you name it. On the other hand, what do you do with your heavy rubbish when the nearest town is over sixty miles away?

As I approached the office, a slight figure in white came tripping down the steps and rapidly walked towards me. Gil was a friend of a friend. When I'd 'phoned him from Lubbock he told me I was welcome to stay with him in Terlingua – indeed, I had no choice if I wanted to attend the Chili Cookoff the following day, since there wasn't a room to be had for fifty miles around. Though he didn't look the part, Gil was a shrewd entrepreneur, despite some false starts. Mercury mining had brought prosperity to Terlingua in the 1890s, and seventy years later Gil had tried to revive a mine, but with no lasting success. He'd left the area for a few years, then returned to establish the trailer park. He was also reviving a cottage industry: making wax from the candelilla cactus, which grows in profusion in Big Bend.

'I thought I'd try to get the industry going again. Make candles. Perhaps ceramics too. There are so many freeze-dried hippies left over from the 'sixties in Big Bend. They like desert life, but there's not much to do down here, and when times are hard they come and work for me.'

To the informality of West Texan couture Gil added a note of eccentricity. His white shirt and slacks were partially covered by a white apron – no affectation, since he does most of the cooking at the adjoining bar and restaurant, La Kiva – and a black top hat. His face had been repeatedly punched by the sun, and his nose had seen better days; over and around his mouth drooped a *bandido* moustache. We walked over to his own trailer, which sat on its own a few yards up a slope.

He gave me a room just by the front door, so I hardly ever had to encounter Gil's large green parrot, whose perch swung over the middle of the living room. On the floor was heavy shag carpeting streaked with parrot debris. As one would expect in a mobile home, the furnishings were cheap and nasty, except for a Caligulan bathroom en suite with Gil's bedroom. My bathroom was more conventional, though colonised by a dozen friendly cockroaches.

'The parrot won't bite you. At least I don't think he will. I moved him in here while I was having a cage specially built for him on the patio at La Kiva. That was six months ago and it's still not ready.' He sighed. 'That's what it's like round here. Nothing happens very fast. Anyhow, so the parrot moved in and I moved out. I sleep here but that's about all. During the day you'll probably find me down at La Kiva or out with the pickup. Put your stuff in your room and come over to La Kiva for a drink. I've got to go down and start the fire for dinner.'

We set off.

'I'm so tired,' he groaned. 'We had a Halloween party down here a few days ago. Adults only. And I charged ten dollars for anyone not in costume. I must say it was fun. I wore a tux a Vietnam vet made for me from old combat material and black satin. *Very* nice. And just as I'm recovering from Halloween we've got half of Texas driving down for the cookoff.'

'Like me.'

'You're no trouble – I hope. Stay as long as you like. It's just that La Kiva has the reputation of being the best bar within a hundred miles and the place gets kinda crowded.'

'Sounds like you enjoy living here.'

'I do. It's the last frontier, it really is. Hardly any of this land is settled – there's little water and few roads. It's beautiful here but I only stay six months each year, and then I go off to some place like San Francisco. But I always like coming back to the desert. It's friendly, we all help each other, and when we don't we have a nice little feud and then shake hands. You can do pretty much what you want down here – people don't give a rat's ass. We know each other but we don't socialize much. You don't give dinner parties in the desert.'

We walked down a few steps and pulled open the heavy cellar door leading into La Kiva. Most of the bar is built as a dug-out, with walls of rock, wooden ceilings, and large redwood tables. The candlelit bar is dark and cosy, but not constricting. Doors lead out onto patios where Gil does the barbecuing. There's even a stage and a pool room in a far corner. ('I don't approve of pool in bars,' said Gil with a sniff. 'That's why I make it hard to find.') He'd recently installed a satellite dish – a rarity in Big Bend – and built a viewing room, with TV and video, as an additional attraction. As Gil dashed about, checking the charcoal, greeting the regulars, haranguing the kitchen help, I realised why he wears his Mad Hatter outfit: he becomes instantly recognisable, to friend and stranger. He introduced me to a group of revellers led by a geologist from Midland, brought me a huge T-bone for my dinner, then left me to the geologists and my own devices.

Keeping Abreast

For some twenty years Terlingua has been the home of the World Championship Chili Cookoff. Throughout the year regional contests are held, not just in Texas, but in other states whose citizens, rightly or wrongly, flatter themselves that they know how to cook good chili. Regional winners then bring their pots and pans to Terlingua for a November weekend each year to compete for the world title, where they are joined by other culinary celebrities such as the winner of the Hell Hath No Fury Women's Chili Cookoff. Early on Saturday morning they set up their stalls and spend four hours cooking and stirring and seasoning. The judges only define the dish minimally: chili has certain essential ingredients, but there's room left for individual embellishments. There are those, though I was relieved not to find them at Terlingua, who insist that a few spoonfuls of diced rattlesnake do wonders for a bowl of red.

The Terlingua contest began about twenty years ago when a brazen journalist claimed in a Connecticut newspaper that he could cook better chili than any Texan – and remember that chili, according to the legislature, is the State Dish of Texas. This foolish boast was challenged by one Wick Fowler and a cookoff was held at Terlingua to settle the issue. That first year, however, no prize could be awarded: the judges declared that their mouths were too badly burnt by the chili for them to be able to decide. The following year the dispute also remained unresolved, since the ballot box containing the judges' votes was stolen by masked raiders.

After a while the contest settled down into an annual event – until this year, when a long-threatened split between two factions gashed open. The principal organizer of the original cookoff was the venerable Dallas journalist Frank X. Tolbert, whose book about chili, *A Bowl of Red*, is widely accepted as definitive. Tolbert resented what he saw as growing commercial sponsorship, though his critics claim his objection arose because he hadn't been sufficiently consulted about which sponsors were acceptable. This year the official cookoff was to take place on the hillsides of Villa de la Mina, five miles beyond

Terlingua to the west, while Tolbert's forces had pitched camp two miles away on the main road.

Which to choose? I consulted Gil. He was in no doubt: Villa de la Mina. Other local people concurred. It wasn't hard to dig out the reason: one sponsor had contributed $60,000 towards an ambulance for the Terlingua Medical Team. Here in the middle of the Chihuahuan Desert, where the nearest hospital is over sixty miles away in Alpine, such a gift was much appreciated by the sparse population of Brewster County (8000 people scattered over 6200 square miles). The locals were bitter about Tolbert's curmudgeonly behaviour, which they regarded as a combination of overblown ego, senility, and sour grapes. By the end of the weekend, the purist Tolbert had attracted twice as many cooks but far fewer visitors than the Villa de la Mina group.

A few thousand people had been funnelling into the Terlingua area all day and well into the night. To warm up the crowd a dance was to be held at Villa de la Mina, and after Gil's excellent steak I drove off to see what was happening. It was drizzling, and by the time I reached the dirt road that led to the site, a powerful storm was in noisy progress. Thunder bounced off the mountains, and pebbles of rain splashed onto my windscreen with such force that the wipers could only bat feebly against the watery scree. The track is rough in the best of conditions, but criss-crossed by fast-moving torrents of rainwater it became not only difficult to negotiate but quite dangerous: dry water-courses can carry ever larger bodies of water down them to create flash floods. In mountainous desert country, it's foolish to park a car in a gully or along a dry creek, even when the sky is blue. A storm out of sight over the next range can send fast-moving slashes of water gushing down arroyos and creeks.

I twisted the car along the stony road, around sharp bends and over steep hillocks. It was obvious that any dance planned for that night was literally washed out. But it was impossible to turn round. A convoy of powerful headlights behind me urged me onwards. Eventually the track broadened, and I was able to U-turn after a quick word with a drenched youth who confirmed that the dance was off, and I splashed my way back to Terlingua. In Gil's trailer I found my host curled up under his duvet watching a Bogart movie on television.

'That's why you bought the satellite dish! So you could watch old movies!'

'Of course. La Kiva is just an incidental beneficiary.'

So deep in the desert, with rain improbably splashing down on the roof and a large green parrot keeping me under surveillance, I watched *The African Queen*.

*

The men stooped over their Hibachis and, as thin shoots of smoke rose into a cloudless sky, coaxed the coals into hot life. From further along the hillside wafted the scent of sausages on the grill. Long-haired women in loose-fitting tunics and dresses clambered out of trailers and tents clutching coffee mugs, while small groups of burly bearded men wearing Harley Davidson T-shirts and holding cans of beer, belched into the soft morning air.

It was breakfast time at Villa de la Mina. Gazing around me, I saw quite how many people had travelled hundreds of miles to this shrine of beef and peppers. Trailers and campers, cars and motorbikes, lined the oval hillside, while down below in a hollow the contestants were getting their pots and pans ready. Hell's Angels parked their gleaming bloated machines next to neat hatchbacks from New Mexico; desert freaks in huge pickups with oversized tyres loomed over Volkswagen-loads of students from Austin.

A small group of men, some with cameras, were yelling into a tent near their own trailer: 'Aw, c'mon, c'mon, let's see 'em!' Moments later two hefty women emerged sleepily from the tent, stringy hair falling lank onto grubby grey T-shirts. The men redoubled their noises of encouragement and spread themselves over the dirt track, blocking the slow-moving traffic. The women shrugged and with a single gesture raised their shirts up to their necks, revealing pumpkin-sized breasts. The men yelled delightedly, cameras clicked, the T-shirts came down, and the women, grinning, retreated, as the men crowed: 'Hey! We blocked the traffic for titty shots!'

The reason why a couple of thousand brawny men cross state lines to be in Terlingua is not because they want to get stoned or get laid, not because they want to drink enough tequila to fill the canals of Xochimilco – though they may well accomplish all this in the course of a sleepless weekend – and it certainly isn't because more than a handful are true chiliheads. No, they come to Terlingua to look at tits.

I made my way down the stony slopes to the arena to inspect the culinary preparations. Sipping a cup of ammoniac coffee, I chatted to the helpful Sweethang Neale, who explained to me the order of events. I didn't take in a word she was saying, as I was founding a mystical order for the contemplation of her name. Chili champs are not shy and reclusive. Their cauldrons thicken a dark meaty lava fierce enough to collapse the roof of your mouth. Taste and texture and important, but so is presentation. Each stall was flamboyantly assembled, for points are awarded for showmanship as well as for gustatory qualities. Bertie Calhoun, the Louisiana state champion, and her assistant wore chef's hats and fake moustaches, clowning cooks stirring a stew in earnest. She let me taste her prizewinning brew.

'Needs a couple more hours until it's good and ready,' she cautioned as she ladled a portion into a paper cup. 'Whadya think?'

'Good, good, not as hot as I expected.'

'Quality's what counts – anyone can throw more peppers in.'

'Is your recipe much the same as a Texan one?'

'No sir. Ah use ground meat. So do most out-of-states. New Mexico, they use ground meat. But in Texas they only use cubed.'

This was important information which I squirreled away for future use.

'I suppose you used cubed meat?' I said to a brawny Texan in a straw hat who was stirring the pot at the Last Gonzo stall.

'Sure do. We won't use any ole beef in our chili. The beef you're tastin' right now costs fahv dollars a pound.'

Not every cook was willing to let aficionados sample the goods, since they needed to keep plenty for the judges, who wouldn't be sampling for another two hours or so. I had no joy at the Bottom of the Barrel or Biting Bullet stalls. At Uganda Chili the emphasis was on entertaining the crowd more than on correcting the seasoning. A team of loin-clothed men in black body make-up and blonde wigs charged round the stall, waving spears and attempting primitive war chants which resembled the yells heard at college football games – which is doubtless where this platoon usually spent its Saturdays.

At the Paine in the Ass stall, chili was also a low priority. On display was a photograph album half-filled with colour snapshots of bare-breasted women; one of the 'cooks' had a Polaroid at the ready, just in case a passing nubile wench ventured a quick flash. On the front of the stand was a blue sticker with the eloquent words SHOW ME YOUR TITS. Some of those wandering about made it equally clear what brought them to Terlingua, as their T-shirts bore the same motto. The man with the camera tried to cajole likely prospects. 'C'mon, honey,' thrusting the album towards anything female on two legs, 'we've gotta lotta extra pages to fill . . .'

Wandering back for another chat with Bertie Calhoun, I was startled to hear a strong French accent emanating from a swarthy man near her stall. The Stetson the man was wearing was a disguise, since Michel was a restaurateur from Béziers with a taste for travel. This year he'd brought his family to Texas. How, I wondered, was a master of bouillabaisse getting on with chili con carne? Michel certainly seemed to like Bertie's and she presented him with a jar of picante sauce to serve as an alternative to aïoli.

Half an hour later I heard booming from the loudspeakers the words, 'Michel, all the way from the south of France, folks,' and looking towards the stage, I saw Michel standing next to the master of ceremonies, Tex Scofield, a heavily built man in a scarlet suit studded with buttons and badges, souvenirs of a hundred other great events and promotable products. Michel was beaming and nodding as Tex told the crowd: 'Michel's gonna be a real strong contender in our Roadrunner contest this year. I want y'all to show Michel and his lovely family how glad y'all are to see 'em here in Terlingua.'

Applause all round, except from me. I know a rival when I see one. I slowly made my way to the stage and casually presented myself to Tex.

'You're from London, England? Is that right? Well, come right up on stage and let me introduce you and enter you for our Roadrunner contest. You met Michel yet? He's –'

'I know.'

Tex flicked on the mike and again asked the crowd for their indulgence. It was still morning and most people hadn't downed more than a dozen beers, so they were brightly attentive. Tex asked me to address the mob and I was happy to oblige. I brought out the trowel.

'I've come all the way from England to Texas to write a book about your great state, and it seemed a good idea to come to the heart of Texas to see the place at its best and meet its finest people. And that's why I've come to Terlingua.'

This flummery went down a treat. Tex slapped my back, then drew me aside. 'Say, Steve, is England further away from here than the south of France. Ah'm not sure.'

'I am. It's about five hundred miles further north.'

'Guess that puts you in the lead.'

'Guess it does.'

There were prizes to be won.

And now for the results. Neither Michel nor I won the Roadrunner Award. We were beaten by a girl from San Angelo, Texas, as she happened to be spending a year in Germany. It was, I told Michel, bad form that the prize had been awarded to a daughter of Texas, when he and I had traversed an ocean and half a continent to risk food poisoning and look at tits. Michel was sympathetic, but we agreed not to create an international incident and to accept our runner-up prizes. Moments later I was acknowledging the roars of the crowd as Tex placed on my head a Dodge Ram Trucks gimme cap which, with its plastic mesh top and frail adjustable strap, is so unprepossessing a piece of headgear as to constitute a veritable anti-fashion. How bizarre, even servile, this American predilection for clothing oneself in advertisement – it's a nationwide con trick to have persuaded millions that a cap or T-shirt with a visible brand name is chic.

At noon stewards called on each competitor and took away samples of their art to the hut above the stage where the experts had gathered to choose the winner on the basis of colour, aroma, consistency, taste, and aftertaste. Claret is scarcely less complex. Chili's origins may have had to do with concealing the fatigue of decaying meat, but these days the ingredients are fresh, and the dish exists as a form of aggression, a macho war against the tastebuds, a Texan denial of refinement and finesse, the generation of a gustatory heat that can flay effete stomachs and induce terminal conflagration in cold-blooded Yankees.

'How do you get to be a judge?' I asked a woman wearing a judge's badge.

'I've no idea,' she shrugged.

Tex had vacated the stage and a band was playing, one of three that was to play through the rest of the day and half the night. Now that the judges were blind-tasting their portions, the crowd was free to ask the contestants for samples, but few people were bothering. Many visitors were dangling their legs over the cliff that overlooked the hollow, and, having opened their beer coolers, were devoting the rest of the day to consuming the contents. Others had made their way back to their tents and campers to grill hot dogs and smoke dope. I tasted twelve varieties of chili and was surprised by the differences between them; moreover, everything I sampled tasted good. My plastic bowl had become quite stained by the time I reached a stall from which rich steamy aromas were rising.

'Can I taste your chili?'

A huge man with a silver buckle holding up his paunch looked blearily at me. 'Yeh, but ya gotta get rid of that Commie chili first.' I wiped the bowl with a paper towel. 'And get that Commie chili off your spoon too.' More wipings. 'OK. Here you go.' He tipped some of the sludge into my pristine bowl.

'Good! Big chunks of meat too!'

'Yup. Got big cows in Texas.'

A scrawny youth came by. 'Hey, you the guy from England?' I nodded. 'Jeez, you're not eatin' that shit, are ya?'

'Yes, it's very good.'

'Hell, I've never gotten strung out on that.'

Another stall was run by a friendly couple from Virginia. I took pity on them. Virginians don't stand much of a chance in Texas – too close to the Mason-Dixon line for comfort.

'This stuff is real good,' said a bulldog of a man. 'Try some.' I did and it was. Not very Texan, but good.

By one o'clock most people were drunk, and it was getting a bit rough down in the arena. Swarms of men formed circles round buxom gals and demanded a view of their bazooms. The girls were coy, foolishly so. Dressed or breast would have been my advice to them; shy simperings would only inflame the boob-crazed men all the more, and it was obvious that the only way these women were going to escape from the press of the circle was by complying with its increasingly urgent collective request. To negotiate was to ask for trouble. One immense-breasted woman lunged for a man's shorts and tried to pull out his penis. He responded with good humour.

'C'mon, honey, no one wants to see mah dick. We all wanna see your titties.'

'Tits, tits, tits!'

'Show, show, show!'

'Go, go, go!'

Eventually the T-shirts would be raised, a huge cheer would go up, cameras would click. Other women took up positions on the cliff, from where they could prove that their mammary glands were larger than their heads without the immediate danger of a mauling by fifty men.

I like tits as much as the next man, but these displays at two-minute intervals grew wearisome, and I climbed up the cliff to enjoy a more panoramic view. There I found Clinton, the geologist from Midland, and his friends, two strapping young men from Dallas, and two couples: Jerry and Annie, aerial photographers, and Andy and Barbara, of no fixed occupation. Clinton invited me to join their party. The capacious Igloo cooler was opened up and I peered into a marina of beer, Scotch, Jack Daniels, and tequila bottles. I stuck to beer.

'We've just about had enough of the cookoff,' said Clinton, in his high eager voice.

'Me too.' Though I was quite keen to stay around till 2.30 to see the wet T-shirt contest.

'We're going to Mexico for the afternoon. Why don't you come along?'

'Mexico?'

'It's only fifty miles or so. We've got two cars. Plenty of room.'

'I haven't got my papers.'

'Aw grunt, don't need none, not the way we're travelling.'

Annie clamped her Resistol hat on my head and we stumbled down the path with the cooler and other supplies and made for her car. I asked how far it was to the border.

'To Boquillas?' said Clinton. 'Aw grunt, about fifty, I guess.'

'Fifty?' queried Annie. 'Nearer a hundred, I'd say.'

'That's OK,' said Jerry, 'we're Americans.'

Clinton sat in the back with me and told stories and drank beer. His open weathered face handsomely reflected a warmth of heart, an eagerness to please. A bachelor of sixty, Clinton, I suspected, had willingly endured a lifetime of manipulation by sneckdraws less scrupulous and more worldly than himself. A desperate gregariousness demanded companionship; the need to invite overshadowed the qualities of who was invited.

Midland was, or had been until recently, a boom town thanks to its site in the midst of the oil-rich Permian basin. I asked Clinton whether he liked living there. Even Texans rarely had a good word to say for the place.

'I love it. Couldn't live any other place. I've had offers but I won't move. Nothing to do there, and the climate's something awful with the dust storms and all, but I like the people. It's real friendly. We visit each other. Like Mel, friend of mine you met last night? He moved into my spare room on June one and didn't leave till October one.' He laughed. 'Aw grunt. Wanna beer, anyone?'

The fifty-mile drive east brought us to the stretch of river opposite Boquillas at about three. A path led past clumps of bamboo and reed to the Rio Grande. Downstream rose the walls of the Boquillas Canyon and behind them were the first flat-topped ridges of the Sierra del Carmen in Mexico. The Rio Grande is usually a sluggish stream, despite its promising name; dams to the west control its flow and much of the water is drained off for irrigation long before it reaches Big Bend. The recent storms had swollen the river: fast-moving grey-brown water swirled by. Clinton made an exploratory foray up the riverbank. Two minutes later he returned. 'They'll be here in a coupla minutes.'

Soon I spotted in midstream a rowing boat in the grip of the strong current; two Mexicans were manfully rowing in the opposite direction to prevent the small boat from overshooting the spot where they hoped to land. The boat pulled close to where we stood and half a dozen passengers clambered out. We took their places while Clinton negotiated the return fare for our group. The Mexicans pushed the boat back into the swift waters and I bade the world farewell until it dawned on me that the silent rowers had a vested interest in their own survival as well as mine. Ferrying gringos across the Rio Grande was a lucrative little business, but chickenfeed compared to what they probably made from more serious smuggling when tourists were snug in their beds. We arrived safely, and Annie and

Barbara hired burros to carry them up to the sleepy village of Boquillas del Carmen half a mile away.

Boquillas used to be a mining village. Its present affluence, such as it is, comes from smuggling, ranching, and fleecing tourists. The place looks rundown, but then most Mexican villages look rundown. The houses were adobe, the roads unpaved; large shady shops contained few goods on their high shelves. Yet there was a new schoolhouse, and plump chickens scrabbled in wire compounds behind most houses. We soon found our way to the leafy terrace of a pleasant cantina, and kept some niños busy fetching us beers and plates of tacos.

Many Carta Blancas later we hurtled back across the river the same way we'd come. Knowing of official consternation in Texas over illegal immigration, I was astonished that it was so easy to cross back and forth without a scrap of identification, even though there was a US border station at Boquillas itself. American citizens crossing into Mexico don't need passports as long as they stay within a few miles of the border. The Border Patrol knows that most people who cross the Rio Grande at Big Bend are tourists, not smugglers or wetbacks. Mexicans do cross the river illegally, but few try it here in the middle of the desert, where you must negotiate hundreds of miles of emptiness on either side of the river.

It had been hot at Boquillas and hotter still in the car driving back. At Terlingua a unanimous decision was taken by the thirsty group to stop at La Kiva for cocktails. Cavorting around my temples was a knot of pain, tied by the sun, lack of food other than morsels of chili, and the four or five chemical-laden beers I'd drunk in the course of the day. As we dropped into the comfortable chairs round one of the redwood tables, Clinton ordered drinks. He was astonished when I declined. I explained I had a headache. He commiserated: 'You must be havin' a sinkin' spell.'

I nodded. 'It's this Texan beer that does it.'

'Gives me a headache too,' contributed Andy, 'but that don't stop me drinkin' it.'

I wanted to crawl off to the trailer and extinguish all consciousness for a while, but that wasn't possible. My car was still at Villa de la Mina, and I had to wait till Jerry or Andy were ready to drive me back there. The preprandial crowd at La Kiva perked up when a guitarist appeared and picked his way inexpertly through some country favourites. Everybody joined in the chorus of 'Up Against the Wall, Redneck Mother' ('He's thirty-four and drinkin' in a honkytonk/Kickin' hippies' asses and raisin' hell'), while I closed my eyes and groaned. Andy was inspired by his thirtieth beer of the day to hail every girl that walked into the bar: if they responded, in any way, he would look to us for applause and admiration.

At 7.30 we moved on. Clinton suggested I join them for dinner at Lajitas, a village ten miles beyond Villa de la Mina. Jerry dropped me off close to my car. I walked down to the hollow to see how the revellers were getting on. The band was still playing and a few hundred people were swaying, stomping and stumbling to the music. The stony ground was covered with squashed beer cans, like empty cartridges on a battlefield. Fires flared yellow on the hillsides as weary campers turned their thoughts to supper. I later learnt that I'd missed scenes of orgiastic depravity while I'd been in Boquillas. In the heat of the afternoon some of the young women had removed all their clothes – on stage. Unable to contain a lust already inflamed by chili peppers, some of the men climbed up after them and took a closer look, at which point the sheriff, previously absent, arrived to unlock the bodies and restore decorum. I'd noticed earlier that there were no police at Villa de la Mina. Since there probably aren't more than twelve law enforcement officers in all of Big Bend, their presence would not have made much of an impression. All Texas knew that ninety per cent of those attending the cookoff would be either drunk or stoned ninety per cent of the time, so why spoil the fun?

Clinton and his party were staying at Lajitas, a tiny village that had been carefully developed by a Houston property tycoon. They were dining at the Badlands Motel, a reconstruction of the old Cavalry Post that had been built there during the days when Pancho Villa was giving banditry a good name in these parts. Here I sampled for the first time a Texan delicacy called chicken-fried steak. The principle of the dish is simple: you take some inferior steak and pretend it's a piece of chicken you're going to cook Southern-style by dipping it in batter before deep-frying it. Not such a terrible idea, but the American love of excess demands that the fried meat is then smothered in 'cream gravy' – a gelatinous white sauce. There are those who travel across Texas in search of supreme chicken-fried steak; connoisseurs exchange the names of favourite holes in the wall where arthritic crones, employing recipes learnt at the dugs of their wet-nurse during the War Between the States, still stir up a cream gravy as smooth as camomile lotion. For my part, I'd think twice about serving the stuff to a dog.

Andy had switched from beer to bourbon and was well away by the time I arrived.

'Come and see us in Dallas,' he urged, handing me his card. 'At least you'll get a free meal,' he added, rather insultingly, as if that might be my principal reason for accepting the invitation. I peered at the card. 'Contractor' it read.

In truth he was a handyman. Like Jerry and Annie, Andy had been a photographer but he'd had a protracted fight with the taxman (which arose from his having neglected to pay any for years – he just hated to see his earnings squandered on the government) and had gone bankrupt. I had grudging admiration for the bravado of the man, grinning his pig-headed way to financial disaster, and now working quite cheerfully, it seemed, as an odd-job man. He was intrigued by England.

'Hey, do you have any niggers in England?'

'Yes, but we don't call them that.'

'What *do* you call 'em?'

'Blacks, West Indians, Asians, whatever.'

'They a problem?'

'No.'

Clinton looked interested. 'Not a problem?'

'Well, only the problems you get with any immigrant community.'

'Like Yankees?' We all laughed.

'What about the maids?' inquired Clinton.

'What maids?'

'Don't you have black maids in England?'

'We have hardly any maids at all of any colour.'

'I'll be darned.' In Texas, of course, it's by no means unusual to have a maid, and chances are she'll be black or Hispanic. Later a well-off housewife in Houston would tell me: 'It's as easy as pie to get someone to clean up your yard or look after your kids. Round here all you've got to do is stand out on the sidewalk and whistle and ten Guatemalans will come running.'

'It's Buck!' yelled Clinton, as a tall craggy seventy-year-old in Western clothes ambled uncertainly past. I'd seen him in the lavatories earlier, spirtling like a horse and snorting and chewing; I'd taken an instant dislike to him.

'Buck, come over here and meet our friend from England.' Clinton explained that Buck was a former border patrolman who'd written a book about his life. Everybody said I simply had to read it if I wanted to understand what life had been like along the Rio Grande over the past forty years. Buck grumbled a bit at being told I had to have a copy, but flattered by the clamour, he plodded off, and came back carrying *Shod With Iron*.

'Whadya say your name was?'

I told him. He took out a ballpoint and scrawled an inscription: 'Branded for Stephen Brook.' He handed the book to me.

'Thank you, Buck. That's most kind of you.'

'Got ten American dollars?'

'What?'

'Ten US dollars? Pounds would do, I guess.'

It dawned on me that he was invoicing me for the gift. The embarrassment was palpable; everybody present, Buck excepted, had assumed the book, which I didn't want, was being pressed on me as a gift. Buck was impervious to all this, just stood there waitingly. I saw Clinton reaching for his wallet – a gesture he'd been performing far too often that day – but I refused to let him pay. I produced the money and handed it to Buck, who counted the notes and sloped off to the bar.

Against my better judgment I later read the book. Buck came over as ornery, opinionated, and prejudiced, but not without sympathy for the plight of the poor Mexican wetbacks who were exploited as cheap labour along the Valley while at the same time they were harassed and pursued by the Border Patrol. Devotees of the following prose style will find much to admire in *Shod With Iron*: 'Losing your gun in the Patrol is as embarrassing as a fart at a pink tea.'

The Dallas contingent staggered off to bed. Clinton was eager for me to join him for a final brandy, but I begged off. He was spectacularly drunk but, even more spectacularly, still on his feet. His determined generosity was heroically sad and I felt oddly reluctant to leave him to his isolation. But I was exhausted, my head felt as if it had been steam-rollered, and I followed my headlights back to Terlingua through the black starry night.

All of Y'All

The puzzle of Texas is that it is simultaneously diverse and unified. Climatically, topographically, economically, the east has no connection with the west; yet the Texans' sense of themselves, their cultural identity, whether formed by a shared passion for football or Willie Nelson or frosted margaritas, links the rancher from San Angelo with the timber merchant from Nacogdoches like mountaineers at different heights yet on the same rope. Education has much to do with it. Texan history is taught in schools and Texans grow up revering common heroes. A heritage compounded of legend and historical fact is communicated to each generation. The historian A. C. Greene felt that being a Texan in America was comparable to being a Scot in Britain.

Big Bend is both unique within Texas – there is no landscape in the state remotely like it – and yet typical of what Texas is all about. If Texas isn't a real place, as Christopher Middleton had suggested to me, it is nevertheless a bag into which all its mythologies have been chucked over the years, forming and preserving a strange potent ragout of fact and fiction and attitude. All those inflated notions that comprised its identity, none of which were without some grip on reality, found an embodiment in the countless square miles of the Big Bend.

There was still, as Gil had claimed, something frontier-like about the place. So much of it was raw, virtually inaccessible, untamable; to live there, simply to pass one's existence in that desert, was not easy, while to prosper there took real determination. However, the necessary self-reliance is mirrored by co-operation and hospitality. Few people can afford, socially or financially, to work at one activity alone. Steve Harris, who helps to operate Far Flung Adventures, which organises river trips, also writes for the *Alpine Avalanche* and assists the paramedical team in Terlingua. Desert life is lived in the midst of immensity and solitude, and at the same time lived with a greater sense of community than in more populous parts of the country. The sense of constraint, of the proprieties that rule Dallas, were refreshingly underdeveloped in Big Bend.

Texas, more perhaps than any other state, admires the entrepreneur, not just the rich man. There are no executives in the remoteness of Big Bend. Self-employment, or a very small business, was how most people got by. There were the river tour operators – at least three companies between Terlingua and Lajitas – and the tough old families who ran the grocery stores and garages in Study Butte and Terlingua, the quirky little businesses set up with an eye on the tourist trade, and the local wheelers and dealers hoping to make a killing, or at least a few bucks, on a property scam. Big Bend has no room for the pampered and dependent. There's little to do – just the occasional party and evening in a bar or a catfish dinner at a small roadside restaurant – and television has only just been brought to the area by satellite. Groceries and liquor and string and charcoal can be bought at one of the trading posts, but more serious shopping requires a sixty-mile drive to Alpine or Marathon. There's an air strip at Lajitas, but the nearest commercial airport is in Midland, 250 miles away.

I was beginning to feel surprisingly at home in this elbow of Texas and kept postponing my departure. My own natural indolence was matched by everybody else's. There was no need to hurry in the desert. The flood of visitors to the cookoff had receded, and everybody was slowing down again. I hung out at Far Flung Adventures. Business was sluggish, and mornings were spent sitting outside the offices in the eighty-degree sunshine, gossiping and fetching cold beers from the icebox. I even found myself growing tolerant of the junk that had so offended me when I'd first arrived. There's no zoning in the desert; if you have property you do as you please on it. Then too the heaps of industrial rubbish were testimony to how the natural forces of the desert overpowered men and women despite their technological expertise. Many structures around Terlingua, and not only the old houses of the ghost town, were abandoned. People had come out here to start projects and had given up. Innocents would erect a hamburger stand by the road and only later realise that they didn't have enough water to keep the place in operation. In Big Bend you must sink wells up to a thousand feet deep if you want to hit the water table, and five out of six holes turn out to be dry.

While idling in Terlingua, I made a number of forays into the Park. One of its glories, and a reason why floaters are so drawn to the area, is the number of canyons on this stretch of the Rio Grande. The Santa Elena, which begins a few miles downstream from Lajitas, is one of the most spectacular. The terror of being almost trapped between towering limestone walls 1700 feet tall, can only be experienced from inside the canyon, and the only way to penetrate the canyons of Santa Elena or Mariscal or Boquillas is by raft or kayak. But it is possible to stand at the lower end of Santa Elena and stroll up a short path that leads into the canyon for a mile. It's likely that one side of the canyon will be glowing in the sunshine with a rich warm sandy colour, while the other side will be in shadow. Where the cliffs jut and turn, cool dark patches will be thrown onto the other side, sun and shade in a slow careful dance. By the water's edge there's greenery, fern and tamarisk, but a few yards from the shore the sand and the mud give way to limestone cliff.

Leaving the canyons, I attempted to drive up the unpaved Old Maverick Road as a short cut. I'd passed the top of the road coming from Terlingua but a sign had declared the road closed. There was no such sign here at the southern end, so I made the turn. The surface was uneven, to put it mildly, but the road was negotiable; there were steep gradients that gave me some trouble – they have to be taken at a reasonable speed in order to get up them at all, but not so fast that you end up with a boulder shattering an axle. After about five miles I came to a dry arroyo which is usually crossed by the road. Not today. Although the creek was dry again, it was filled with debris and sediment and mud from the recent storm. There were no tracks on the far side of the creek bed. I took that as a signal to turn round. A creek on a closed road was no place to be stuck in the mud. It might be hours, or even a day, before another vehicle came by. I made the bumpy drive back to the paved road and turned towards Cottonwood.

As its name implies, this is a grove of magnificent cottonwood trees, some a hundred feet high. They are less common than they used to be along the creeks and the Rio Grande, as many were hacked down by settlers in the last century; cottonwoods make good mine shafts and roof beams. Nearby is squat, flat-topped Castolon Peak, only half the height of the Chisos Mountains a few miles away, but an impressive volcanic remnant all the same: much of the sheer mountain is composed of compressed ash of a great range of colour, from white and grey to dirty pink, colours that shift in hue according to the light and time of day. Other volcanic formations along the sides of Castolon resemble petrified wood.

It was afternoon by the time I took the steep road that leads up to the Chisos Basin. The elevation down by the river is about 1800 feet; up at the Basin it's 5000. The sudden increase in height accounts for natural features that make Big Bend so absorbing to naturalists. Above 4000 feet or so, scrub and creosote bush give way to woodland, thick with pinyon pine, juniper, oak. Yet the growth patterns won't let you pretend you're now in a mountain forest. Even in the comparatively moist woods of the Chisos, cactus flourishes: century plants and giant yucca and sotol. A range formed when molten rock was squeezed through the earth's surface, the Chisos loom out of the desert like Gormenghast. To this day the elevation and eco-climate of the Chisos preserve plants and animals that are unique. Hundreds of bird species, more than in any other American park, live or winter here. The desert below is home to coyotes and the wild pig they call javelina, but up in the Chisos Mountains live cougars and mountain lions. You expect desert to be well stocked with lizards, wolf spiders, snakes, kangaroo rats, banded geckos, and innumerable species of stridulating insects, from unique grasshoppers to busy millipedes, but the Chisos's height and vegetation give Big Bend a range of flora and fauna unmatched elsewhere. In addition to the rare lion, the highlands shelter two species of deer, the Sierra del Carmen whitetail and the mule deer; and peregrine falcons and golden eagles sweep from the peaks down into the canyons.

In the late afternoon the Basin appeared suspended in a light of the most extraordinary clarity and depth. But it was already too late to hike to the Window, a V-shaped gap in the mountain wall that, especially at sunset, presents a spectacular panorama to the west and south. Moreover, at over 5000 feet it was far cooler than it had been down in the desert and I wasn't equipped for further drops in temperature. I reluctantly returned to Terlingua, where I found Gil in his trailer arguing with the parrot and filling an ice bucket.

'Have some champagne?'

'Sure. What are you celebrating?'

'The end of the cookoff. They've all gone away.'

'Why celebrate? The cookoff must be good for your business.'

The cork flew. The parrot hopped. 'It makes me some money, but let me tell you I earn every damn cent. I can't stand most of the people that crawl down here every year from the cities. They're flashy, they're noisy.'

'You're not exactly bashful yourself, Gil.'

'Yes, but I need to put on a show. And if I'm going to work this hard I'm gonna have some fun too. Don't think I'm interested only in making money and buying fancy things. I'm glad to be away from places like Dallas where people really care about what car they're driving. Not here. I know a guy who inherited, well nobody knows, maybe fifty million. He's got a lot of land around here, a 727, a Lear jet, a helicopter. I've never seen him wear anything except khaki, and he drives beat-up old cars.'

'Perhaps he's just cheap.'

'No, he comes down from Houston, where he lives most of the time, because here he can get away from all that show and display. You know, I used to do all that shit when I lived in Dallas. I went to country clubs and the right restaurants, but it's not important to me any more. I like cities. I like good living. I like spending money and having a good time – I'm not against any of that, but I won't compete with that shit. I don't need to. I'm not rich, but I have enough money to do what I want. It's my choice. But in Dallas it's not a matter of choice. The women wear all that jewellery, the men drive Mercedes cars, they join the right clubs, have the right people over to dinner. They only do that in order to get on – this champagne isn't too good, is it? What the hell – have another glass? Just help yourself. I'm too tired to move.

'I'll tell you something you may not know about Texas. Just because you drive a Mercedes or a Lincoln doesn't mean you're rich. It means you need people to think you are. Most of these guys in their fancy cars are salaried, they're dependent on oil or insurance companies that write their pay cheques. They may have a lot of stuff – a big house and fancy cars and a boat – but you can bet your ass they're making large payments on every damn thing they have. But in Texas people don't really respect you unless you're working for yourself. There's a higher regard for some guy with a small business who's making it on his own than there is for some jerk of a high-paid executive who probably doesn't own property, and wealth in Texas is based on land. I'm not just talking about ranches – it's urban property just as much these days. I buy land too, though I've been selling off anything that doesn't have water on it.'

'How many acres have you got?'

'I've no idea. I keep buying and selling so it's hard to keep track. Anyhow, we don't talk about acres down here. We talk square miles.'

'Do you own a square mile?'

'More. A square mile isn't much land in the desert. That oilman Robert Anderson's got 550.'

*

In their heyday the mines of Terlingua and Study Butte formed the second largest mercury mining operation in the world. About half a mile off the main road are the ruins of the old mining town. The houses are almost all roofless now, some no more than crumbling walls providing a surface for cactus to nudge. Squarely built in yellow stone or adobe, they look bleached after a century of unprotected exposure to the heat, which in summer can reach 110 degrees in the shade. The layout of the small town is plain to see, and the larger, more substantial houses were built higher on the slope away from the road.

Old Terlingua is far from deserted, though it's called a ghost town on the maps. Mobile homes incongruously slide into lots between the ruins, and though about a hundred years have passed since the original town was built, even in its ruinous condition it looks more permanent and robust than the portable dwellings of its present-day inhabitants. I stepped carefully through the small cemetery, keeping an eye out for rattlers. It's poorly maintained, perhaps not cared for at all. The graves are marked either with a mound or cairn topped with the simplest of wooden crosses, or with a small dignified stone tomb shaped like a cradle. This tightly packed huddle of Mexican graves was more visited by lizards than people; though apparently untended, it remained intact in this inhospitable yet beautiful spot. Even here, my consciousness lightly grazed by melancholy and thoughts of death, I looked around me at the landscape and the stone, so harmoniously touched by the crisp morning light, and I was hard pressed to think of a good reason to leave Terlingua.

*

The cases of beer bit into my arms as I carried them from the Lajitas Trading Post to the bed of the pickup. The guide, Gay, whom I'd met a couple of days earlier in her other role as La Kiva barmaid, also insisted we take plenty of ice and fresh water with us. Food too. We found everything we wanted at the trading post, an original structure dating from the founding of the cavalry post in 1915. It's popular with tourists too, not just because this shabby old hut is crammed with just about everything, edible or otherwise, necessary for survival in the desert, but because tethered outside is whiskered Clay Henry, the alcoholic goat, who not only downs bottles of beer and whisky in multiples, but completes his parody of human frailty by suffering from hangovers the next day. The morning after a bender, Clay Henry grows irascible and has been known to tear down the wall to which he's tied with a chain. I kept my distance.

I'd been trying ever since I arrived in Big Bend to organize a raft trip, preferably an overnight float down Santa Elena. But now the cookoff was over, there were too few tourists about to get a group of river runners together. Steve Harris of Far Flung came to the rescue. Gay was taking out a private party, some friends of hers from Wichita Falls, and they all said I was welcome to come along. Since no money was involved, I contributed supplies instead.

The logistics of floating are complicated, chiefly because your take-out point is likely to be ten or fifty miles away from your put-in point. That means two cars: a vehicle to carry the raft, and a second one with a team to drive the emptied pickup to the take-out point and leave it there for the rest of the day. For even the shortest trip a rubber raft has to be loaded with oars, lines, lifejackets, first-aid kit, and waterproofed bags for personal possessions, not to mention the ubiquitous beer cooler. I met my hosts at the Trading Post and in between purchases we got acquainted. Johnny was the wild man of the group, a scrawny plumber with heavy black eyebrows and a bandit's moustache; growing more and more weary of Johnny by the hour was his girlfriend Glenda, a court reporter. Ernie, pudgy, good-natured, stood in Johnny's shadow, and was accompanied by his equally unprepossessing wife Sharon, a policewoman. They'd come down from Wichita Falls, a deservedly maligned industrial city in the north of the state where, they explained, they led modest humble lives most of the year – until the first week of November, when they'd break out and head down to Terlingua for a long weekend of riotous living. How this rather rough crew came to know Gay, a shrewd and self-possessed young woman of quiet intelligence, never became clear.

Our put-in point was about fifteen miles west from Lajitas along the beautiful Camino del Rio, the river road that runs as far as Presidio, offering from its turns and slopes ravishing views of the river and the empty mountains beyond. Johnny felt compelled to drive as fast as possible, whooping and yelling whenever the fancy took him. That wouldn't have mattered much except for the curious conditions in which I found myself. There was room for no more than three in the front of the pickup, two others were in the second car, and I had to pile onto the bed of the pickup. No problem about that, except that I had to share the space with, or rather beneath, a large rubber raft. Sandwiched on the bed of the truck, I did my best to avoid sharp corners – unlike Johnny, whose instinctive reaction on encountering a sharp corner or steep hill was to slam his foot down.

'Shit,' I heard him bark, 'if I'd known that hill was coming I'd have had my foot down on the floor four miles back.'

It was noon by the time we were carrying the craft down to the edge of the river. To launch it we had to cross a strip of deep mud. Shoes and socks came off, and we sank almost up to our knees in thick warm sludge as we hauled the raft into the shallow water and stashed our supplies. It was a pleasant sensation, and I began to understand what attracts ancient marchesas to once fashionable spas.

With Gay at the oars we drifted down towards the entrance to the Colorado Canyon, which differs from the other Rio Grande canyons in that it wasn't eroded through limestone but through lava; its 1000-foot cliffs reveal an extraordinary range of colour, pinks and puces, browns and blacks. The Colorado is well supplied with rapids, all manageable, so much so that although Gay took us through the first ones herself, she turned the oars over to the inexperienced Johnny and Ernie later in the day, and with the minimum of instruction they coped well enough. On a placid stretch of river I leaned back in the stern and closed my eyes, listening to the jabbering of the water. A hand touched my arm, shook it. A familiar herby aroma tickled my nostrils. I opened my eyes to see Sharon with her hand outstretched, proffering a smouldering joint of the good weed marijuana.

'Thanks,' I said, accepting, and inhaled deeply. As I passed the joint on to dozy Ernie, something occurred to me. 'Hey, Sharon, as an officer of the law are you about to arrest me for this and throw me into some foetid Texas penitentiary? I'm prepared to confess about the parking tickets if it'll reduce my sentence.' She smiled and shook her head.

'We just wanna have ourselves some fun,' interjected Ernie, who even in mid-fun sounded closer to catatonia than rapture.

'Fun?' screamed Johnny from the bows. 'Hell, we're gonna be raisin' a lot of hell before we're through with this river.'

We stopped for lunch on the Mexican side. Gay knew a side canyon where we could beach the raft and find comfortable rocks on which to sprawl. The river, clotted with sediment, is always brown and muddy, but a few yards up the side canyon Gay showed us a tinaja, a small clear shaded pool. The mountains and mesa are studded with them, and without them much of Big Bend's wildlife could not survive. Johnny was thrilled. 'Man, this water is crystally clear,' and climbing onto a high rock he dived headfirst into the limpid water, and then treated us to a full minute of colourful cursing on the theme of the frigidity of the water. Ernie was down on the beach trying to photograph the expedition.

'Hey!' we heard him yell. 'Turn around so's I can get a picture of all of y'all.'

In Southern parlance 'y'all' can be addressed to a single individual; when addressing a crowd the term can be left unadorned or enriched by an additional 'all'. What nourishing mouthfuls of language, flush with redundancy, one can hear in Texas, words stumbling over each other, vowels endlessly elongated into dipthongs like verbal rainbows, containing elements and ghosts of every vowel sound known to the human race, including a few that, like the Big Bend mosquitofish, are unique to Texas. I heard some of the drawliest Texan noises in Waco and central Texas, and sampled rich linguistic mousses in the wilds of West Texas. A Texan accent in full throttle was to me – though not to most listeners – one of the joys of being in this place. A ripe Texas sound – part drawl, part whine, emerging from some strangulated corner of the throat – was an arrowroot that could thicken into minimal dignity the declarations of even the most doltish of its citizens. I refer, of course, to Ernie.

We floated on. Johnny maintained his chorus of whoops and screeches and appreciations of the natural world.

'Shee-it! What the fuck's that?' he screamed, pointing at a stately bird on the shore.

'A blue heron,' I murmured, watching it disappear in terror at the sight and sound of its admirer.

'Fuckin' fantastic!'

Fortunately he didn't spot the turtle which was bobbing away as fast as its tiny flippers could propel it from the disruptive presence of our fat rubber raft, now jingling merrily to the sound of fifty empty cans of Budweiser. Johnny's other idea of fun was to leap up without warning and extemporise a little dance, shaking the raft and wetting us all. In the course of one of his more hair-raising cavortings he lost his balance. I must, I suppose, instinctively adhere to the ancient liberal notion that man is essentially good. Why else would I have reached out and grabbed Johnny's ankle, when nothing, to my rational mind, would have given me deeper pleasure than to see him tumble into the Rio Grande? As a result of my thoughtless good deed, I instantly became his buddy, which meant he felt at liberty to punch my arm and slap my back at will.

Putting the raft in the river had been a messy business, but nothing compared to the mudbath we took bringing the damn thing back on shore. Our take-out point was on a fairly shallow beach but the road could only be reached up a steep path which was as smeared with mud as the beach itself. The ascent was not simple: it's easier to slither down than up, all the more so when one's hands are full of equipment, clothes and bags of rubbish. Furthermore the raft had to be rinsed clean while still in the water, and then carried up the path without letting it drop into the mud again. Up at the roadside manic Johnny and moony Ernie were delegated to ferry buckets of water up to us so we could wash our legs and arms. Drivers tooling down the Camino del Rio started with astonishment at this bunch of drug-crazed river runners, whose top halves were in recognisable flesh colours, but whose lower parts were a thick elephant grey.

Johnny thought this hour-long operation a terrific hoot, which persuaded the rest of us that he must be too pissed to drive. Johnny, good lad, agreed, so I had the doubtful pleasure of sharing my cramped cave under the raft with the demented though affectionate plumber while Gay, still a model of poise after the burden of a whole day devoted to keeping us from drowning, drove us safely back to Lajitas.

I thanked these kind strangers again, then drove back through the dusk to Terlingua and stopped in at Uncle Joe's Cafe. Apart from myself, everybody there was local. Good, I thought to myself, the tourists have all gone. But no, the door burst open, and two drunken men in ponytails, clutching cans of Coors beer, came reeling in.

'Hey man, this is far out, this is neat! Far out!'

Did people still talk like that? Apparently so. No one else in the café paid the slightest attention to the two indecorous drunks, and moments later they left of their own accord and disappeared back into the desert, which, serene and immutable, can absorb anything.

Alpine

When I eventually left Terlingua, it was along the Camino del Rio, and it was good to be able to see the view this time. The road plunged up and down hillsides and cliffs, but began to calm itself as I approached Redford, a sleepy hamlet guarding the irrigated fields sloping down to the Rio Grande. Some miles beyond, on the edge of Presidio, is the remarkable Fort Leaton, which dates from 1846. This rambling adobe structure, though fortified, was built as an old trading post. There have been Spanish missions at Presidio and Mexican Ojinaga, on the other bank, since the seventeenth century, and when Ben Leaton came to Presidio in the mid nineteenth century, he was by no means the first Anglo settler to arrive. The trading post has been much restored, but it remains a most lovely building, its low buff-coloured walls enclosing about forty spacious rooms, many of them interconnected, and a large patio. On this warm but not especially hot morning, the shuttered windows and the adobe walls kept the rooms wonderfully cool. Some have been renovated and are used for exhibits, but I preferred to stroll through the empty rooms for which no use had yet been found, and to let my imagination populate and furnish them. The placidity of the old fort was misleading; much of the time it must have been crammed with traders, travellers, bandits, and itinerant soldiers. Now it was half-museum, half-shell, and the shell, blank rooms looking out onto the small desert garden on the outside, or opening through small doorways into a sun-washed patio, was far more eloquent than the museum.

Presidio, a few miles to the west, is a dump. I don't think anyone ever has a good word to say for this dusty little town of 3000 people. It droops on the margins of Texas like a wilting wallflower. Across the river lay Ojinaga, ten times the size of Presidio, and as always happens along this border, there is constant movement back and forth, much of it legal, but the Border Patrol keeps a vigilant eye on this human ebb and flow. From time to time, the balance tips the wrong way, at least to official American eyes, and illegal immigrants, whose presence is positively welcomed at harvest times, are bundled back over the international bridge.

Presidio's chief claim to fame is its extreme and unremitting heat. For about a month each summer Presidio is the hottest place in the United States. Even on this November morning the thermometer was in the mid-eighties. The main streets, paved only in the centre, can never have been attractive; dreary flat-roofed cement-block shops and office buildings are fronted by functional metallic awnings to provide shelter from the sun. Presidio, which was never prosperous, has been further drained by the devaluation of the peso. Many of the shops are empty or boarded up. Most trading takes place not in the main street shops but from old garages and shacks close to the bridge. In these makeshift trading posts you can buy old clothes, mattresses, lavatory bowls, old air-conditioning units, baskets, anything.

I wandered into Mary's Café for a cup of coffee. The café was as drab as the rest of Presidio. Three border patrolmen ambled in and sat down. A glum Mexican girl took their lunch order, and while they were waiting I strolled over and asked whether I could join them. Their response was a collective half-nod, half-grunt. Politely, I asked them about their work. Again collectively, they shook their heavy heads. It was 'against policy' for them to discuss their work with strangers. As patrolmen who deal not just with illegal immigration but with smuggling and other criminal activity, they weren't about to pass any information, however trivial, to a stranger. I'd have to consult their supervisor first, they told me. That was the end of that. I removed myself with a smile and returned to my booth, leaving them to their crossword puzzles and enchiladas.

The river road ends just beyond Presidio, and I headed north through the desert. Given the poverty of the soil, I was surprised to see that vast tracts of land, neatly fenced, were evidently working ranches. Very few cattle were visible, but from time to time a small group could be seen gathering in wonder around a green stalk. Earlier in the century ranches had extended much further south than they do today, but overgrazing killed off the grasslands that were essential to profitable ranching. The Park Service has successfully replanted in certain areas, especially on higher ground, but it's unlikely that ranching will ever be a commercial operation again in the desert.

The destruction of the grasslands was a salutary reminder

that desert should not be equated with absence. Although Big Bend teems with animal and bird life, not to mention innumerable species of insect, it remains desert, parched and inhospitable. It's a landscape of denial: lack of moisture is the deprivation to which every other feature of the desert ecology must accommodate itself. That the desert should be so full of life is a constant surprise to us; yet the sustaining of that life is a deeply delicate matter. Entire species of grasshopper live and breed only under the shadow of certain plants. Remove the latter and the other, inescapably, perishes. The balance of nature is an old familiar notion, but in so arid a climate that balance is even more finely tuned than elsewhere. A century plant flowering for its one and only time after fifty years, or the bright yellow petals of the rock nettle nodding from a canyon wall, these are wonderfully moving sights, not just because they present parables of endurance and show us beauty in the midst of seeming negation, but because only through the intervention of that unpredictable commodity, moisture, are wildflower seeds coaxed out of hibernation to reward the onlooker with flounces of colour and rustling greenery.

All life, from the near extinct mosquitofish to adaptable mankind, must struggle to survive here, and in retrospect one can only wonder at the folly and greed that plundered the resources the desert had so frailly to offer, and thus diminished significantly, though not catastrophically, the life and variety of the desert. The once wooded Chinati Mountains are now bare. Where once, to the south, there had been grasslands there is now creosote bush, its tentacular taproots rummaging down through the desert floor to suck up moisture, its sour taste repulsing the animals that might otherwise have feasted on its proliferation. Although its presence discourages wind erosion and provides hospitality to insects and rodents, scrappy creosote bush is no substitute for generous grass.

For miles as I drove, both sides of the road were lined with a profusion of wildflowers. Moisture from the recent rains had gathered in the gullies that run parallel to roadways and germinated the seeds that lay in wait. There were vivid yellow baileya plants, as thick as bushes, and clumps of purple sage. I drove for fifty miles more up Route 67, past the old mining town of Shafter, through the arid landscape so spectacularly bordered with rococo swashes of yellow and purple and green, and up onto what in more temperate climates would be called heathland: more scrubby, less obviously dessicated than the flatter land closer to the river.

The road led to Marfa, a highland rather than a desert town, 4700 feet up in the foothills of the Davis Mountains. The large Frenchified courthouse, which seems far too big for the administration of a county with no more than 5000 inhabitants, dominates the leafy main square as if it were the headquarters of Toyland. Marfa is self-possessed, neat to the point of gentility, low-key but not without pride and style. In contrast to Presidio, Marfa looks prosperous, and the charmingly eclectic Spanish Colonial Paisano Hotel has been converted into a smart little shopping mall. The cast of *Giant*, which was filmed nearby, was housed in this pretty structure. What, I wondered, did James Dean do to pass away the time in Marfa?

Fort Davis, twenty miles to the north and even higher in the mountains, has a similar feel to it, though perhaps a bit more rough at the edges. The fort, established in 1854, was kept busy for thirty years until the surrounding Apaches, who harassed settlers and travellers crossing the mountains on the Overland Trail, were finally vanquished. The Second Empire pretensions of the Marfa courthouse seemed more incongruous than ever in these remote mountains when set beside Fort Davis's modest yet more dignified monuments: the Limpia Hotel, still in use, and the old bank building in the main square, both built sturdily from local stone. On the other side of the street is a drugstore that claims to serve the best Cokes in Texas. I went in and ordered the *spécialité de la maison* from the cheerful wench who divided her time between the soda fountain and the counter opposite from which she sold candy to kids and cold cream to their mothers. I eagerly drank the potion. It tasted just like Coke.

Visitors drive up to the McDonald Observatory a few miles to the north in order to inspect at close quarters one of the largest telescopes in the world. An equally good reason for the excursion is to enjoy the splendid view over the Davis Mountains. Because the valley below is itself over 4000 feet high, the vista from the 6800-foot-high observatory is not so much down as across, over great green waves that roll towards the horizon. Given how close the mountains are to the desert, it's astonishing how verdant they are, soft and billowing rather than craggy and Dolomitic, though with peaks rising to over 8000 feet the Davis Mountains are not lacking in drama. A highland Scot would, I suspect, feel reasonably at home there.

It certainly doesn't feel Swiss around here, and the small town of Alpine, some thirty miles southwest from the observatory, seems oddly named. The Brewster County seat, Alpine is home to about three-quarters of the population of this largest of all Texan counties, which, as the guidebooks never let you forget, is bigger than Connecticut and Rhode Island combined. It's a college town, with a small museum, and I was visiting Adalberto Garcia, who teaches English and Spanish at Sul Ross State University, and his wife Jo Ana Sanchez, a psychiatrist. As their names suggest, they are not natives of the region. Berto was born in the Lower Rio Grande Valley and comes from one of those families, Mexican in origin, that for decades have worked the land on both sides of the border; with his lean dark face, and an emphatic black moustache, Berto looked distinctly Mexican, whereas Jo Ana's ethnic origins would be harder to identify at a glance. Born in Los Angeles and raised in New Mexico, she seemed more American than her husband. But both were Harvard-educated and bilingual.

I asked Berto about Sul Ross University. He spoke highly of its animal science and geology schools and told me it's said to have the best rodeo school in Texas. Sul Ross is geared to what most West Texans do for a living: ranching. More academic pursuits, such as reading and writing, were not a high priority. 'It's not just that they use grammatical constructions that are wrong, they use some that don't even exist.' His dark eyes gloomed downwards. 'I guess most of the students go to college to play sports. I wish I could show you some of those scripts. They're depressing.'

'They're not depressing,' said Jo Ana sharply. 'They're pitiful. I wonder how the hell those kids are going to survive in the world.'

I asked Jo Ana about her patients. Was mountain craziness different from city craziness? She told me she found as much stress out here as she did in the cities. Not surprisingly, much of it took the form of depression made more acute by isolation.

Alpine is no border town, and I wondered what it must be like for this Mexican-American couple to live in a community dominated by white families. Jo Ana told me that Mexicans and Anglos had their own clubs, their own Veterans posts. Socially, the town was divided. Most Mexicans in Alpine worked at menial jobs. There were a few middle-class Mexicans, mostly teachers and gas station owners, but she and Berto and the pharmacist were the only well-educated Mexican-Americans in the area. I wondered whether things were beginning to change.

'No, not much,' said Berto, shaking his head and stretching his long legs out under the table. 'There's not much friction between the communities because Mexicans know their place, and they're tolerated as long as they stay there. The Anglos don't need to oppress them. I keep hearing Mexicans say 'I'm not supposed to . . .' and so they don't. They're reluctant to move up the social scale, even when the opportunities are there. They fear the disapproval of the Anglos if they appear too pushy, and, though I hate to say it, there's also pressure from their own community to stay put.'

*

That night the temperature dropped to about 40 degrees, and a brisk wind was blowing. For the first time since coming to Texas I had to rummage through my case for a sweater. A norther had swept down across the mountains, and weather reports predicted it would remain cold and blustery all day long. Driving east out of Alpine I passed a couple of motels near the campus. Both had a large sign that read: OWNED BY NATIVE TEXANS. This is a coded reference to the Indian families who have moved into the motel business in Texas and other central states. I'd heard resentment voiced at the Asian presence from individuals who were convinced that Indian owners were often inclined to cut corners and allow motels to run down. In my experience Indian-run motels were neither better nor worse than any others, but that the hostility was widespread was unpleasantly clear from the signs in Alpine.

The cold front pursued me eastwards, through Marathon and along the uninterrupted 55-mile stretch of treeless prairie to Sanderson. When I stopped to check the map I could feel the car shaking as 40 mph gusts flapped around it. Beyond Sanderson was more desert country, with tall ocotillo and yucca on all sides; near Dryden a large tumbleweed loped over the road. And just beyond Dryden I spotted in my rear-view mirror a fast-moving police car with its characteristic flashing red light. It had been a while since my last encounter with the species – with the delightful exception of Sharon – and it was high time I broke a law or two and gave the cops something to do. I pulled over. The cop ambled up, leaned down to window level, and graciously tipped his hat.

'Seems to me like you were goin' jest a bit too fast along that stretch of road.'

There was no point arguing. I'd been doing at least 65. 'You're probably right, officer. On these long stretches of straight road my attention sometimes wanders.'

He nodded. My capitulation paid off, and he let me off with a warning. Nobody in West Texas drives at 55 in open country. To do so could add hours to a long journey, and there are few short ones in the West. It's hard for even the police to feel that a steady high speed on straight empty roads is much of a threat to public safety.

I was in Langtry by lunchtime and it was warming up. I made the obligatory stop at Judge Roy Bean's Jersey Lily Saloon, which looks authentic and is, though you can't buy a drink there. Roy Bean was an entrepreneur and barman, but he's remembered for the justice he dispensed from behind the bar. He became known as 'The Law West of the Pecos', died in 1903, and was committed to celluloid by Paul Newman. Langtry is not far from the joint Mexican-American Amistad Reservoir, a popular base for water sports and hunting expeditions, so this part of Texas is much frequented by tourists. I was glad to have seen the old saloon, but more interested by the lovely desert garden planted next to it; here I could identify some of the cacti that had left small darts in my flesh after careless strolls into the Chihuahuan Desert.

The road presses east along the Rio Grande through some lovely country, and the Pecos River Bridge near Comstock vaults the river at a height of 273 feet. To the southwest, in Mexico, lies the Serriana del Burro, while immediately below are the vertical cliffs of the Pecos Canyon. Prehistoric tribes once lived here, and they have left rock paintings and other marks of their settlement. At the other end of the reservoir is the friendly town of Del Rio. What gives this border town its charm is its unexpected greenery, for the rest of Val Verde County is as arid as any other region in West Texas. On the edge of town is a small park that encloses the San Felipe springs; its abundant waters, up to ninety million gallons a day, irrigate all Del Rio and much of the surrounding land.

I dawdled down Hudson Drive, where wealthy ranchers have built their town mansions over the years. Large Spanish and Colonial style houses sit squarely on lawns moistened by sprinklers, and the road itself is shaded by large cottonwoods and pecan trees. Further north I'd been paying a few dollars a bag for pecans; here they could be had for nothing. Along Hudson Drive at least a dozen Mexicans were filling plastic buckets with windfall pecans. At the end of the street was the domaine of the Val Verde Winery, which was celebrating its centenary. The Qualia family has grown grapes here and made them into wine since 1883. I went in to taste the results of a century's experience. Perhaps after another century . . .

Further east, on a small road south of Bracketville, I paused at the Seminole Indian Scout Cemetery. Founded in 1872, this secluded graveyard is the burial place of the scouts who assisted the US Army during the Indian Wars. Their unsophisticated graves are marked either with simple crosses or with a broken slate scratched with a name or inscription. Many of the epitaphs are semi-literate, with capitals inserted in the wrong places: FeBruary. I deciphered the crude markers over the flat graves of Clarence Warrior, Mary Bowlegs, Carolino Warrior. Some of the graves are modern, but the surnames are the same as on the nineteenth century crosses; the scouts' descendants still maintain the cemetery until it becomes their turn to lie in it.

After Bracketville the landscape changes. Growth identifiable as vegetation appears, and so do sheep and cattle who bury their snouts in it. Turning north towards Camp Wood I soon found myself climbing into the Hill Country, which is the southeastern portion of the Edwards Plateau. The Plateau extends as far west as the Pecos River and as far north as the prairie country beyond San Angelo and Midland. Here on the edge of it is some of the loveliest country in Texas: limestone and granite hills, gashed by gorges sunk by fast-moving rivers, unroll eastwards as far as Austin and San Antonio. First-rate hunting and fishing draws vacationers here every summer, many of them Texans, and they return as hunters in the autumn.

Shortly before I reached Leakey (pronounced Lakey) I

spotted a deer crossing the road. It was the beginning of the hunting season, no time for any creature with four legs to be admiring the scenery. I pleaded, I yelled, I implored, until the deer finally loped off into the wood. Then I drove on to the hamlet of Rio Frio and looked out for the white flag that would identify the driveway that led to Camelot.

Rio Frio Mio

That the Knights' seventy-acre ranch was called Camelot, that
their favourite cow was called Guinevere and their most potent
bull Excalibur, intimated that their approach to the rural life
had its frivolous side. Jerry Knight had been a property man in
Houston and at the age of forty and with his second wife Susan
on his arm, had left the city and moved to this small spread in
Rio Frio. While it was true that they were not dependent on the
profits from the ranch to keep the larder stocked, the Knights
were hardly typical city people who'd made good and then, in
accordance with Texan ways, bought themselves a house and
cow. Susan had grown up in Rio Frio and her mother still
owned a neighbouring ranch, so for her it had been a homecoming, and the surrounding hills and farms were well stocked with
relatives, including the black sheep of the family whom she
refused to let me meet, though I did glimpse him stumbling
across to his barn in what I took to be one of his daily alcoholic
stupors.

I'd met the Knights at La Kiva, where they had reported to
me on the more disgusting goings-on I'd missed at the cookoff.
No traveller in Texas, they'd insisted, could claim to know the
state unless he'd visited the Hill Country, which of course I had
every intention of doing. Two minutes later I'd willingly
committed myself to going to stay with them at Camelot. A
princely estate their ranch is not, but it's comfortable and
pretty. The house is shaded by magnificent trees, a 100-foot
pecan and a colossal fig, and down in the village grows, fat and
old, the second largest oak in Texas. Because Camelot is not
primarily a commercial undertaking, Jerry was experimenting
with growing blackberries, plums, and peaches, and he also
raised cattle, Nubian goats, and chickens.

We seemed very far from the West Texan prairies, where
seventy acres could only support two or three cows. A Camelot
cow needs only a couple of acres. Jerry had a dozen or more
cattle of various breeds, and he introduced me to them all,
commenting on their personalities, their partialities, their
eccentricities. There was animal life in the fields and more
animal life in the house and on the porch. Five cats dozed on

battered garden furniture, waking periodically to ambush each other, and two dogs patrolled the house and paths. The large brown weimaraner had just given birth to seven puppies.

'We found homes for two of them,' said Jerry, 'but I had to get rid of the rest. I sent Susan down to the mailbox this morning and when she came back I'd sent five pups airmail to heaven.' But not without a sentimental gesture, for in a corner of the garden was a pet cemetery, which was already alarmingly well filled with dogs, cats, two parrots, and a monkey.

There was barbecued brisket – perhaps it was monkey – for dinner. Women cook but men barbecue. There was no doubt, then, about who burnt the meat. Embarrassed, Jerry came in from the porch carrying a lump of beef masquerading as a boulder of coal. The edible chunks were very good indeed, and the sharp taste left by burnt corners was washed away by the first of many margaritas we downed that evening. Susan found the mishap hilarious. Indeed, hilarity was her principal mode of expression, and it was aided by a fine sense of comic timing. She was sturdily built, a bit overweight, unlike Jerry, who was positively dapper, a trim, good-looking man, quietly sure of himself. They both loved to talk, but – and this is less common among Texans – they were good listeners too, full of curiosity.

'I can't help speaking out,' said Jerry. 'It's always been my nature.'

'Except you like to give people advice whether or not they're asking you for it,' interposed Susan.

'That's perfectly true. In my opinion, it's my duty to tell people what I think, especially if I think they're wrong about something important. Don't you think that's right?'

Which inaugurated the first of many debates on matters ethical, cultural, philosophical.

'That's all very well,' said Susan, not disposed to take too much pomposity from either of us, 'but with your big mouth, Jerry, you keep getting into trouble.' She turned to me. 'We had a neighbour down the road who's not too popular with the other folks around here, but Jerry thought he was right about something and spoke up for him at a town meeting. Big mistake. And the other thing he did was to tell a joke at a party that some people said was sacrilegious.' (Jerry was coaxed into telling me the joke, which was more innocuous than some jests I've heard from accredited clergy.) 'Since then a lot of people in Rio Frio and Leakey have more or less stopped talking to us.'

'Surely not . . .'

'It's true,' affirmed Jerry, not without pride. 'This is a very tight community, which is both good and bad. Hell, the judge in town was the guy who ran the grocery store. Everybody knew him and everybody knew how far you could go. We kind of regulated ourselves. It was almost like a family mafia around here, but it worked. Things are changing now, there are new people moving in, but it's still true that if you want to survive in a community like ours you have to play by the rules. We've had quite a few families move in over the past few years, and a year later many of them have gone.'

'Forced out?'

'No, no. Nobody pushed them. But if you don't fit in, you'll find, for instance, that nobody's gonna sell you land. I mean, nobody's gonna tell you to leave, but you'll soon find that you don't want to stay around any longer. I'll be honest with you. We're not too keen on outsiders. You've heard people say that Texans don't much like folks from out of state? Well, most people here don't even like the folks from the next county.'

'People who don't fit in, are they ignored or actually discriminated against?' I asked delicately.

'You mean do people hate blacks here? No, they don't.'

'That's because there isn't a single black family in Real County,' added Susan, not irrelevantly. 'Not one. That's why we have no discrimination! Remember, Jerry, one time a black family did move in?' He nodded. 'They left after six months. So now we have none again.'

'Which is the way most people want it.'

*

I slept in a small cosy caravan near the barns, and the next morning, when I spotted signs of life at the ranch house, I walked over in search of coffee. My hosts greeted me cheerily. In the same solicitous spirit Twink the weimaraner came bounding up to me. Casually, I reached out a hand to pat her shapely head, and she responded by sinking her teeth into my arm. Susan went pale. So did I. Fortunately the damage to my sweater was greater than to my arm.

'It's those puppies,' said Susan, full of apologies. 'She's all nervous because of her babies. She's never gone for anyone before.'

For my protection Susan insisted Jerry take me out of the house for a drive. Meandering through the village we passed a small pickup truck driven by a young man of obviously Mexican appearance.

'How ya doin', Diego?' shouted Jerry, and the Mexican waved back.

'A wetback?' I asked.

Jerry nodded. There were plenty about, most of them farm labourers. He told me how Diego had appeared from nowhere two years ago and had knocked on the door of a rancher called Ed. He was looking for work, he said, and Ed took him on at eight dollars a day, plus room and board. Ed was so pleased with Diego's work that a few weeks later he raised him to ten without even being asked. The wetbacks have the reputation of being good workers, and ranchers do their best to keep them. Ed, for instance, drives Diego across the border once a year so he can visit his relatives and a few weeks later Diego walks back to Leakey. Walks? Walks.

Even with cheap wetback labour, ranching, Jerry insisted, was a lousy way to earn a living. To start off, you'll buy a cow and a calf, and then haul them back to your ranch. Then you must pay for inoculation, for worming, for high-protein breeder cubes, salt, and other supplements. Hay costs three bucks a bale. A few cattle may die. When a calf's ready, you take it to auction, but from the sum it fetches the rancher must deduct the auctioneer's commission and transportation costs. 'If you're showing a profit at the end of all that,' said Jerry, 'you're damn lucky. And I haven't even begun to figure in the cost of land, labour, fencing, farm equipment.'

In his view, the middlemen – auctioneer, trucker, butcher – make money, but the ranchers don't. Squeezed for cash, ranchers unload fast; with too much beef on the market, prices drop like anchors. Most ranchers supplement their income by selling deer leases at five dollars an acre during hunting season, or they peddle hay and repair fences. They stay on their land because they value the way of life, not because they're prospering. The large farming subsidies dished out by Congress fall into the pockets of large corporations rather than small ranchers. Only the largest operators, who buy land for investment or in hope of exploiting mineral rights, can afford not to work the land.

'It's the small rancher who works to feed America and his life is being made more and more difficult. There comes a point where he may not think it worth his while to stay in business.' That point is often reached when the rancher realises he can get between two and six thousand dollars an acre for his land. Excitable developers are queuing up for prime 'recreational' land in these beautiful hills, and many a rancher has traded in his gradually vanishing business and his fading way of life for a large cheque.

After lunch, Susan, still fretting over Twink's assault, took me over to visit her mother. Susan's broad humour, her forthright manner, her simple gutsiness, hadn't prepared me for what I found. I knew that Susan came from a fairly wealthy family, that her father had been the local sheriff, that her grandfather had made a small fortune from oil, though his money, like a French farm, had been endlessly divided among generations of descendants. We walked up the drive to a lovely hacienda-style ranch house, beautifully cared for, sumptuous in a discreet way, and were greeted on the porch by her mother, very much the grande dame in an elegant dress, her white hair drawn into a bun. Although it was a warm day, a log fire was blazing in the living room; the doors onto the porch were left open, wastefully but sensuously blending fresh Hill Country breezes with the steady heat of the fire. We talked about local history, about books which Susan, an avid reader, thought her mother would enjoy, and about the dipsomaniacal uncle nobody would let me meet. It was a call rather than a visit, with a precise beginning and all the formalities of leavetaking.

Such graciousness was new to me in Texas. Money, I had observed, was either flashed about in the form of cars and jewellery, or put aside as an asset essential to well-being and status but scarcely affecting how one lived one's life. At this lovely ranch house, money had been translated into pleasing furniture and tasteful decoration, a style of living awash with comfort, a house and garden tended by a servant or two – and into leisure as a way of life, not without its own industriousness, but conducted with the ease that only money could make possible. As Susan and I walked down to the river through her mother's fields, I remarked how very differently she and Jerry lived from the quiet stylishness her mother had adopted.

She nodded. 'That's because when I was growing up here I was the little rich girl, and I spent my youth trying to live it down. I didn't feel it as an advantage. To me it got in the way. I wanted to be like the other children in the county, not different from them.'

After crossing so many dry creeks in the Big Bend, it was a joy to stand on the banks of the Rio Frio and watch the water gush splashily over rocks and deviously around clumps of weed. The pebbles on the river bed shimmered up through a surface dappled by the shade of the large cypress trees that leaned over the bank. It was a beautiful spot and, in its conjunction of white limestone hills, swiftly moving water, and an abundance of vegetation, both cultivated and wild, was entirely typical of the Hill Country. In no sense was it a domesticated landscape, and that gave a suitably Texan feel to it, yet its scale was more manageable, easier to accommodate, than the vastness of the Piney Woods or the High Plains or the desert.

Later that afternoon I drove south to Uvalde, a pleasant town that spreads itself attractively around large plazas and along broad streets. It took me some time to find the Grand Opera House, chiefly because I was not expecting so fulsomely named a structure to be scarcely bigger than a modest two-storey mansion. I don't believe much opera has been heard here recently, but theatre companies do stop by. Uvalde doesn't have the air of a cultural centre; instead it frolics outdoors. There's excellent deer and turkey hunting nearby, and canoeing and rubber-tubing down the many spring-fed rivers that flow through Uvalde County. It's ranching country too, and just north of the town former Governor Dolph Briscoe owns half a million acres. While in town I replaced the tequila I'd polished off the night before and returned to Camelot with two cases of beer for my hosts.

Uvalde County is wet, but Real County, where the Knights live, is dry. I couldn't believe that in terms of mores the populations of the two counties differed that much. Jerry agreed it was hard to figure out. His neighbours in Leakey liked their drink as much as anyone, but whenever it comes to the vote, Real stays dry. 'The reason is that if liquor was available here in Leakey, lots of men wouldn't be able to keep telling their wives they were going down to Uvalde for the evening and wouldn't be back till late.' So it wasn't religious scruple, but a kind of marital strategy.

We dined early, as one does in so many parts of the United States. Just before Susan served the pot roast, the door swung open and a tall bearded man in a Stetson and elaborate boots strode in.

'Hey, Larry!' Jerry greeted him. 'This is our friend from England, and I've told him all about you, how you're a real cowboy. So sit down and have some dinner with us.'

'Aw Jerry, can't do that. Judy's expectin' me back for dinner about now.'

'She can wait a while.'

'Oh no, she can't. See, I'm cookin' tonight.'

'In that case, have some pot roast with us and we'll wrap up a piece for you to take back to her. That way you don't have to cook, and Judy gets herself a damn good supper.'

'Hell, Ah don't know about that,' muttered Larry, sitting down. He was a Texan, and sounded it; he'd worked as a cowboy in Montana and as a bartender in Dallas. His appearance, his dress, his accent, his work, all combined to make him a copybook Texan. I admired his belt buckle, a brass slab engraved with the eloquent words HUMPIN' TO PLEASE. He immediately took it off and gave it to me, drowning out my protestations.

Larry was right to be apprehensive. As his teeth sank into the pot roast the door swung open and a petite dark woman walked in clutching a baby. Yes, it was Judy and, surprisingly, since Judy couldn't have been a day over forty, her grandson Chad. Larry was her second husband, and consequently step-grandfather to the infant. Judy was distraught, but none of us showed any patience with her. All was well, everybody would be fed, there was enough beer for all Rio Frio.

'Judy?' said Jerry, wearying of her lament that it would be easier all round if Larry would come home on time. 'Judy? Will you just sit yerself down, shut up, and eat your dinner with us?'

'You do that, honey,' Larry nodded, and she did.

Ten minutes later the door opened again – 'Told you Rio Frio was a friendly place,' murmured Jerry to me – and four women walked in. They were all blonde, identically blonde. I stared in wonder. The eldest was Yvonne, another forty-year-old grand-mother, and she was in high spirits.

'Yvonne got married a coupla days ago,' Larry told me.

'Remarried you mean,' said her daughter Renee, slender and sexy, hand on hip, pouting as if it were a way of life.

'Sit down, sit down!' welcomed Jerry and Susan.

'Can't!' said Yvonne and Renee in unison.

'Why not?' Larry wanted to know. 'You guys, what y'all doin' tonight, dressed up all pretty like that?'

'We're going to Uvalde for the dance,' said Renee. 'George Strait's playing, and I'm gonna find me a rich man.'

'Look no further,' said Susan, sliding the tequila in my direction.

'You the man from England?' asked Renee. I nodded. 'I knew a guy from England. He wanted me to go back to England with him. Said he'd buy two plane tickets, he'd take Mother too if I wanted. But I thought, oh no, he's just gonna get me up in that plane, then he's gonna try something funny on me, and I'm gonna have to push him out the plane. I told him I never been out of the state of Texas and I was gonna stay right here. Then he said he just wanted to be friends with me, wasn't gonna try anything funny. So I said, if you just wanna friend, go and find someone else.'

In the meantime Renee's five-year-old daughter Leather was risking death by cooing at the puppies in the other room. Renee's friend Kim, an eternal sixteen, all her sap ready to rise, was gnawing on her tightly set lips; she clearly didn't want to miss a note of the concert, and wanted to be on her way.

While Judy ate, young Chad had been passed to Larry, who was conducting some Texan experiments on his step-grandson.

'Larry!' yelled Renee. 'Don't you give that little baby any of that beer now. Hell, Ah was raised off of a Lone Star bottle, so I'm almost an alkie mahself.'

'We better be goin',' said Yvonne, oblivious to the shadow her daughter had cast on her reputation as a mother. En masse, the blondes said goodbye.

'Sure was nice to meet you,' Renee said to me.

'You too. I happen to have two plane tickets to London . . .'

'Get her out of here, Yvonne,' said Jerry, though whether he was protecting Renee or me was unclear. And so they left. Chad was now transferred to the lap of the replete Judy, while Larry pursued the baby's education.

'Nowaz,' he said very slowly, pointing at his own nose. 'Show us your nowaz.'

Chortling Chad obliged.

'Hay-edd. Show us your hay-edd.' Chad stabbed his cheek with his finger.

Judy took over. 'Bullet. Show us your little bullet,' she instructed, pointing at the infant groin.

'Hay-ell!' interjected Larry indignantly. 'Don't you call it that, honey, otherwise that little booger's gonna grow up thinkin' you put that darn thing in your gern and shoot it.'

After all the visitors had gone, Jerry and Susan and I sat up late into the night. While I made myself well-diluted margaritas, they drained the beer lake I'd hauled from Uvalde. They told rambling stories, especially Jerry, tales of graveyards and strange happenings. Tales of the supernatural led us to dialogues concerning natural religion, and as the clock struck midnight at the ranch in Rio Frio, Texas, the three of us, surrounded by sleeping cats and a pyramid of beer cans, talked of pantheism, the afterlife, and the meaning of honour.

Ain't Nobody Feelin' No Pain

On the edge of the University of Texas campus in Austin hunkers a lumpish white box with a heavy-lidded roof placed as a slab over the top. Its monumentality is fitting, since this is the Lyndon Baines Johnson Library and Museum, a repository not only of presidential papers but of presidential legend. There are seven such libraries in the United States, and it says much about the presidential system that it has become virtually automatic for holders of that office, however undistinguished their tenure may have been, to arrange for the perpetual glorification of their administrations. It's the man and his accomplishments, such as they were, that are celebrated, reflecting alarmingly how in the United States executive power rests in the hands of a single individual, while party and policy and cabinet count for little.

Not that I begrudge LBJ his mausoleum. Like most of my generation, I had loathed him in office because of the obscenity of the Vietnam War. Yet I couldn't help holding him in awe for his sheer brilliance as a politician, and as the years have gone by that admiration has grown. Johnson, a very traditional Southern politician, steeped in wheeling and dealing of the shadiest kind, in league with powerful vested interests, cajoled Congress into some of the most radical legislation since the New Deal. That some of it was over-ambitious, and that Johnson usually neglected to find a way to pay for his legislative largesse, certainly tarnishes that achievement; it doesn't negate it.

The personality of the man appeals to me too. Unlike many other Presidents, he at least had one. His Texan earthiness, his boundless vulgarity, his monstrous ego, they bunched together as the expression of a man who was both defined by the small world he'd emerged from and yet was able to fill and outgrow each office he occupied. Flawed he undoubtedly was, but splendidly vital. His sentimentality about his humble origins kept his populist sympathies alive; Nixon's sentimentality about equally humble origins allied him to the rich and powerful at the expense of the poor, thus setting the tone for a conservatism based on greed rather than any Burkean vision. Such essential meanness of spirit that has now become a political norm was, I'd argue, alien to Johnson. But perhaps that's a sentimentality of my own. Nevertheless, it was with a strange mixture of awe and loathing that I stepped into his Library.

The first two floors are given over to glass-caged exhibits of memorabilia: photographs, newspaper clippings, quotations from speeches, personal possessions. It's an exercise in hagiography rather than information, with all the holy relics on display. The view of history that is conveyed is an unrevised Johnsonian version. The brief account of the Tonkin Gulf incident that led to congressional approval of the escalation of the Vietnam War blithely ignores the long established fact that the Administration's account of that incident was in all significant aspects a pack of lies. It may have been naive of me to expect intellectual honesty within a seven-storey genuflection to an imperial statesman, but since the Library was built by a great university and squats on its campus one does hope for more than duplicitous pieties. The next floor opens out into a great cube of a room, and at the far end, to a height of five storeys, rise behind glass the red boxes that contain the presidential archives. 31 million items are conserved in those acid-free boxes, enough material to tie the most diligent historian in knots for a decade.

About fifty miles west of Austin, deep in the Hill Country, is Johnson City, where one can visit the President's boyhood home and other places associated with his early life. I did go there, but couldn't face another white frame house filled with rocking chairs and chintzes and photographs of spectral settlers. I was more interested in visiting the LBJ Ranch, some fourteen miles further west. Although the ranch is now a National Historical Park, Johnson's widow still lives there much of the year. A stretch of the Pedernales (pronounced Purder*nar*less) River courses through the estate, which is spread over 2000 acres of the river valley. Visitors are taken round in small buses, and since the roomy but far from ostentatious ranch house is still occupied it is not possible to do more than glimpse the exterior as the bus trundles past.

The guide intersperses his comments with tapes of Lyndon nd Lady Bird saying a few words about some of the places we e being shown. Johnson's public manner was never appeal-With his tie straightened and his language cleaned up, he emerges as solemn and ponderous. The Johnson who said that Gerald Ford was too dumb to fart and chew gum at the same time and who discussed affairs of state with his advisers while grunting on the lavatory felt constrained in public to act presidentially. Yet when he most sought dignity he showed it least, and it's the vulgar, devious, brawling, back-slapping, manipulative, cajoling, foul-mouthed Johnson who paradoxically commands respect. I grew irritated by the slow drawling account of his schooldays or whatever other drivel he'd taped for the adoration of posterity, and was bored by the short traipse through the one-room schoolhouse that was part of the tour.

LBJ, in true Texas tradition, had bought up the land his family had once worked; so the associations of the ranch are not limited to his presidency. One of the stops on the tour is the house where in 1908 baby Lyndon was born. Well, not quite. The original three-room cabin was torn down decades ago; in any case, although LBJ had spent his babyhood there, at the age of five his family had moved to what is now commemorated as the Boyhood Home in Johnson City. Pilgrims need shrines, and so Johnson reconstructed the old cabin. To be fair, he originally did so to provide a guesthouse for distinguished visitors to the ranch while he was President, but after his retirement and the opening of the ranch to the public he milked the place for all it was worth. Gleefully the guide told us that 'the President', referring to him as though he were still alive and sitting in the Oval Office instead of buried in the lovely shady family cemetery near the river, used to drive up while tourists were admiring the ersatz homestead and lie in wait for them in the small garden at the back. As the tourists emerged he'd pounce, peddling signed copies of his turgid memoirs. The guide certainly found something endearing about this story of the multi-millionaire ex-President making a few more bucks on the side, but it eluded me.

So did the appeal of Fredericksburg, still a centre of the large German community that emigrated to Texas. In 1846, when Baron Meusebach brought his colonists out here, this spot was deep in Comanche territory, and, as should be clear by now, the Comanches had a low tolerance level for white settlers. Yet Meusebach succeeded in negotiating a treaty with the Indians and his community thrived. Fredericksburg remains a reasonably intact example of an early Texan town. (Here too the longest recorded chicken flight took place: 256 feet.) On either side of its broad main street are gingerbread houses with canopies and balconies, the very charming octagonal Vereins Kirche of 1847, and other structures built more robustly from local stone. Fredericksburg is not content to exist simply as a pleasant and historic old town; instead it feels obliged to proclaim its individuality at every corner. An old house can speak for itself, but not at Fredericksburg, where it has to be labelled with a creaking 'olde worlde' sign with bogus anti-quated lettering. Plump tourists, no doubt authentically German, ambled along the Main Street eating soft ice cream and gluttonously emptying bakery windows. I left them to it. (Travellers based in Austin who are considering a drive out to Fredericksburg can save themselves the trouble. Just west of the capital you will find Fredericksburg Village, a small shopping precinct behind tall colourful wooden façades in a mock-Teutonic style. Why drive a further seventy miles to its namesake when you have a toytown version on the doorstep?)

If Fredericksburg is a community that's losing its authen-ticity by tarting itself up for the diversion of tourists, at least Enchanted Rock, despite its Disney name, cannot easily be spoiled by commercial depradations. About twenty miles north of Fredericksburg, the rock is, quite simply, an immense pink breast of granite, rising 500 feet into the air and covering an area of 640 acres. Like the best breasts, it supports no veg-etation and the great naked rose expanse slopes down into the surrounding landscape of oak and cedar. At night, the rock, which was a sacred place to the Indians, creaks and groans as its mass contracts in the cooling air. This is still a place of mystery, enduring and disturbing.

Luckenbach, a few miles to the other side of Fredericksburg, is a far more cheerful spot. It's as much an invention of the tourist industry as Fredericksburg, but much more entrancing. With a population of 25 (some days 3), it scarcely makes it onto the map. There's not much to the hamlet, which lies in a hard-to-find Hill Country dip. There's a dance hall, a garage, perhaps three small houses, and an unpainted general store. Luckenbach was rescued from nonentity by a local humorist th the fine name of Hondo Crouch, the village's mayor, police , sheriff, and, indeed, owner. His bust in front of the store is the village's principal monument. Crouch's greatest inspiration was to hold a world's fair here. Then in the 1970s Waylon Jennings wrote a song about 'Luckenbach, Texas', Jerry Jeff Walker recorded a double album dedicated to Hondo Crouch, and now every sentient Texan in the world knows about the place, and many manage to puzzle their way to it down unmarked roads – unmarked because souvenir hunters tear down any signs bearing the magic name, so the local authorities no longer bother to erect them.

The rickety old store, which is also a post office and bar, is the Hill Country's answer to Washington Square. In the garden at the back a few dozen young men and women were sitting in the mottled sunshine sipping beer and quietly picking at guitars, though the sound was often drowned out by the whoops of grackles lined up on the branches of ancient trees. The warm November afternoon had drawn everyone outdoors, except for half a dozen chickens that scurried along the floorboards of the store. The place is a joke but a good one, and what a triumph to have made a tourist attraction from a clapped-out hamlet that has nothing to offer. Waylon Jennings put his finger on the secret of the place when in his song he wrote that 'in Luckenbach, Texas, ain't nobody feelin' no pain.'

*

WILLKOMMEN! say the billboards, and that's an order. No, I wasn't back in Fredericksburg, but in New Braunfels, another German settlement some way to the southeast. The town was founded by Prince Carl zu Solms-Braunfels, who, unlike his courageous deputy Meusebach, left Texas his name rather than his person, which he removed back to Germany shortly after he'd dumped his band of colonists. The Prince certainly chose a good spot for his community, which settled just beyond the Balcones Escarpment, on fertile land close to the lively Guadalupe River. The town preserves some old churches, the wood and limestone Schmitz Hotel, with its three storeys of porches handsomely overlooking the main square, and the sturdy brick Faust Hotel, with its charming tile-floored lobby crammed with potted plants and velvet couches and cooled by broad fans suspended from ceiling lights. There is a scattering of gingerbread houses, and some decent German restaurants and bakeries. In Landa Park, very close to the town centre, the

Comal Springs fill pools and a lake, and lovely trees and shrubs line winding trails.

WILLKOMMEN! shrieked the billboards, because the annual Wurstfest was in full swing that weekend. Where three or more Germans are gathered together, there's either an army or a beerhall, but the tribes that descended on the Wurstfest were in pacific mood. Americans have this strange way of honouring their ethnic heritage by parodying it. Stock items from the ragbag of national characteristics are totemized. In Boston, the large community of Irish descendants shows an intense patriotic fervour, a devotion to the colour green almost as fervent as their adoration of the Virgin Mary, that would baffle a true Irishman were they ever to meet one. The past has been sentimentalized, turned into a cupboard of stage props.

The same is true of the Texas Germans. Emblems have been plucked as if from travel posters, and then paraded as badges of identity. The casual visitor to the Wurstfest will observe that all *Mädchen* don peasant costumes and wear pigtails and red ribbons, that all German men sport feathered Tyrolean hats and lederhosen, and that the national dish is sausage on a stick. Yet even those costumes were parodied; those scarlet Tyrolean hats were far too dinky for the bulbous heads they covered.

There are two things to do at the Wurstfest: eat and listen to music. Stalls offered pretzels, potato pancakes, strudel, smoked beef rib, and the other delicacies that keep Germans slim. Sausage on a stick too, of course. And Mexican food at Jesse's El Dorado Café for those unable to stomach endless variations in the key of dough. In Das Grosse Zelt (the Big Tent) and Das Kleine Zelt (work that out for yourself) was a continuous serenade by the Bavarian Village Band, or Oma and the Oompahs, or the Canyon Middle School Polka Band. In Das Kleine Zelt I endured for ten minutes a recital by a prize-winning local accordionist, who was doing his best to whip up the modest crowd of pretzel-chomping burghers into a frenzy of hand-clapping. Later in the day the vast Wursthalle, a barn the size of an aircraft hanger but thoughtfully equipped with a number of bars, opened for dancing to the Cloverleafs and for listening to the singing of Myron Floren, much-loved star of the Lawrence Welk Show.

In a corner of the Wurstfest grounds they were conducting preliminary rounds for the Sausage Dog Show, where your pet dachshund could win ze prize for its close resemblance to knackwurst. Oh, how easy it is to have fun when you're German! Yet the faces that passed by as I munched my – yes, I confess – sausage on a stick – didn't express much glee. Those men in their lederhosen and kneesocks and red waistcoats and daft little hats had no fiery mountain gleam in their eyes; instead they offered to the world greying hair, greying faces, uncertain bellies, and prominent knees. The womenfolk came in two styles: hefty and blowsy, or, less attractively, pinched and sharp, with the straps of their peasant dresses hanging loosely over bony shoulders, their hair coiffed and curled and lacquered into solid place, and enamelled faces that reflected the light.

Even outside the Wurstfest grounds the travesty continued, a permanent feature of tourist-conscious New Braunfels. The local language, if signs and ads can be trusted, is pidgin German. An arrow outside the grounds directed officials to the Kleine Office, a store just off the main highway announced itself to be Opa's Haus of Steins. A standard pancake parlour was transformed into a Pancake Haus, and the sign was in straightened-out Gothic script. The culture had been fossilized, and it seemed strange and sad that it had been allowed to happen, for although the German immigrants had in most respects happily dived into the American melting pot, the community had, more than most, preserved its language and cuisine. The best of the German heritage in Texas is to be found in pit barbecues and in the smokehouses where first-rate sausages and smoked meats are sold. The Wurstfest was a mockery of a culture – not a culture that at the best of times stirs my affections, but for all that a culture that deserves better than the vulgar nonsense that New Braunfels offers. The Germans themselves have a word for it: *Dreck*.

Forget the Alamo

'Will you have some chicken-fried steak? It'll only take a second in the microwave?'

Lethal rays resurrected the limp meat and the cream gravy, and I was soon perched at the kitchen counter tucking in to my favourite dish. It was, unquestionably, better than the stodge I'd been given at the Badlands Hotel in Lajitas.

'I'm so glad you called me. I was hoping we'd have a chance to visit with you when you came to San Antonio. I'm just so sorry Bernard is sick. I'd love you to meet him. I'll show you around the house, and we'll check in on Bernard.'

Once again I was given the Texan household tour; no nook was to be left unadmired. In the sunken living room she showed me some paintings on the walls, examples of Western art, not a genre I care for: Panhandle sunsets and cowboys and cactus and full-throated skies.

'This one here is a Millard. That name may not mean much to you.'

'I'm afraid not.'

'He's one of our most famous Western artists, very highly thought of. Do you know that this very painting was featured last year in a leading art magazine?'

'Really?'

'I swear to you. And do you like this one?' She pointed to a small painting of some distant pillars.

'Yes I do.'

'That's one of my paintings. I'm sure you recognise the subject.'

'Let me see now . . .' Panic – from which LaVerne rescued me.

'It's the Dallas skyline.'

'Of course it is! I was thrown for a moment by the perspective.'

She nodded. Lining the stairs and all along one wall of her bedroom, which was awash with pastel draperies and billowing cushions, were photographs of LaVerne during her earlier career as an actress; articles about her work as performer and director had been framed at eye-level and I was invited to read them while she went to see whether Bernard was well enough to receive me. He was, and I was ushered into his room, where, looking a little peaked, a handsome skinny teenager lay sprawled in his shorts on his bed.

'Hello, I'm sorry to hear you're not well.'

'Oh, but he's much better,' intervened LaVerne, 'and he says he's going to come down in a few minutes. See you downstairs, sweetheart.'

I'd met LaVerne at Terlingua, and as seemed to happen at the end of every conversation there, however slight, it had resulted in an invitation. Not, in this case, to stay, but to get in touch so she could 'visit with' me. Recently divorced, LaVerne was testing the waters of singlehood again, and the world seemed full of possibilities. With me she discussed more projects and plans than most people could accomplish in a lifetime, let alone the next year or two. She wanted to travel, to direct, to produce TV programmes, to continue her studies as a painter. She bounced ideas off me as we sat in the kitchen waiting for Bernard to descend.

He came down and, with little prompting, went into the living room and sat down at the grand piano. Rippling tuneful music in the style of Superior Free-Form Nightclub poured through the open door.

'That boy is so talented,' said La Verne.

'He certainly is.'

'Would it surprise you to know that what you're listening to are his own compositions?'

'Good Lord. That's very remarkable. Does Bernard want to be a musician?'

'Oh no. He wants to go to Yale to study math and then he's going to be a tax lawyer. I wish you could meet my other boy, Shelby. He's only twelve but he's adorable. I always say that Bernard wants to change the world, Shelby just wants to love it.'

The doorbell rang and LaVerne went off to answer it. I wandered about the kitchen, peering at shopping lists and reading notes magnetically pinned to the refrigerator. Above the Snoopy telephone was a small framed homily in the form of a letter which concluded: 'My Dad sends His love. I want you to meet Him. He cares too.' It was signed, 'Your friend Jesus'.

LaVerne returned with a dark and very handsome young

man in tow. Mario, I rapidly learnt, was an Italian model and it just happened that he had his portfolio with him. While LaVerne went upstairs to change into something glamorous, Mario showed me a few dozen photographs of himself wearing expensive clothes. Mario was so vain it was endearing. LaVerne coyly suggested to me that he had been her lover: 'Isn't he gorgeous? I'm going to write a book called "Italian men – why every woman should have one – for two weeks". Isn't that a good idea?' It seemed, though, that Mario's passion had cooled and he was far more interested in taking Bernard off to the gym for an all-male workout while I was out with LaVerne.

San Antonio remains the most Spanish and Mexican of Texan cities. A small border town such as Presidio or Roma may be more Mexican in the sense that it reflects more accurately the impoverished life of a present-day Mexican village, but the Hispanic quality of San Antonio is more positive: cuisine, pace, architecture, fiestas – these are all enlivened by a relaxed, sunnier attitude to living more typical of indolent Mexico than buttoned-up north Texas. In Dallas pedestrians cringe obediently before Stop lights on street corners even when there isn't a car in sight. In San Antonio nobody gives a damn. If you think you can make it to the other side of the road without injury, go.

Yet San Antonio is not an exclusively Hispanic settlement. It was inhabited by a few hundred Spaniards in the eighteenth century, and priests and large numbers of tame Indians occupied the missions that stretched from San Antonio's Alamo south towards the border. The first real colonists were Canary Islanders, who soon ran up against the powerful missionaries, not to mention the local Apaches. By the 1790s, however, the missions were in decay and were later secularized. German immigrants began to pour into San Antonio and their influence is still evident today in the names of stores and the once luxurious Menger Hotel. The rich merchants who built the splendid mansions that crowd King William Street, just south of downtown, were mostly German or of German descent, though the architecture doesn't reflect it.

Despite this mixed heritage, the third largest city in Texas is overwhelmingly Mexican-American in atmosphere as well as population. Well over half the city's million inhabitants are

Mexican; for over twenty years San Antonio's staunchly liberal congressman has been Henry B. Gonzalez, though his reputation as Texas's most prominent Mexican-American politician is being eclipsed by that of San Antonio's dashing young mayor, Henry Cisneros. The separatist ideology that marked much Chicano politics in the 1960s and 1970s has died down, and Cisneros, for all his youth, is no radical. Capable, business-oriented, he is thoroughly typical of the upwardly mobile Mexican-American determined to make his way in and through society just like any other American citizen.

Although Hispanic styles of architecture are common, if not abundant, in the wealthy northern suburbs of Olmos Park and Alamo Heights, these are predominantly Anglo enclaves. The vast majority of the Hispanic population lives in more abject circumstances in the southern quarters of the city in what must be one of the largest barrios in the United States. Driving down to the missions one morning I passed a small building that announced itself to be a Discoteca Pentecostal, which said much about the blending of cultures in this attractive and open-necked city.

I strapped myself into LaVerne's mile-long sedan and we purred down McCullough towards the city centre. Other than Austin, a typical college town, San Antonio is the only Texan city where the downtown area is bustling after dark. We parked and then strolled into Market Square. There's still a daytime market here in one section, but most of the square has been turned into a pedestrianized precinct with shops and restaurants occupying the old commercial buildings. Small galleries specialize in the more elegant examples of Western art and Indian weaving and ceramics. Some shops sold piñatas, the Mexican dolls *de rigeur* at any festivity in San Antonio. The core of the piñata is a clay pot filled with toys and sweets, and festooned with paper streamers and decorations that transform it into a bull or donkey or Santa Claus. Filled in Aztec times with gifts for the exacting gods of pre-Columbian America, piñatas now fulfil a more frivolous role at celebrations of all kinds.

Even in late November, it was still warm enough to sit outdoors at one of the Market Square restaurants. As we walked between La Margarita and Mi Tierra, which share the same broad alley, I could smell and hear the sizzling *fajitas* being brought out to the tables on hot platters. *Fajitas*, which I made a point of eating as often as possible in southern Texas, are succulent strips of marinated skirt steak cooked with onions and served with tortillas. Mi Tierra is as much a café as a restaurant and stays open twenty-four hours a day. Its bakery sells a variety of Mexican sweetmeats: sugary things done to fruits and vegetables. The place was packed, and LaVerne assured me that even in the small hours of the morning Mi Tierra is never deserted.

Walking towards the centre of San Antonio – and walking is the obvious way to get about in downtown San Antonio, a statement no one could make about, say, Houston – we came to one of the many bridges that cross the river. The San Antonio River has been diverted in the downtown area to form a network of canals. By the side of most of these bridges are steps that lead down to the Paseo del Rio, a complex of footpaths that follow, usually on both sides, the windings of the river. Over the years the San Antonio had become a noxious verminous stream after drilling for wells had sharply reduced its flow. Then in 1939 the city fathers blocked a plan to pave over the river for use as a highway, and instead set about transforming the river-banks into a chain of walks and cafés and gardens. The fine hotels, whose fronts face the busy downtown streets and whose backs spill onto terraces that abut the calmer Paseo, exploit the charm of the waterways without detracting from it.

As we sat sipping margaritas at a small outdoor café, I asked LaVerne whether most of the good restaurants in San Antonio were close to the Paseo del Rio.

'Many of them are. But this is a big city. Restaurants are spread out all over town. There's an interesting place to the north of the city called the San Francisco Steak House. The food's quite good, but people go there to see a girl who every half hour or so climbs onto a kind of trapeze and swings through the dining room and tries to kick a bell that's hung from the ceiling.'

'You're joking.'

'No, it's true.'

'Have you ever been there?'

'Been there, sweetheart? I used to be the girl on the trapeze.'

*

Remember the Alamo! Hard to forget it in San Antonio, where the unmistakable broad silhouette of the old Spanish church has become the emblem of the city. Tourists flock in their thousands to wander about the church and the beautiful gardens planted with oaks, catclaws, pecans, and chinaberry trees, recalling, with the aid of permanent exhibits, the tragic events of March 1836. The siege of the Alamo is presented as a triumph of independent Texas over autocratic Mexico. It is indeed hard to have much sympathy for the brutal Mexican dictator Santa Anna. Yet it's quite important to remember, as one wanders through the shrine and gazes at the portraits of the heroic defenders of the Alamo – James Bowie, David Crockett, William Travis, and the other 150 men – that the siege was a disaster, an appalling defeat, falling not far short of mass suicide.

Bad luck played its part too: men who should have remained at the garrison in San Antonio were drawn off, thanks to divisions in the Texan military leadership, to capture distant Matamoros on the Rio Grande, a foolish ill-planned expedition that led nowhere. Expected reinforcements never arrived; San Antonio was many miles away from other settlements with the capacity to send fighting men to beef up the garrison. Moreover, the occupants of the Alamo were unpaid, badly clothed, badly fed. That some of them wandered off is less surprising than that so many stayed, especially when one considers that a large number of those who perished at the Alamo were not Texans at all. There were twenty or so Englishmen, eleven Irishmen, and a sprinkling of Danes and Germans, all with a variety of motivations for being present: some were aspiring colonists, hopeful of obtaining large land grants in independent Texas, others were adventurers, others idealists keen to have a crack at Mexican tyranny. The defence of the Alamo was, in some sense, though not perhaps as fully as Texan collective pride would have us believe, a defence of freedom; the mythology of the Alamo that equates the siege with a heroic struggle for liberty and independence should not blind the visitor to the recognition that almost two hundred brave men died to little purpose. The garrison could have escaped before the vindictive Santa Anna unleashed his superior forces on the Alamo, but Travis and his men decided to stay put. 'God and Texas,' wrote the defiant (foolhardy?) Travis, 'Victory or Death.' They got Death.

A few hundred yards away stands the uninspired nineteenth-century cathedral of San Fernando, and there I stood respectfully before the tomb that contains the remains of the heroic defenders. I later discovered that I had been fooled, that years ago the corpses had been disinterred and conclusively shown to be not those of the heroes of the Alamo. Myth, here as elsewhere in San Antonio, rides roughshod over truth, blurring the realisation that what happened in March 1836 is infinitely more poignant, exasperating, stirring, and heartbreaking than the bland simplicities substituted by the legend-makers.

Although the Alamo is the best-known mission church of San Antonio, there are four others close to the city, all of which give a clearer idea of what the original eighteenth-century missions must have been like. The Spanish missions were more than religious centres; they were also agricultural outposts where the priests taught tractable Indians European farming techniques. Two miles south of the Alamo stands the imposing Mission Concepción, built from beautifully weathered tufa stone and surrounded by tall palm trees. Harmonious carvings decorate the façade, and the crossing is capped by a small dome. Some frescoes in the small baptistery have been further embellished by visitors, and on May 28, 1913, Marie from Victoria, Texas, scrawled her name across the base of the Crucifixion.

The most impressive of the missions is San Jose. Not only is the church, with its elaborate façade, a fine one, but the spacious compound survives in more complete form here than at the other missions. Indians lived in sets of rooms built along the inside of the compound wall; these and other buildings survive: a lofty granary, a mill, the roofless ruins of the monastery. Old prints make it clear how heavily, and adroitly, San Jose and the other missions have been restored from a state of ruin.

Few coachloads make it to the Espada, on the outskirts of the city. It's the most peaceful of the missions. The rebuilt chapel is modest, less grand than San Jose; few florid carvings here, just sturdy wooden benches and simple whitewashed walls. A mile away is the Espada Aqueduct, the only surviving Spanish aqueduct in the United States. Water still flows, albeit sluggishly, along the gentle curve of the arched structure just as it did in the 1730s, and I spent a tranquil few minutes standing nearby, staring down at the minnows darting about in the

Piedras Creek and at the ants that were pouncing on my sandaled feet for lunch. Dragonflies flitted over the water. Standing there in the ninety-degree sunshine, it was hard to convince myself that I was indeed in Texas. I was standing among the leavings of a European culture, scarcely modified at all by the exigencies of a New World. Here was a history that predated Texas, and yet Texas had absorbed the heritage of its Spanish and Mexican past and transmuted it into that lively cultural hybrid the world knows as TexMex. In the peaceful structures of the Espada, its mission, its dam, its aqueduct, that old pre-Texan world quietly breathes on.

*

San Antonio, already blessed with a lovely climate and an unaffected charm, also supports as many museums as most museums have rooms. In addition to the fairly new Museum of Art, there's the Witte Museum, amply stocked with American furniture and Indian artefacts, as well as local exhibits and four historic houses moved there intact. The largest display of horns in the world may be inspected at the Buckhorn Hall of Horns. Not satisfied with rooms filled with antlers, stuffed bears, narwhal tusks, and a famous chandelier made from over 4000 horns, the museum authorities have added a Hall of Fins. Just as singular is the Hertzberg Circus Collection, with 20,000 items including a genuine fragment of the wedding cake once sliced by Mr and Mrs Tom Thumb.

Close to the city centre is La Villita, a small neighbourhood of compact stone houses and adobe cottages, many of them built by German and French immigrants who came to San Antonio in the nineteenth century. By the early 1920s La Villita had become a slum. In the 1930s, instead of tearing the place down, Mayor Maury Maverick took the enlightened step of closing the area to traffic and conserving it, with the happy result that visitors can gain a fairly clear idea of the conditions in which ordinary Texan immigrants lived over a century ago. The small houses with their plain porches have been converted into restaurants and workshops used by weavers, glass-blowers, candlemakers, and other *soi-disant* crafts people. Most American cities with a history to conserve do so with a heavy hand, but throughout San Antonio, with the one exception of the Alamo, buildings and districts have been converted not only with delicacy and sensitivity, but with imagination too. La Villita is not fossilized; it is re-used, as is the Museum of Art, stylishly transformed from a brewery. The missions too are largely rebuilt, but only a well-informed or highly observant visitor would be aware of it.

Nearby is the Spanish Governor's Palace of 1749. A palace it's not, but it too has been impeccably restored and furnished to show how those in authority lived in what in those days was a very remote colonial outpost. If the palace is typical of other Spanish officials' residences, they seem to have lived rather well. With its chapel, handsome dining room, spacious kitchen, cool floors and ancient beams, the house, though far from luxurious, is dignified and comfortable. Unlike the palace, the Majestic Theater isn't a historic monument, but it ought to be. It's one of the most theatrical of theatres, a marvellous old building, both sides of the stage piled high with absurd yet magical structures: loggias, lights glimmering in Moorish windows, balconies, and behind them cedars and palms, while above the whole fantastical extravaganza spreads a deep dark sky filled with twinkling stars. Never mind the play, go and see the theatre.

However, the dominant mode of San Antonio is not drama but an undemonstrative refinement, nowhere more evident than at the fine McNay Art Institute. Like the celebrated Gardner Museum at Fenway Court in Boston, the museum was the brainchild of a rich, determined local matron. Mrs Gardner went to the trouble of reconstructing a Venetian palazzo in Boston, while Mrs McNay, rather less rich, contented herself with a beautiful Mexican-style mansion built around a flower-filled patio and set on a hillock among 25 acres of lush gardens.

The Institute was being thoroughly used when I was there. A party of small children was checking the crevices of Maillol's *La Nymphe* in the elegant new sculpture gallery, while in another room a dozen permed middle-aged women were arguing about the physical charms of a crop-haired young woman in a painting by André Derain.

'I think she's cute, real cute,' piped a stout woman who should not have been wearing tartan slacks.

'She don't look too sexy to me,' contributed a gruff dotard, the only man in the group, who sat in a chair clutching his cane.

A chorus of disagreement rose from the women, and one of

them said: 'Bartley, I guess that's one thing men and women ain't ever going to agree about.'

'That's right, ma'm.'

*

It would have been pleasant to linger in San Antonio, but I heard the call of the hinterland and plunged back into the scrub. I drove for an hour and there it was, outside the tiny city hall, a strawberry, seven feet tall. Poteet is strawberry capital of Texas and has erected this statue to its most important crop. I touched it, then driving east, came upon the village of Fashing. Curious name, I thought. Could it have been founded by homesick immigrants from Munich recalling the annual booze-up they would never again experience? I found one of the useful historical markers placed wherever a town or spot on the landscape has left a dent in Texan history, and all was made clear. Fashing wasn't founded by Germans at all, let alone those with *heimweh*, but was a small farming community established in 1915, at which time it was named Hickock. But the US Post Office objected to this name (why?) so the hamlet was renamed after a favourite product, Fashion Cut Plug Tobacco. The founders of Fashing did well: the community has become the only commercial producer of uranium in Texas.

In San Antonio I'd spent some enthralled hours at the Institute of Texas Cultures, which documents and demonstrates the contributions of twenty-five ethnic groups, including such unexpected nations as the Lebanese and the Wends, that flowed like tributaries into the mainstream of Texan life. The Institute had sparked a curiosity that was drawing me to these early rural settlements. Immigrants had travelled, often under perilous conditions, to a remote territory that offered large tracts of land but little else, and I was curious to see how they'd put down new roots. I'd spent the previous night at Castroville, settled in the 1840s by a band of Alsatian colonists led by Henri Castro. Laid out on ample lots are stone and wooden cottages, simple, graceful, functional. A few houses on a lane by the Medina River had old wooden shutters; otherwise there were few clues to the national origin of the settlers. It was pleasant to stay at the Landmark Inn, a simple old hotel that had been in use almost since the village's foundation. As the sun had dipped down over the mulberry trees, I'd sat on the verandah in a rocking chair and looked out over the garden and the old mill. This must be one of the few spots in Texas that feels more like New England. Still, Castroville disappointed. Why I imagined it would be filled with narrow streets overlooked by high gabled buildings with shutters and painted inscriptions I don't know, but there it was. I'd conjured up a mental image of old Alsace in southern Texas, and it wasn't there.

Nor was Panna Maria like Cracow, even though it's the oldest Polish community in the United States. Silesians fleeing Poland in despair after the failure of the 1848 revolution had come to this spot about fifty miles southeast of San Antonio, led by a monk who had already spent some time in Texas. The names on the tombstones close to the Gothic Revival church were Polish, to be sure, and the small stone cottages grouped nearby may, for all I know, resemble the cottages of Silesia. Yet nothing about Panna Maria felt Polish. Again my expectations were all wrong. It was absurd to imagine that I would find wizened babushkas at their spinning wheels in open doorways, while kasha stewed in blackened pots over wood-burning stoves. Panna Maria was little different from any other agricultural hamlet in Texas. The immigrants had not fled Poland in order to recreate it five thousand miles from home in Karnes County, Texas. The old ways became as well concealed as a strong poker hand.

Nearby Helena used to be the county seat but, like Jefferson, fell into rapid decline when the railway failed to pass through the town. The dilapidated courthouse is now a dilapidated museum which contains nothing of interest – which is why I found it fascinating. In dusty cabinets were displayed, in disarray, old photographs, spectacles, hymnals, clothes, books, minerals, dolls in faded lacy garments. Helena was a rough place in the nineteenth century: trade wars between freight haulers led to frequent duels and killings. In the courthouse museum, however, none of this is apparent; instead the brittle exhibits record the tedium of everyday life in rural Texas. Only in the grounds is there a reminder of that lawlessness: the village jail, which is, quite simply, a rusty iron cage, scarcely large enough to accommodate a single well-built offender.

*

When I'd lunched at the country club in Dallas, Sam had said to me with pride: 'Y'know, when Carmen was still in school she was the Come and Take It Queen.'

As I was absorbing this curious piece of biographical information, Carmen had snapped: 'Sam, how can you be so crude! Saying that without explaining what it's about!'

The explanation was disappointing. Carmen had grown up in Gonzalez, a small town that had been much involved in the war against Mexico. When the Mexican army approached the rebellious town, its citizens dragged out a small cannon, originally donated to Gonzalez for protection against Indian raiders, and fired the first shot of the Texas revolution. COME AND TAKE IT, the soldiers printed on a flag that flew beside the cannon, and from that time on those four words have been the town motto. Each October Gonzalez celebrates its Come and Take It Days, and many years ago Carmen had been its beauty queen.

The town is broadly laid out around two main squares; in one of them stands a statue of a Confederate soldier, facing north just in case the enemy should ever return. Despite its Mexican name many of Gonzalez' citizens are of German descent, including Miss Corinne Remschel, a former schoolteacher whose grandfather had never spoken a word of his native tongue from the time he came to Texas. His lumber business had prospered and he had built the large rambling frame house where Miss Remschel still lived. She greeted me at the front door and took me into a breakfast room. It was brighter here than in the shadowy front rooms, and there was a pleasant view onto the small garden around her house, with its large old trees.

Miss Remschel travelled a great deal and seemed to live quite lavishly for a former teacher. She then explained that she had inherited some farmland to the north of town where oil had recently been found. Almost overnight she had become rich in a typically Texan way. Her lawyers had drawn up the necessary documents, and the royalties began to flow as regularly as the oil. The slump in prices, she said regretfully, would diminish her income this year, but the sum she mentioned was far from trifling.

'That's a beautiful tree,' I said, pointing to a huge pecan that was brushing the screens with its branches.

'I got a real good crop this year. Would you like a pecan?'

And she pushed a well-filled bowl towards me. I selected a nut and the bowl was then withdrawn.

I didn't stay long. I had quite a long drive ahead of me north to Taylor, and hopes of being granted a second pecan were fast fading. I was going to Taylor for a single reason. The local Chamber of Commerce promotes this town near Austin with the hopeless slogan TRY TAYLOR . . . IT'S GREAT. Let me help out. Try Louie Mueller's, skip the rest. Most aficionados would agree that Mueller's is one of the very best barbecue restaurants in Texas. Best and least attractive. The second-class waiting room at Preston Station has more charm. Mueller's is a large cavernous room, bare of decoration and with walls painted school corridor green. The only furnishings were large square tables and plain chairs. Customers are not invited to linger; this is working man's food, to be eaten rapidly during a lunch break or immediately after the day's work. Behind a long counter at the end of the room stand huge blackened ovens. I picked up a tray and the counterman lined it with a paper sheet.

I ordered brisket and sausage. The counterman removed a large joint of beef from the oven, carved me two generous slices, weighed them, then slapped them down on the paper. (No plates.) Then he extracted a sausage from the oven and added it to the brisket. He scribbled the amount owed on the paper, and after ordering a beer I paid and carried my lunch off to an empty table. The food was wonderful. Lunging greedily into the meaty sausage with my plastic fork, the damn thing broke.

A man at the next table smiled sympathetically. 'They don't make 'em like they used to.'

City of Bunnies

Arriving in Dallas the next day, I parked in the driveway of Sam and Carmen's house, stepped across the road to collect the key (my hosts were away for a couple of days), then let myself in. I heard barking from the side porch. Of course: the dog, a rottweiler bitch who'd just had puppies. Rottweilers are much prized brutes, even more vicious than weimaraners, and in Texas that month there were two bitches, one from each horrible species, who'd given birth, and I just happened to be staying with both sets of owners. Since my wardrobe still bore Twink's autograph, I was taking no chances. I'd been told the dog had been locked out onto the porch with her babies and I strolled confidently into the adjoining den so that the creature, still growling and barking, could get accustomed to the unfamiliar presence in the house.

'There's a good dog,' I said soothingly, keeping my distance from the porch screens.

'Yap,' replied the bitch, and the next thing I knew the door was swinging open and the brute was leaping towards me. This was no time for heroics. I ran for it, slammed the door behind me, and paid another visit to the neighbour, who then returned to the house as an advance guard. The dog was impounded. I'd rather have a gorilla in the house than a rottweiler.

*

Dallas, spreading out over the last century from its original centre, has touched hands with about thirty other townships, such as Irving, Richardson, Garland, Arlington. Eventually the townships found themselves surrounded by the expanding city, into which they were tucked like forgotten letters in a drawer. The towns retain their formal independence, though such crucial resources as water are administered by Dallas for the entire Metroplex – a suitably ugly term for the metropolitan area that sprawls for over thirty miles from shabby Mesquite in the east to the decorous outskirts of Fort Worth in the west. After years of bickering between the two major cities of the Metroplex, they finally kissed and made up over the construction of the Dallas-Fort Worth Airport, which, strategically situated between the two, has brought even greater prosperity to this part of Texas.

These towns had their histories, but no one cared to preserve that past until recently, and for the most part the efforts have come too late. In Dallas the grandest residential areas a century ago were close to the downtown area. Ross Avenue was lined with resplendent mansions, but only one has survived. Some fine houses, spreading out under broad eaves, still look onto Park Row and South Boulevard. Here the Jewish merchants, whose names are still synonymous with the best shops in town – Marcus, Sanger, Zales – lived in properties so grand that easements specified that each house must contain quarters large enough for seven servants. This area, only a few blocks from downtown, is now a black middle-class enclave, and many of the houses have been bought up and restored with the incentive of generous tax advantages.

Swiss Avenue and Munger Place, boulevards rolling into East Dallas, were built in the 1920s and contain the largest group of prairie-style houses in the United States, many of them designed by Frank Lloyd Wright. Yet this district was almost razed to the ground ten years ago. Hank, a local restaurateur, born in Dallas and fascinated by its early history, remembered East Dallas a mere dozen years ago. 'It was a disgusting neighbourhood. These single-family houses were back-zoned to permit multiple occupancy, which meant they were turned into rooming houses owned by absentee landlords. There were lots of totally trashed houses here. The city didn't care. They were happy to see East Dallas deteriorate so they could tear it down and turn it over to developers. What saved it was the determination of individual homeowners who weren't prepared to see this unique neighbourhood turned into freeways and high-rises.'

Another East Dallas resident, a journalist called Jack, confirmed what Hank told me. 'In fighting those demolition plans a lot of people became politicized. Of course, local determination to resist the developers was seen as just a shade away from communism, reminiscent of northern-style decadent ward-heeling politics.' This local activism spread to other parts of the city. Glen Lakes, which Carmen had shown me, had not been built that long ago but already developers were hoping to tear it down and build homes even more expensive than those already there. At meetings the residents instructed their councilman to vote against demolition schemes.

'He was just an errand boy for the developers,' explained Jack, 'and said he couldn't vote against the scheme. Then a businessman stood up – and remember these are lawyers and merchants living in Glen Lakes, not acid-dropping hippies, which is the way the oligarchy perceives East Dallas – and he undertook to raise a million bucks in one week and would spend every penny, and I quote, "to make sure you never get another fucking vote in your life".'

For local activists the enemy is the 'oligarchy' that in their eyes still controls Dallas. Until the mid-1970s the city was run by a group of conservative businessmen, who formed the Citizens Charter Association to endorse candidates for council elections. Until 1975 council members were voted for at large, that is, by city-wide election and not on a local district basis. Such a system clearly favoured a wealthy clique that could select candidates sympathetic to its interests and then boost them through their newspapers and advertising campaigns. In 1975 the courts ruled that the system had to be changed, and most of the at-large districts were replaced by single-member districts, which were much more responsive to local pressures and interests. The oligarchy's power was diminished though hardly obliterated. It could no longer assume that it could get its own way.

Far north Dallas may have been colonised by the nouveau riche, and East Dallas may be newly settled by liberals, journalists, and other suspect people, but for those who can write half a dozen noughts on a cheque without thinking twice, the Park Cities, Highland Park and University Park, remain the most desirable places to live. When they were founded about fifty years ago in what were then remote outskirts, the city fathers were unwilling to embrace the new suburbs within the Dallas boundaries. It would mean providing services and schools, and the council decided it wasn't worth the trouble. So the two cities incorporated themselves, and the city of Dallas, unable to benefit from the enormous tax base provided by these prohibitively expensive houses, has been kicking itself ever since.

On either side of Turtle Creek, a brook that meanders through Highland Park, lies a narrow strip of well-tended park, shrubs and rocks and lawns, flanked on both sides by Lakeside

Drive. Truffling this pastoral scene are some of the most handsome mansions of Dallas, set among grandfatherly trees and harsh local grass. Lakeside nudges Beverley Drive; here brick walls and proud gates conceal equally large houses from the vulgar gaze. Like any very rich suburb, it's a sheltered world and the password is money. Skilful landscaping and bright sunshine give stiff dignity and warmth to these miniature estates built in one of two architectural styles: Colonial and pastiche.

The sleek hierarchical orderliness of the Park Cities has no counterpart south of downtown, where skyscrapers give way to a bruised spattered area of warehouses, run-down frame houses, and farmers' markets, where shrewd households come at weekends to stock up on cheap fresh vegetables. On a particularly grubby and rutted side street I drove past a man lying motionless in the gutter. Children were playing nearby, so I assumed he was a familiar fixture, a local drunk who routinely slept off his hangovers on the street. On one of the doors leading into a windowless brick office building was a small poster showing the barrel of a shotgun pointing out. Beneath the image were these words: NEVER MIND THE DOG. BEWARE THE OWNER.

Crossing the Trinity River, one of the least noticeable waterways to flow through any major city, I found myself in West Dallas. A few miles away rose the downtown skyscrapers, moated by the leisurely river. Here, though, street after street was filled with rubbish: garbage in the gutters, fast food containers and styrofoam boxes and rotting chicken legs left where they'd been discarded on front lawns. Even the low unpainted frame houses were junk, squalid shacks that seemed only barely habitable. Porches were sagging with rot and the weight of household goods consigned to the verandah. One ancient Chrysler had lost its wheels but still retained the vestiges of a bumper sticker that read: WELCOME TO TEXAS. NOW GO HOME.

West Dallas, or large swathes of it, is a slum, and in part its poverty lies not in the absence of goods and possessions, but in their superfluity. Most of what was possessed – whether a 1950s Buick with fins, or an immense refrigerator, or a couch with protruding springs and stuffing – no longer functioned, and so around many of the shacks spread an entire junkyard of material objects that their owners had rejected, and of material objects that had rejected their owners. I came to Lakewest housing project, a small development of bungalows and two-storey brick blocks, most of which were defaced with graffiti. Lakewest looked like an abandoned POW camp. About half of these unsavoury and ugly buildings had been boarded up. The rest should have been.

*

While West Dallas, ignored, stagnates, North Dallas booms. The area east of the Park Cities is home to a vast community of young professionals, single and divorced, who spend the evening hours driving up and down streets such as Greenville Avenue, block after block of bars and restaurants and discotheques. The recession has bypassed Dallas, and the city's YUPs (Young Urban Professionals) have money to burn.

Shannon Wynne set the tone for Dallas's night life when he opened a fashionable bar called Nostromo and then a club called Tango, an old bank building on Lower Greenville which he'd cleverly converted into a multi-level disco. Although he substantially redesigned some of the interior so as to provide ample space for dancing, he'd also left other features intact, such as the old bank vaults, now filled with space invader machines. Wandering into Tango one evening I found myself walking purposefully down a long corridor, wondering where it led to, and saw coming towards me a most intent-looking man. Only when I collided with the mirror at the end of the hall did I realise I'd been approaching my own reflection. Bashed and abashed, I left.

Tango has an uninviting exterior, so Shannon Wynne, with a freakish humour uncharacteristic of Dallas, had the bright idea of commissioning six ten-foot-high dancing frogs from a local artist, and he placed them on the roof. Floodlit, the jolly frogs could be seen from many blocks away and, overnight, Dallas knew where Tango was. The city authorities, however, were less amused. The sign control board, entrusted with the serious mission of preventing excessive sign pollution, took action, maintaining that the frogs constituted an advertisement. Not at all, retorted Wynne; they are Art. Wynne lost, and it seemed clear that the frogs would have to hop off. At that moment a journalist wrote up the story for the *New York Times* and soon after that the city reversed its decision, probably because the Dallas city elders couldn't bear the thought that New Yorkers were laughing at them.

I had a chat with Shannon Wynne during a quiet moment mid-afternoon at Nostromo, a bar so chic that the building, in contrast to Tango, carries no identifying sign of any kind. Wynne, the Dallasite with the reputation of being one step ahead of everybody else in the restaurant game, was not, as I'd expected, a stylish middle-aged man in a white suit with a flamboyant cravate and a silver cigar case. No, he was a tall, lanky man of thirty with long hair and the intensely preoccupied manner of a mathematician searching for a lost square root. His tension seemed related to a mania for detail, for getting things right. We had coffee and then I accompanied him on his routine tour of Nostromo to check that everything would be in order by the time it opened. When he found something not in place, or not done to his satisfaction, his staff were sent scurrying off to remedy the matter.

Wynne controls everything. 'I design my bars, I choose the menus, I pick the clothes my staff wear.' There were large pictures on the walls, giving a welcome dash of colour to the decor, which was hi-tech white and clinical. 'See those paintings? I keep changing them. I like to keep my places current. The bar looks strange when it's empty like this. It'll start to fill about 7.30, and by 11.00 it'll take ten minutes just to cross the room. One reason it stays popular is that I recently opened up a place at the back. I'll show you.'

He took me through a door into a small room, with little in it other than a dancing area in the centre and two levels of booths surrounding it. The colour scheme was a stylish grey and black, and into the walls were set panels of coloured etched glass.

'This is the Rio Room. It looks good, I think. I used that coloured glass to give it a swampy look.'

'What's the difference between Nostromo and the Rio Room?'

'A thousand dollars a year, that's the difference. The Rio is a private club.' He saw me wince and nodded. 'I think it's a lot too. People join for status. Young businessmen like to be seen here, they can show off to their girlfriends and each other. The place has the feel of a very exclusive nightclub. Nearly everybody drinks champagne.

'Dallas is different from the rest of Texas. It's the New York of the Southwest. Its sophistication isn't new – it was probably Neiman-Marcus that started it, and that store's been going almost eighty years. It's a self-conscious city. People who've never set foot in Texas know Dallas. They know about Neiman-Marcus, the Kennedy assassination, they watch that stupid soap opera on TV. Nowadays Dallas is acting like an international city. Houston, which to be honest is just as international, still behaves like Cowtown. It's garish. Dallas isn't. Dallas now has the third largest fashion industry in America and it's a big convention city. The newcomers have made a difference too. They've brought in lots of money, and while some of them force native Texans into a stronger sense of being Texan – all that urban cowboy stuff – others bring a real sophistication to the city.'

*

It was indeed Neiman-Marcus that first established that Dallas was more than a hick town, and the famous department store is still flourishing. Although it has tried to transplant its gracious character to its other stores in Texas and beyond, it's still the original store on Main Street that best conveys its quality. The displays are elegant and uncrowded, and shoppers are generously provided with comfortable chairs and sofas into which they can subside to catch their breath between writing cheques. I did wonder, though, whether it's tactful for the sales staff to be, on the whole, better dressed and groomed than the customers.

This year the chosen people for their National Fortnight extravaganza were the lovable German *Volk*. Entire rooms within the store had been converted into beerhalls and toy fairs, a market place, a street bazaar. Blonde women with pigtails thrust small bottles of 4711 toilet water into my hands. Leading fashion designers showed off their creations; there were exhibitions of 1920s prints, old photographs, antique beer steins. Special restaurants, from a simple Wursthaus to a grander establishment, had been set up. It was exceptionally well done, though it did give me the creeps. The German heritage, as exemplified in New Braunfels, was bad enough, but this was the real thing. On an upper floor a Lufthansa band (accordion, bass, drums, harmonium) lumpishly ground out traditional melodies. A large crowd gathered to listen, and they whooped and swayed to the music. The bandleader spoke.

'We will now sing a song about ze cuckoo,' he began patiently, discerning that he was addressing an audience akin to a geriatric kindergarten. 'Whenever you hear me say "Cuckoo!" I want you all to say, like an echo, "Cuckoo!"' And they obeyed. I looked pityingly at the ranks of grown men and women shouting 'Cuckoo!' at each other, and reflected that they were only following orders.

It's the Christmas book that connoisseurs of conspicuous consumption associate with Neiman-Marcus. It was in 1959 that Stanley Marcus began to advertise preposterous gifts in his annual catalogue; that year it was a Black Angus steer, delivered alive or in steaks. The following year he began the His and Hers section, and offered a pair of airplanes. As a gimmick it was brilliant, and Marcus even sold some of the items. From the current catalogue (circulation 1.5 million) I ordered the pear-shaped natural yellow diamond ($250,000), the three-quarter length Russian lynx coat for my moll ($125,000), two Chinese Shar-Pei puppies ($4000), and a bottle of Private Reserve Barbecue Sauce (a snip at $14).

Having left the store, I stood obediently at the kerbside waiting to cross Main Street to where my car was parked. Rumbling towards me was a bus. Nothing unusual about that, except that this bus was painted pink and had ears three feet high. Over the radiator were painted whiskers and buck teeth. The sign above the driver's window announced that this was a Hop-a-Bus, one of eight pink vehicles with bunny appendages that have been in service since 1978.

I was surprised at first, but then I remembered what everybody had been at pains to tell me: Dallas is a very sophisticated city.

The High Society of the Holy Ghost

Church and class are as closely linked in the United States as in Britain. The Episcopalians are socially the most respectable, but they don't count for much in Texas, where Southern traditions of church membership remain dominant. Methodism isn't looked down on, and even Baptism, not a grouping with much cachet elsewhere, is acceptable. Socially ambitious Baptists must choose their congregation carefully, for Southern Baptism is a church of many houses, and individual pastors still define through their preaching the line that they wish their flock to follow and set the social tone of the congregation.

Baptists tend to be fundamentalists who favour clean living and lay stress on salvation and a personal relationship with Christ; they also baptise by the full dunking method. Yet there are as many variations on these basic themes as there are individual churches. At Second Baptist in Huntsville, I'd heard the Sunday sermon given by Dr Larry Patton. The pastor spoke of Judas, of hearts hardened against God and the need to change them, and he spoke fervently of the importance of a personal relationship to Christ. 'You must know Jesus Christ to be a Christian!' he declaimed. Yet, and this was a liberal streak in the austere setting of a Baptist church, he was against bullying preachers. He told of a preacher who not long ago soaked a dog in kerosene and set it alight and threw it in the trash to demonstrate to a Sunday school class what happens if you don't accept Jesus. Dr Patton's congregation murmured their disapproval; it was generally agreed that dog-burning was carrying things a bit far, and doubtless the issue was fervently debated at the meeting of the Senior Keenagers Klub that took place immediately after the service.

The Big Daddy of Southern Baptist churches is First Baptist in downtown Dallas. The largest Baptist church in the country, it has a membership of about 20,000. Its pastor, the Rev. W. A. Criswell, is a most eminent man: meetings are held in the Criswell Building, and he has put his name to the Criswell Study Bible. The pastor is well known outside Dallas too. During the 1960 presidential campaign, one of his parishioners, the immensely rich H. L. Hunt, circulated 200,000 copies of a sermon in which Dr Criswell had said: 'The election of a Catholic as President would mean the end of religious freedom in America.' On another occasion, when the issue of integration was being hotly debated in the South, Criswell declared: 'If I had a liberal hair in my head, I'd pluck it out.'

When I attended First Baptist, Dr Criswell was up on the rostrum but, as a patriarchal figure, he took the back seat while younger ministers led the service. Tom Melzoni greeted us from the platform, blessed the church football team, and welcomed a group of out-of-town evangelists who'd dropped by to 'join our worship experience'. I was surprised when the lights began to dim, leaving only a pale blue glow behind what seemed to be a glass panel above the choir. A moment later a robed minister walked slowly into the aura followed by two women in white sheets. The blue glow, it dawned on me – I'm sorry to be slow about this, but I'm not a regular at Baptist initiation rites – was water. After a brief catechism the women, one at a time, held their noses and down they went. They came out dripping but saved, then sloshed their way out to the changing room. Each to his own ritual, to be sure, but it didn't strike me as a very dignified way to make contact with the divine.

Dr Criswell now rose. He's no tent preacher. White-haired, of course, and wearing a dark suit with a chic red handkerchief in the breast pocket, he had a soft deep voice and a manner that radiated complete self-assurance. He introduced the preacher. Chuck Colson, he told us, was a born-again Christian, whose conversion he compared to that of Saul, Augustine, Luther, and Wesley.

We all remember Charles Colson, Nixon's burly little helper in the White House. To ensure Nixon's re-election, he would, he declared, 'walk over my grandmother if necessary'. In charge of dirty tricks, chubby Chuck spread false information to defeat a liberal senator, compiled the notorious 'enemies list', was indicted for his part in the break-in at Dan Ellsberg's office as well as the Watergate cover-up, and proposed firebombing the Brookings Institution. That's all in the past, of course, and while in prison, where he so richly deserved to be, Colson 'came face to face with the living God', wept, and hasn't looked back. Born again, he became a proselytising Christian and founded a Prison Fellowship Program to spread the Word among convicts.

He began his address with a joke. Sermons at First Baptist are so popular they are usually taped and made available to the public, and Colson remarked: 'Isn't it nice that in the Christian world we know we're being taped in advance?' That won an uneasy chuckle from the congregation, most of whom, I imagine, were still wondering why people had made all that fuss over Watergate. The sermon was stirring stuff, about his acceptance of Christ, about how governments can't alter much in the world because all problems are fundamentally moral ones that can only be changed if hearts are changed. (In his days as White House hatchet man, Colson had hung a plaque in his house that read: 'If you've got them by the balls, their hearts and minds will follow.')

In his peroration he'd called on us to make, or reaffirm, our commitment to Christ by coming forward to the platform. Past where I was sitting moved a teenage girl, tears wetting her cheeks, led by her mother. At the front of the church I could see the white hair of Dr Criswell bobbing up and down as he and Colson greeted those who approached. There was a good crop of souls harvested in First Baptist that morning.

*

You can learn a great deal from a parking lot. At Word of Faith charismatic church out at Farmers Branch, a distant Dallas suburb, Cadillacs and Lincolns were interparked with Chevys and Datsuns. Some worshippers were wearing their best double-knit suits, but many others had come in open shirts and jeans. Mexicans and whites and a sprinkling of blacks filled the varnished pews. It was noticeable that in a church that banged the same ideological drum as many of the more ferociously right-wing political groups in the country, the congregation was as mixed as any I'd seen.

The fan-shaped auditorium swept row by row down towards the fern-filled platform. The words JESUS CHRIST IS LORD were emblazoned over the stage, on which were planted the Stars and Stripes and the Lone Star flags. To the left of the platform a band – piano, brass, drums, guitar – was tuning its instruments. The service opened in the traditional manner with an appeal for money.

'The tithe,' pleaded Pastor Robert Tilton, 'belongs to God, it's a tenth of how God hath prospered you. You're sowing back into the Kingdom of God. If you're not giving your tithe, it's a curse, it's stealing. Let's put God in first place, put Him above your finances.'

The offering envelope by my chair bore the quotation: 'Honor the Lord with thy substance' and allowed the donor to direct a cheque to either the TV station, the building fund, the missions, or to Pastors Bob and Marte Tilton. That's fair.

Word of Faith is a popular church, not just with Farmers Branch folk, but with viewers nationwide. This very service was being televised. 'Up in the balcony,' the pastor told the viewers, 'we have one hundred 'phones, and one hundred helpers manning those 'phones, and we're ready to receive the calls from those of you who want to meet Jesus.'

Onto the stage came a black woman, a singer. Five years ago, she told us, she'd been declared terminally ill, but here she was still among us, 'a living and walking miracle'. An extremely good singer, moreover, and she and the band screwed up the tension a few more notches.

There was no liturgy. Pastor Tilton simply winged it: 'We don't have a set service here at Word of Faith. Here we're moved by the Holy Spirit.' The Spirit suggested it would be nice if a plump man called Chuck joined the pastor on stage. Chuck was popular with the crowd, he had a way with prophecy, and Tilton took him into overdrive by asking questions about faith and deliverance and all the rest of it. Whenever Chuck overheated, Tilton would raise his hand, clutching the mike in the other, and feverishly intone, 'Abaka tababaka abaka akakakatana'. A few minutes later both of them had reduced their utterances to gibberish, scattering their discourse, such as it was, with key words such as: anoint, praise, deliverance, Word, salvation, Glory of the Lord, Thy gifts, spirit, revelation. While the Pastor was concluding one of his brief fits in tongues, Chuck summarized the experience for those of us listening: 'When you're praising God and He's delivering, then you're living in the High Society of the Holy Ghost.' The congregation grew increasingly excited by what the Lord was doing to his ministers on that stage, and people would stand and raise their hands into the air, like human antennae hoping for better reception of the Holy Spirit.

You don't have to speak in tongues to talk nonsense. The call to prayer, printed in that Sunday's information sheet, was equally opaque: 'We believe that more and more we WILL commit to be in Your Word and ALLOW it to become Spirit and Life to us. *Thank you* it dwells in these richly in all wisdom. It does not depart out of their MOUTHS, thus bearing much fruit and success with its seeds, which don't return void when sent forth. THANK YOU Sir that as they look into it, the MORE of Your DIVINE NATURE & LIFE is formed in them. THANK YOU, it is their counsel, shield, buckler, powerful weapon in battle. It is a lamp unto their feet and a light unto their path.' In such wild opacity do the rantings of, say, Abiezer Coppe live on.

The theme of the sermon was defeating worry. The solution, of course, was faith: the promises of the Bible will bring deliverance to you. It was a case of 'the survival of the spiritually fit'. Pastor Tilton quoted from a hymn: 'The Lord will make a way for me', and then sang it over and over and persuaded us all to join in. In front of me sat a gum-chewing little man and his demure wife, far too pretty, I thought, to be wasted on Ratso, who, during the fiftieth airing of 'The Lord will make a way for me' punched a man sitting on the other side of his wife, and snarled 'Believe it?' The man hastily nodded and Ratso turned away satisfied. During spiritually urgent moments he and his wife would hold hands and clutch each other.

Finally, those in the congregation with a problem were asked to stand, and people next to or behind them were asked to place their hands on the shoulders of the afflicted. Then we all prayed and spoke in tongues and went home for lunch.

Don't think the day was over at Word of Faith. Oh no, and I was back with the rest of them at seven that evening for the Special Mountain Moving Miracle Service. We began with half an hour of singing:

'Oh I love you Jesus
Oh I love you Jesus
Oh I love you Jesus
Because you first loved me.'

But the introduction of that different last line taxed us too severely, so succeeding verses consisted of just the one line repeated four times:

'I love you Jesus . . . (×4)
He is coming . . . (×4)
I am ready . . . (×4)
I'm rejoicing . . . (×4)'

The lines grew shorter and shorter with each quatrain, requiring the singers to plug the missing syllables with wails and moans. It was obvious to me that the intensifying excitement of this incantation – these slogans were scarcely hymns – was less religious than erotic, and the words reinforced it. The mood was set for a seventeenth century Love Feast.

After about twenty minutes we reached the end of that particular road. From the stage came the instruction. 'Let's give the Lord a big praise!' Clapping and cheering, pounding of drums, and more cheering as Pastor Tilton himself loped onto the stage. He asked for requests. The most popular number proved to be 'Let God arise, and the enemy is scattered', a piece so jaunty it had the congregation jumping up and down as they sang.

'I want you all to shake hands with the folks around you! Greet your brothers and sisters!' I'd deliberately placed myself in a remote row, but it soon became clear I wasn't going to be able to evade fellowship. A woman with a large cross round her neck came bearing down on me from two rows behind and offered her hand. She looked grim. 'I'm not crazy,' she said, 'I just love Jesus. I can see the look on your face,' she added to my embarrassment. True, I felt surrounded by freaks, but I hadn't wanted my discomfort to show. It showed. We shook. Handshaking wasn't over. Evangelist Don Stewart was the special guest that evening, and he began by asking each of us in the congregation to shake hands with three people and say to each, 'The Devil is a liar.'

Next he enacted an Old Testament story by asking four well-built men to come up on the stage and impersonate devils. Then Don illustrated how they were overcome by forces of good. He did this by pushing them to the ground and removing their watches and wallets which he later, much later, returned. It was like a scene from a justly neglected Miracle Play.

Speaking of miracles, Don then produced from a shopping bag the following products: Miracle Whip, Miracle Grow (plant food), Miracle Margarine. 'I found all these products in the Seven Eleven on my way here. You want me to tell you why I bought these items? Well, my friends, if you can have Miracle Whip and Miracle Grow, tell me, just tell me, why we can't have miracle healing!'

But we could have miracle healing! That's why we'd come from all over Farmers Branch to spend two hours in church. Don invited anyone in need of a miracle to come forward. Were they, I wondered, all first-timers, or had they been through this on previous occasions when the miracle just hadn't taken? Miracle, it seemed, was loosely interpreted. Don was offering to treat not just physical ailments such as arthritis, but financial difficulties too – and who was free from those? Women sobbed as Don asked Jesus to heal and the Devil to depart. Whether both parties obliged on this occasion I can't say, but some fortunate worshippers who'd experienced mountain moving miracles on other nights came forward to testify. A woman's wonky back had been sorted out, and she showed us she could touch her toes. Another said her ingrown toenails no longer troubled her, and a third said that although doctors had pronounced her infertile, Pastor Tilton had pointed at her during a healing service a month before, and now she was pregnant . . . Now wait a minute, ma'm, he just pointed at you? With what?

Self-reliance is seen as one of the great Texan virtues. It's not peculiar to Texas, of course; it underpins the entire American dream, but Texas, with its strong pioneer tradition, is marked by it to an extraordinary degree. Many Southern states are miserly when it comes to dealing with the poorest, weakest members of society, but then many Southern states are circumscribed by their own relative poverty. Texas, though, is rich and stingy. If you don't survive, it's your own fault, and fundamentalist Christianity confirms the justness of your failure. Pastor Tilton had referred to the survival of the spiritually fit; Social Darwinism is alive and well in Texas.

His wife Marte, as dapper and svelte as her husband was sleek and handsome, writes in a Word of Faith publication: 'Christians have come to be very successful people in America. Man was instructed in Genesis to take dominion over the earth and subdue it – to totally master his circumstances. And many of us have learned to do just that. We learned how to take authority in the realm of health, finances, etc.' I dare say those offerings envelopes played their part. Again and again, in print, in person, over the countless religious radio and TV stations, it is drummed into millions, mostly people at the poorer, less well-educated end of the social scale, that the individual alone is responsible for his or her success, that the role of the community, especially any governmental role, should be minimized.

One of America's most popular evangelists is the Texan Kenneth Copeland, whose weekly televised service attracts half a million viewers. When, from the comfort of my bed, I watched him preach, he was appropriately addressing himself to the problem of feeding the needy. The Lord, he assured us, would provide as he always had done, with loaves and fishes and manna. It was, he said, 'supernatural feeding'. The Lord would provide, and do better than 'the miserable job the welfare agencies have done'. The evangelist Marilyn Hickey took the viewers with her to Ethiopia one morning, where she'd embarked on a mission to the starving peasants of that unhappy country. She'd handed out some food, certainly, but we were to note with pride the number of Bibles she'd been able to distribute. The Lord will provide. One of her printed sermons concludes: 'What did God make us to be? WINNERS!! You win, because God made you a winner.' By implication, if you happen to be one of the losers, tough shit.

No Problem, No Problem

Steve was waiting for me at the bar of On the Border, a popular Mexican restaurant, where I was to join him and his friend A. for lunch. A stockbroker, cautiously peering over the ramparts into middle age and not liking what he saw, Steve bristled with a restless enthusiasm for good living. He would grow morose if he weren't within groping distance of a beautiful woman, but he arranged his life so that this hardly ever happened. He was chatting to a lawyer called Ron Kessler, and introduced me. Kessler used to be chairman of the Dallas County Democratic Party and suggested I come past his office for a chat later in the week. A waiter told him his table was ready, and as he moved off he said to me: 'Steve is one of the smartest guys I know. And here comes A., who's one of the ugliest. How ya doin', A.?'

'What does A. stand for?' I asked politely, as he approached the bar.

'A. stands for asshole,' replied Ron, as he squeezed by the object of his banter and slapped his shoulder. A. didn't seem to mind.

'A. stands for A.,' explained Steve. It seemed contrary to the Texan spirit to christen a child so minimally. A. was serious, bearded, answered my questions carefully, whereas Steve was more lackadaisical. Lunch and two bottles of Chablis were higher on his list of priorities. As we consumed a bowl of unforgiving jalapeño peppers, his complexion grew more florid, and with his round face and wavy hair he began to resemble a miniaturized Teddy Kennedy.

If Steve and A. are to be believed, then Dallas should be renamed Eldorado. It was a city beyond compare. Opportunity beckoned as frequently as whores in Hamburg; anyone with business skills and a bit of luck could make money. Because only ten per cent of the city's economy is energy-based, Dallas had avoided the recession which had stung its rival Houston so badly. City government is run on a city manager basis, not by an all-powerful mayor. Consequently it's run, like all of Dallas, as a business, with competitive bids and everything above board. Fraud on any large scale was virtually unknown. It all sounded too good to be true, but more dispassionate observers I talked to later were unable to disagree.

The nachos and chimichangas were beginning to coagulate in my stomach. I pushed the remnants away and attempted to fissure the congealing mass of starches and cheeses and avocado with libations of acidic white wine, but with little success. My hosts looked at their watches; it was time to return to their offices.

'Say,' said Steve, 'you busy Friday evening? Good. I'm going to ask a few people over to my house, have a small party, introduce you to some people. Got a date? No? Well, I'll just have to invite some beautiful women too.'

*

He was as good as his word. That Friday evening there they were. Ripe Texan bodies that would look a trifle heavy or constrained in jeans or tight-fitting clothes swished softly beneath silk blouses and dresses. Billowing sleeves rippled down to the elbows couching lightly tanned arms that tapered towards wrists often too delicate for the heavy gold or coral bracelets that encircled them. Yet their hands tended to be larger than expected, with meaty fingers admirably structured for the broad rings and multiple stones that clustered around them. More jewels glittered below the neck, and pendulous earrings hung like tassels below the streaked cascade of well-tended hair. Elegant pointed shoes tipped sleek shapely legs lightly gauzed by seamless stockings. The women had names like Lucy and Sandi and Janie, and they worked in investment or real estate. They were indeed, most of them, beautiful, though they had laboured to be beautiful. Each had been schooled to graciousness. Flirtation was frowned upon; a professional self-presentation was all they felt was required of them. If Steve was trying to impress me with how many lovely women he could summon after only ten minutes on the 'phone, I was impressed. Few of them stayed more than half an hour; they hurried off to dinner with young, or not so young, men in three-piece suits who also worked in investments or real estate. Their place was taken by a fluttering swarm of couples.

Steve's house differed from others I'd seen in Texas. Not here the empty expanses of bookless living rooms that were never occupied except on public holidays; nor the mahogany slabs of dining tables in rooms too grand actually to be used as places to eat. Steve's was a townhouse, one in a row of new, tightly packed brick houses, stylishly designed and, in his case, stylishly furnished. Over his bed, which was large enough to accommodate all the Dallas Cowboys Cheerleaders, was a broad gaudy canvas filled with dream images and wispy naked women. Nobody knew what the painting was about, including its owner, who took his guests on tours to inspect the elusive masterwork. It was art, it was daring, it fascinated the liberated, and mildly disconcerted the strait-laced.

Trays of smoked salmon and canapés were brought from the kitchen – who had made them? – and Steve reappeared regularly with bottles of creamy champagne.

A youthful market analyst told me he'd only been in Dallas for five years. 'I married native, though,' nodding towards a large-boned blonde palming a dozen smoked almonds. 'The other day I told Bobbi Ann I was beginning to feel like a native myself, and you know what she said? "Don't push your luck."'

A young Rubens in a superbly cut red and black silk dress told me, 'My Daddy named an oil-well after me,' then cruelly added: 'I must be going now. I have a dinner engagement.' Before drifting off the infanta passed me like a baton to a small woman of middle age.

'My husband,' began Jean, as if to win my respect by association, 'is the finest land developer in the state of Texas.' And she beckoned to a tall lean man with a small chiselled head. Less formal than the other men present, he was wearing a plaid shirt and boots; on his belt a hefty brass buckle bore his initials. Clay had property interests in a number of places, but right now, he told me, he was spending time in Austin where he, in partnership with former governor John Connally and an even more discredited politician, Ben Barnes, was developing a 1500-acre site. I'd been wanting to meet Connally, and Jean must have caught the gleam in my eye.

'Clay, it would be good for Stephen to meet John, wouldn't it?'

'Sure would.'

'He's a remarkable man,' affirmed Jean. 'I bet you'd find that interesting.'

'I'm sure I would. Could you really arrange it?'

'No problem, no problem,' said Clay, waving his glass.

'We like cars,' Jean said from nowhere. 'We collect them. I don't want to be unkind about your country, but we bought the '83 Rolls and were so disappointed. Both of us were. It doesn't ride nearly as smooth as some of the older models. My favourite is the '72 Bentley. That's my special car. Do you know the '72?' I shook my head. 'Oh, it's a beautiful car. We have another Bentley too.'

'That makes three. Any more?'

'Yes. We have six Mercedes and three other cars just for getting around in.'

'But where do you keep them?'

'Here and there. We have a house in Dallas, and another in Lakeway near Austin – oh, I love Lakeway, it's so beautiful there – and we have a place near Santa Fe. I think I like our place in Lakeway best, but Austin isn't as nice as it was a few years ago. It's getting too big.'

'Wouldn't have anything to do with land development?' intervened a lawyer. Jean, doubtless unaccustomed to having her tyres let down, seemed taken aback. I transferred my attention to the sly lawyer, but he soon abandoned me to a dour doctor called K. I was coming to deplore this custom, so marked in Dallas, of neglecting to name your children and leaving them with skimpy initials. K. wanted to know all about the book I hadn't yet written.

'Have you read McMurtry, Dobie?'

'No. I know who they are, but I haven't read them.'

He looked affronted. 'Well, I think you should if you're thinking of writing about us.'

'But I'm trying to write my book, not theirs. Plagiarism comes easily to me, so I'm keeping away from anything that might colour my judgment.'

'How can you write about a place you know nothing about?'

'Oh, I do read books that give me information. I need it. But not the observations of other writers. I'll read people like McMurtry when I've finished my own book.'

'Let me tell you something,' began K., 'my suits are probably older than you –'

'I wouldn't be surprised.'

'– and in my view those guys tell it like it is. You come all the way from London for a couple of months – well, yes, let me tell you, however observant I might be, I couldn't write about London, wouldn't even try to, after I'd been there only three months.'

'And I wouldn't try to diagnose a liver complaint.' Yes, it was a non sequitur, but it threw Dr K. long enough for me to be able to escape. I moved off to talk to Bob, silver-haired, portly and friendly. He had, Steve informed me, retired at twenty-nine, though he still kept his hand in, like everybody else, by dabbling in property.

The party was drawing to a close. I went in search of Clay and Jean; I needed to know how to get in touch with John Connally. Clay held his head high and looked discouraging. 'Trouble is, John's gonna be in Hong Kong for the next two weeks.'

'That's fine. I shan't be in Austin myself for at least two weeks.'

'Look, I'll give you a number that will get you through to his PA. Be persistent, and you may get through. That's all I can do.'

This was not the last time I would come across a failure to deliver. People would casually promise to arrange all sorts of things, but when pressed to come up with the goods, they were often unable or unwilling. 'No problem, no problem,' Clay had assured me. Was it a brag, and no more? Had it been bad form, Texan-style, for me to raise the matter again after it had floated by?

*

'What are your plans for today?' drawled Carmen as I reached for the coffee pot.

'I'm going down to the Kennedy Memorial for the ceremonies,' I said, feeling curiously apologetic. I knew many people in Dallas were weary of being reminded that theirs was the city that had witnessed the assassination.

She leaned her elbow on the formica counter and turned to me. 'Well, I guess you ought to go and take a look. It's just that we're all so sick of it. Here in Dallas we've been trying to live this down for twenty years now.'

Even Dallasites committed to perpetuating the memory of JFK were in sympathy with that view, and this was to be the last time the assassination would be commemorated. In future, at the request of the Kennedy family, his birthday rather than deathday would be honoured.

Two blocks away from the School Book Depository from which Oswald 'allegedly' (according to the circumspect historical marker on the building) shot the President, Philip Johnson's Kennedy Memorial occupies the centre of an otherwise vacant city block. The Memorial takes the form of a roofless white box with two slender entrances leading into the space the walls enclose, and in the middle of that space is a simple black granite slab with Kennedy's name spelt out in gold.

It was drizzling when I arrived, but by the time the ceremonies began at noon the sun had emerged and the day grew steadily more humid. The participants slowly took up their places in front of the white walls of the Memorial: a choir and wind ensemble to the left, and many rows of dignitaries to the right, and facing them all, on a raised platform, about 150 representatives of the world's press. I'd arrived early because I assumed there would be a large crowd gathering to remember, for one last time, that terrible day in 1963. To my surprise, there weren't more than a few hundred people at the Memorial, a thousand at the very most, of which 250 were guests or press.

At noon the choir launched into a dreadful musical prelude consisting of harmonized excerpts from Kennedy's best-known speeches. Invocations by religious leaders, black and white, Christian and Jew, followed, and then a series of speeches. Former Senator Ralph Yarborough, who had been in the motorcade when the shots rang out, spoke passionately about the unfulfilled liberal promise offered by JFK, and how we must strive to be true to those ideals. The delivery was fervent but the words were stale, all that leaden rhetoric about 'rekindling the flame of hope'. Congressman Gonzalez from San Antonio, wearing a startling green suit, was the next politician to approach the lectern. His speech too, like all the others that followed, radiated sincerity yet lacked conviction.

I became restless, stopped listening, watched the faces of the mixed crowd around me. Everybody looked slightly melancholy, slightly bored; when JFK's speeches were quoted, when his youthful ardent qualities were recalled, we would all nod or gaze thoughtfully at the ground for a moment, but there were few tears, few aches. It wasn't hard to know why. Twenty years had passed; so much had happened since those hopeful days in the early 1960s. It is easier to cherish and honour achievement than promise; those of us present were nursing memories that were growing fainter with every year. Liberalism as a political philosophy was outmoded; in a slick heartless age, even those who, in American terms, stand to the left of centre, steer clear of the old notions that are now derided as mere sentimentality inappropriate to a realistic view of social relations. As we stood around the Memorial, the life of the city went on all about us, and our participation in the predictable ceremony seemed increasingly without meaning. The performance of an Irish ballad much loved by the late President seemed wildly out of place in bustling Protestant Dallas. Politics and memory do not embrace; sentiment, however deeply felt, seemed irrelevant, mere lip service to ideals long atrophied.

Afterwards I joined the small queue of people shuffling towards the interior of the Memorial; there we'd pause for a minute or two in front of the black stone, on which a few roses and slender bouquets had been forlornly thrown. Then I walked over to the Hyatt Hotel for the luncheon organized by the local Democratic Party. I sat down at a table with a group of politicians and journalists, and tucked into chicken breast stuffed with what appeared to be more chicken and doused in melted Kraft American cheese. Next to me sat a man wearing boots with stitching as elaborate as circuitry. He was, he told me, a magistrate with plans to run for an elected judgeship; hence his participation in this political event, showing his party loyalty. We talked about my wanderings, and he told me he'd grown up on Pitchfork Ranch, where his father had been the cook many years ago.

From the platform there were invocations and speeches, of course. The mayor, Starke Taylor, spoke in a lacklustre way on behalf of the city. 'We've tried to make Dallas a better city and I think we've succeeded.' Riveting stuff. Everybody clapped. Finally, the lights dimmed and a portrait of JFK flashed on to a screen while we sat through a tape of the last speech he ever gave. The quality of the recording was so poor that the words were inaudible; we gazed into our coffee cups, waiting for it to end. How many times in one day could we be asked to go through the rituals of remembering?

Yet, as I walked back into town, I couldn't help resenting the difficulty of recapturing what had indisputably been a great tragedy. It felt bizarre to be so unmoved, to walk past the very building from which the murderous shots had been fired, and to feel so little. I came to the spot in front of the depository where the road slopes down towards the underpass. It was here that the bullets struck the President. Onto a lamp post that stood a few feet away from the spot, somebody had crudely taped a bunch of flowers. Attached to the bouquet was a scrap of paper on which was scrawled: 'We miss you, Jack.'

On the kerb sat two women, talking to each other about that day. One was Hispanic, raised in Chicago, now living in Dallas; her family had worshipped Kennedy, though she herself was too young to have any memory of the man. The other woman told me she'd witnessed the assassination. As a child of three, she'd been perched on her father's shoulders and heard the shots ring out; she recalled the confusion, the daze, and twenty years later she still seemed dazed. She'd been here at the very same spot for an hour or two, trying to recall what her uncomprehending infant eyes had seen, trying still, after all this time, to come to terms with the murder. It was here, listening to the two voluble young women, that I felt moved for the first time that day; it was in the vivid pained memories of ordinary people, intimately rather than publicly recalled, that the shock of the event had taken root.

*

A less painful commemoration followed a few days later: Thanksgiving. At noon I drove north up the uncrowded expressway past the fashionable department stores of North Park and on to the LBJ Freeway, a ring road which at this point gives access to expensive chain hotels and to the architecturally inventive Galleria, Dallas's newest temple of consumerism. And still the city spreads northwards like a stain, in a continuous act of dispersal. On a gentle ridge some miles beyond LBJ I came to a new development of homes, some houses only recently completed. These were not the monotonous bungalows of the less affluent suburbs, but capacious 'custom homes' with their cathedral ceilings, wet bars, wood-burning fireplaces, and split-level layouts. Alleys behind the houses led to garages, so that the hydromulched lawns wouldn't be slashed by driveways. The houses were all of slightly different design;

there was a family likeness, but the developer had studiously avoided repetition.

I was a few minutes early and took a stroll along some of the empty streets. This was the most northerly street in the development, and there was a view over fields to the township of Plano (a community famous for its recent epidemic of teenage suicides) a mile or two beyond. Here, then, was the edge of Dallas – for that week. I knew that if I were to return six months later many of those fields would be staked out with surveyors' poles while bulldozers levelled and concrete mixers churned.

There were twenty of us for lunch, mostly family members who had come from afar: Don's relatives from Fort Worth and Waco, Carole's from Erie, Pennsylvania. Don was Texan, but not Carole, who was a northerner of Russian ancestry. When I mentioned that I'd been to Russia a couple of times, she said: 'My family all came from Russia but I could never go there. I just couldn't set foot in that satanic, atheistic country.' Her choice of words was revealing. Sam and Carmen were regular church-goers but I didn't sense that their religious feelings ran very deep. In the case of Carole and Don, their Christian commitment seemed paramount. She told me that she, like Don, had been divorced, and in her solitude one day she prayed she would meet a good Christian man; before long her prayers had been answered and she'd met Don. It was evident that they didn't simply profess their religion, they lived it. Their commitment was not ostentatious, not the waving of moral flags, but it was thoroughly pervasive.

The house was elaborately furnished. Over the fireplace hung a large oil portrait of Carole. Corridors were enlivened by a set of curious oils depicting the British royal family. Religious mottoes proliferated, even on the refrigerator door, and there were well-thumbed study Bibles strewn on the kitchen table. Don showed me round every room in the house, shoe closets included, and the garage with its two gleaming Cadillacs nose by nose. Before we sat down to lunch Don asked us all to join hands while he said an improvised grace.

The meal was a typical Thanksgiving feast, turkey with all the trimmings, and a succession of pies to follow. Across the table from me sat Dave Eichelberger, a golf pro from Fort Worth, and this intrigued me, since I'd just finished reading Dan Jenkins' novel *Dead Solid Perfect*. Its hero is Kenny Puckett, a golf pro from Fort Worth. Discreet questioning confirmed that Dave could not have been the model for Kenny. He is a fortunate man.

After lunch some of the more elderly relatives enjoyed a brief coma on the living room sofas, while the more youthful guests were transfixed by the afternoon football game on TV. The rest of us clambered into Don's cavernous Cadillac and he took us to see his new offices. On the way there Dave's wife, a real estate broker, mentioned that she had a client on the lookout for an apartment building priced at between five and ten million. Don thought for a minute, then told her he probably knew just such a building that was about to come on the market. Even on Thanksgiving afternoon in North Dallas, repletion and celebration don't get in the way of hatching business deals. The offices of Don's international trading company were pleasant enough, bright, cheerful, roomy. A small bronze plaque near the main entrance stated that these offices had been opened in September 1983 and 'are dedicated to the Glory of God.'

*

I'd bought a ticket for the Dallas Opera, and when I mentioned this to Carmen she told me she and the girls were going on the same evening. She suggested we drive down to Fair Park together after dinner. Sam, no opera fan, would not be joining us. At dinner we talked about the recent establishment of Martin Luther King Day as an annual public holiday. Opponents had stressed the cost to the government and industry of instituting yet another paid holiday, a view Sam endorsed.

'Just another way for the government to waste our money,' he grumbled.

'Do you know who Martin Luther King was?' Carmen asked her younger daughters. The twelve-year-old knew, but little Cecelia didn't. Carmen explained.

'He got killed,' Sam said, adding, 'Civil rights people usually do.'

The women disappeared to find their fur coats and a few minutes later Carmen was easing the big Mercedes out of the drive. We were on our way to see *Carmen*. 'I want my girls to be able to say that their mother Carmen took them to see *Carmen*.'

By Dallas standards it was a cold night, and I remarked on the unexpected chill.

'To tell you the truth,' said Carmen, 'I'm kinda glad it's turned cold, because now we can all claim we're wearing our fur coats to keep warm.'

Half the opera-going women of Dallas were similarly freed from any pangs of conscience they might otherwise have felt, and a small acreage of fox and mink and lynx enwrapped the slender shoulders and long bodies of a few hundred matrons of all ages. The production was unworthy of such glamorous patronage. I know *Carmen* as a medium-length and fairly snappy piece. But some misguided producer had had the conscientious but foolish idea of restoring long cuts and all the original, and tedious, French dialogue. Consequently, although the curtain rose at eight, it did not make its final descent till after midnight, by which time about half the audience had gone home. Was this philistinism or good taste? I wondered. Had I been on my own I too would have left early. The five of us sat it out. Mary Elizabeth occupied herself during the interval by reading through the entire list of contributors to the Dallas Opera to see how many of them she knew personally. When we left I helped Carmen find the right Mercedes – so many to choose from – and half an hour later we were back in North Dallas.

*

Dallas, it seemed, went through the motions of acting as if it were a lively cultural centre, only its heart wasn't in it. The city was fundamentally stuffy, at root philistine. The Dallas writer A. C. Greene didn't disagree. 'In many ways Dallas is culturally unexciting. It prefers to rent culture rather than produce its own. It doesn't trust its own judgement and that makes it fairly unadventurous.'

Jack agreed that Dallas was philistine, strait-laced. 'But just because it's a Southern Baptist town doesn't stop it from being fairly sophisticated. Still, Dallas is a very conservative town. I wasn't here at the time, but I heard that in the late 1950s there was a move to throw the Picassos out of the art museum because someone had discovered that Picasso had been a Commie. It's curious: they're building a new art museum, as you know, and there's been a tremendous amount of discussion about the new building, but not a word has been said about what they're going to put inside it. They're just assuming that a lot of folks in North Dallas will have a bunch of extra art around that they'll just hand over. And most likely they will. Oh, I meant to ask you. How was *Carmen*?'

'Dreadful. There was some booing at the end.'

'Booing? At the Dallas Opera? Why, that's a tremendously encouraging sign.'

The Finest Amenity Accoutrement in the Metroplex

Where, I asked Jack, were the hundreds of thousands of blacks in Dallas? North of the river I'd only met one, and she was the maid.

They were numerous but quiet, he said, and there was a reason for that. In the mid-1960s the city was still segregated. So the black organizations, eager for change, went to see the oligarchy that still ruled the city and presented it with a number of scenarios. One was called integration. Another was called rioting. The black leaders pointed in the directions of Watts and Newark, and the oligarchy soon got the point. Rioting is bad for business. It didn't take long for the oligarchy to acknowledge that integration was the better package for Dallas. In no time at all the city was integrated; word went out and that was that. If a garage owner continued to offer segregated lavatories, he'd get an admonishing 'phone call from the banker on whose loans he depended. Before long the whole city fell into line. So painless was the transition that a forceful black leadership never had a chance to emerge out of a power struggle such as other cities had experienced in pursuit of integration. That weakness persists, though Dallas has one prominent black politician, Elsie Faye Heggins. Jack told me to go and see her.

So I did. I found her in a conference room conducting one of her weekly evening meetings at the Martin Luther King Center in the entrails of black Dallas. About forty people were present, and every place was taken. I stood by the door trying to look inconspicuous – not easy, since mine was the only white face not just in the room but for a mile around.

A small man with a red bow-tie was holding forth about Jesse Jackson and voter registration. Councilwoman Heggins sat motionless at the end of the table, a bulky presence with rouged cheeks and straightened hair. I couldn't assess her age. Fifty? Sixty? The little man spoke for a few minutes more, carefully building his remarks to a rhetorical climax. As he sat down someone shouted: 'Preach it, brother, preach it!' A brief argument followed, and then Mrs Heggins, speaking in a painfully deliberate way, changed the subject.

'We have to network to get the people out,' she declared. 'They're not going to respect the black community till we all come out and vote at city hall. They don't respect us because they don't think they have to.' The discussion continued, but my unexplained presence proved distracting. A young man in a suit got up, walked to where I was standing, and said: 'What media you with?' I briefly explained; he nodded and returned to his place. The meeting shifted to statements made by witnesses to a police shooting, and a committee to investigate the incident was set up. Then Mrs Heggins, to my surprise, asked me to identify myself, which I readily did. When all business had been completed, she rose to her feet and addressed me.

'At the end of these town hall meetings we have a custom of joining hands and singing.'

I nodded energetically to let her know that was fine with me. We all stood, joined hands, and launched into 'We Shall Overcome', many verses of it. Then we hummed the stirring melody while above our voices a preacher intoned a prayer. He finished and we resumed singing. When it was finally over, the man in the bow-tie came and introduced himself; he ran a security operation. He was quite a dandy, with his three-piece suit, highly polished black and white shoes, and a small enamelled US flag on his lapel. Henna had reddened his short crinkly hair, giving him a slightly mad appearance. He talked to me – no, he talked at me – about the urgent need for a unified space command, with America, Russia, and Europe teaming up. That was the coherent thought; the elaborations upon it were unintelligible. Then he turned his thoughts to the plight of the black community.

'Know something, man? There are no black-owned banks in South Dallas. Isn't that something? It's rape, man, rape, the white folks come into the ghetto and take our money and run.'

I wanted him to develop this theme, but it was no use. He began a verbal tarantella, about Kennedy and King and how their spirit was still with us. He compared Elsie Faye to Robert Mugabe. 'Just like Zimbabwe, first we had to get rid of the Muzorewas round here.'

Eventually I managed to sit down by the weary Mrs Heggins. She'd had a long day, and I promised not to detain her long. She grumbled about the proposed redistricting of the city, which she construed as a deliberate plan to prevent her re-election. Why, I asked her, was the black community opposed to DART, the mass transit plan for Dallas, which ought to benefit the minority communities in the city?

'Should be that way,' she nodded, 'but it's not. Just look at this map. See where most of the rail lines are going? North, to the white suburbs. Very few lines are going south to serve the black neighbourhoods. DART shortchanges the black community. We pay the same taxes as the white community but they get the best services. We want them to scrap the plan and start over, which is what happened in Atlanta where they had the same scenario. They won there and we can win here.'

I later asked Jack whether Mrs Heggins was right to reject this half loaf.

'She has a point,' he said. 'The main reason people support DART is because it allows growth to continue in the outer suburbs. Providing a service to the poorer sections is not the principal justification for its construction. So you did get to see Elsie Faye. How did you get on?'

I told him about the meeting. 'What astonished me was that at the end we all held hands and sang "We Shall Overcome". Very touching, of course, but I wanted to interrupt and say: "Wait a minute! This isn't the 'sixties in Selma anymore! This is the mid-'eighties. The world has changed. *De jure* segregation is a thing of the past. The struggle is a different one. Cut out the old songs!" Of course I didn't dare.'

'I know what you mean,' said Jack. 'The white folks of North Dallas think of Elsie Faye as a mad monster, a firebrand, but the truth is she's hesitant and timid. Put her on the platform at a black political meeting in Detroit or Newark and she'd be hooted off the stage in five minutes.'

*

Foremost among Dallasites who thought Elsie Faye was born of the debil was my relative Lamar. Yes, I discovered kinfolk in Texas. My family tree, if anyone cared to draw it, would resemble a shrub rather than a lofty pine, but at the far tip of its thicketry I found a twig on which I could hang the names of relatives so remote I never had any expectation of meeting them – until I came to Dallas. One evening I found myself in the living room of a modest suburban house, sipping drinks and exchanging politenesses with my most distant cousins. Lamar was a semi-retired builder, aching for the day, now imminent, when he could shut the door on Dallas and move into his new lakeside home near the Oklahoma border. His wife, delighted to learn that I preferred wine to bourbon, proudly brought out a bottle of her favourite Lambrusco and poured me a thimble full, which she fortunately refilled from time to time in a battle against evaporation. Every few minutes Lamar would hitch up his blue Bermuda shorts and pad out to the patio to attend to the barbecue.

'Lamar makes the best barbecue in north Texas,' Marlene confided. It was a boast I'd been hearing in every Hibachi-owning household in the state.

It was good: an immense and quite flavoury steak cut into strips to ensure that within five minutes it would be stone cold. The Lambrusco began to drip more freely, and Lamar's bourbon twinkled around the ice cubes. The talk turned to politics.

'I just don't see,' said Lamar slowly and smilingly, with a sense of certainty that no evidence could presume to shake, 'why the government should provide welfare of any kind.'

'Any kind? The very old? The very sick? The mad?'

'My view is that people should provide for themselves. When there's real need they should turn to their families or perhaps charities. I pay a lot of taxes and don't see why they should be given away to Mexicans who swim over the Rio Grande or northerners who drive down to Houston, can't find a job, and then turn around and ask the state to hand over my tax money. Now is that right?'

'Stated that way, possibly not.' I restated it my way.

Marlene leaned towards me. 'Lamar's very conservative,' she remarked approvingly. 'We all are.'

Lamar went on: 'To me it just seems plain wrong that some unemployed guy on welfare, who doesn't pay a penny in taxes, should have the same voting rights as myself, who works hard, builds up a business, and pays a helluva lot of money each year in taxes. I ask you, is that just?'

He was, I realised, restating an argument revived from the dead by the richest Texan of them all, H. L. Hunt, who at one time earned a million dollars a week from his oil empire. He also wrote reactionary tracts and subsidized radio programmes so right-wing that to label them conservative is to slander that political philosophy. In his novel *Alpaca*, for instance, Hunt argued that the voting power of a citizen should be in direct proportion to his wealth, a sentiment that Lamar clearly endorsed fully.

'I'm crazy about animals,' remarked Marlene out of nowhere, and we talked about dog-fighting instead.

*

When, soon after, I went to see Ron Kessler, the Democratic politician I'd met at On the Border, he did his best to reassure me that my primeval Republican relatives were not representative of political thought in Dallas. Texas, he conceded, was a conservative state, but not the preserve of fossilized Republicans. The state was still nominally Democratic – it had only elected one Republican governor this century. In national politics Texas used to ally itself with the Southern Democrats, good ole boys and dim-eyed wattle-necked small-town lawyers with minds as stubborn as their jaws, men who once elected to Congress could spend the rest of their lives blocking legislation and drinking Wild Turkey in their offices every afternoon. The Southern Democrats were so conservative they could match any Republicans when it came to sneering at the unions, hating communism and singing hallelujah every time the defense budget was quadrupled. Southerners, with their long memories, didn't need to be reminded that the Republican Party was the party of Lincoln, their bitter opponent.

Yet the occasional liberal such as Ralph Yarborough scraped through the primary, usually because the Stone Age vote was split. The big cities harboured liberal Democrats, people whose brains hadn't been boxed in by blinkered Baptists, but they were thin on the ground. Texan Democrats had seen nothing inconsistent in voting Republican during presidential elections, especially when the Democratic candidate, as in the case of McGovern in 1972, was considered dangerously left-wing. The election of a shrewd conservative Republican senator, John Tower, in 1960, and Governor Connally's switch to the Republicans in 1973, helped to restore the fortunes of that party in Texas. Rural conservative Democrats began to lose ground to urban voters, who tend to be either Republicans or moderate

Democrats. In some cities, and Dallas was one of them, Kessler reminded me, it was socially acceptable to be a Republican, and for many people which party you joined was more a question of expedience than principle.

Nevertheless Kessler insisted there were genuine differences between the parties in Texas, even though most Texans were united in their loathing for social services and their indifference to, or their unwillingness to pay for, decent housing and public education. Democrats support the Equal Rights Amendment; Republicans do not. Democrats are opposed to tuition tax credits; Republicans are not. Texan Democrats are unwilling to be too conservative lest they alienate the important black and Mexican voters.

The 'phone rang. A major property developer was at the other end of the line. 'Say,' said Kessler, 'I have to go down to Houston tomorrow night for a dinner to honour' – he mentioned a political luminary – 'and I would sure like to be able to take along a cheque from you to show how much you appreciate the great job he's doing. You'll send it over? That's great. I appreciate it.'

As Kessler was showing me out, we ran into a shirt-sleeved lawyer from his firm in the company of an elderly man whose glasses were unevenly balanced on his nose. His jacket and trousers were shabby, and the knot of his loosened brown tie was slung halfway down his shirt.

'Hey, Trammell!' exclaimed Kessler, exuding bonhomie. 'How ya doin'? Want you to meet a friend of mine.' And he introduced me to Mr Crow. I'd heard about Trammel Crow. He'd grown up in working-class East Dallas, and made his way into the property business by building unglamorous warehouses. Gradually he prospered. The 5-million-square-foot wholesale Market Center along Interstate 35 had been built by Crow, and he paved the way for Dallas to become a leading fashion centre. In 1975 he almost went bankrupt, but the banks didn't force him out of business because they knew no one else could run his empire, and before long Crow had pulled himself – and the banks – out of trouble. Nowadays Crow doesn't use banks. His touch is so sure that if he decides he wants to build, the investors come flowing in. Hank told me that immense wealth hadn't changed Crow. 'Trammell lives in a large house, but he doesn't live opulently. He's still an unpretentious guy, and a brilliant businessman. Trammell just wants to have a good time and own half the world.'

Unpretentious? Not only that, but a disgrace to the fashion industry. Trammell gripped the arm of the shirtsleeved lawyer at his side, and with his other hand jabbed me in the chest. 'Steve, I wanna tell you something. There are all kinds of lawyers. Counselors, regular attorneys, bondsmen, and springers. This guy's a springer.' I had no idea what he was talking about.

Back at the house I mentioned to Carmen that I'd met Trammell Crow.

'Some years ago his son, Trammell Junior, married one of the Hunt girls,' she said. 'I thought that was a real shame, money marrying money like that. They should spread it around a little. Could use some of it here.'

'You're not doing so badly,' I said, recalling that Sam had returned the previous evening gloating over how much money he'd made that afternoon – though, prompted by Carmen, he did concede that the windfall represented only a fraction of the sum he owed the bank.

'Oh, I'm very materialistic, I know,' conceded Carmen. 'There are things I want, such as more jewellery. Sam may have spent the money already – he's just ordered a new Mercedes – but that's not going to stop me.'

It was not, after all, unhealthy or preposterous to believe that the purpose of wealth was its enjoyment rather than its pro-pagation. Display, in materialist Dallas, validated the efforts of the menfolk, who toiled in their air-conditioned offices to provide the means for their wives to inform the world that the labours of their husbands had been profitable. Objects of high status could deck a marriage with splendour, and Sam's Mercedes could provide the right setting for Carmen and her jewels, just as Carmen's jewels would ornament the cave of the car's interior.

'Seems to run in the family,' I said, a touch impudently. 'Mary Elizabeth sounds quite certain that she's going to be given a car for her sixteenth birthday.'

'Well, she's going to be disappointed. If anyone round here is going to get a neat new sports car, it's going to be me.'

*

I got lost. Many do. I was trying to get to Las Colinas, Texas's answer to Milton Keynes, but instead I was zipping along the Airport Freeway, one of the most desolate strips of highway that Texas has to offer, and there's plenty of competition. What made it so depressing was its unfinished look. Many lots alongside the freeway and its access roads were already filled with offices, used car lots, non-smoker hotels, gas stations, and tents called JESUS, but in between these dreary adjuncts to civilization were ploughed-up holes in the ground staked with property brokers' billboards of jazzily lettered signs announcing that the moonscape to your left was in fact THE FUTURE HOME OF CALVARY CHURCH OF CHRIST.

Somehow I got to Las Colinas, a 12,000-acre site at the northern edge of the Metroplex, strategically situated only fifteen minutes from downtown Dallas – unless you're travelling with me – and ten minutes from the DFW Airport. Fifteen years ago the site was, most of it, ranchland, the property of Ben Carpenter, president of the billion-dollar Southland Corporation and son of John W. Carpenter, the industrial magnate who won immortality when a freeway was named after him. Carpenter knew well that ranchland close to an international airport was a wasted resource. Texans think big, but Carpenter thought bigger than most. He simply resolved to build a new city. It's not finished yet – the year 2000 is the target for completion – but it's well under way. New towns have sprung up elsewhere, but what's different about Las Colinas is that its shaping and financing are controlled by a single individual. Dallas has its share of oil tycoons, but perhaps that familiar totem should be replaced by the property developer. Dallas seems to spawn men such as Crow and Carpenter, who operate on a scarcely credible scale of ambition and daring. Later in the day I'd be meeting one of the younger breed of property millionaires, Sherwood Blount, whose shrewd dealings in increasingly valuable parcels of North Dallas land had made him very rich very fast.

I drove by the Las Colinas Country Club, where the green around the first hole is shaped like the state of Texas, on past the 350 acres that remain of Carpenter's Hackberry Creek Ranch, and up towards Corporate Drive and Executive Drive in what will be the Office Center. Then I headed back towards the Urban Center; here Las Colinas Boulevard circles the artificial 125-acre Lake Carolyn (Carpenter's sister), and close to its desolate shores I parked. It's unfair to remark that much of Las Colinas resembles wasteland; there are another fifteen years to go before the jury returns to give its verdict on the success, financial and aesthetic, of Carpenter's vision. In its final form Las Colinas will have a downtown office and entertainment district larger than that of Dallas, 125 acres of film production facilities, six residential villages, and extensive landscaping. But if the city fails to attract major corporations to fill the large office blocks going up in the Urban Center, it will be in trouble. The master plan envisages a population of 50,000 by 2000; so far 10,000 residents have moved in. 'As a total living environment,' the publicists ensure potential purchasers, 'the villages of Las Colinas offer a rainbow-hued sampler of distinctive homestyles – with the finest amenity accoutrement in the Metroplex'.

The amenities are indeed lavish: private policing, computerized alarm systems, golf courses, riding and physical fitness centres are on the doorstep, and a generous 3500 acres are set aside as parkland. Carpenter has even built a nursery to ensure the annual replacement of 400,000 flowers. He also laid down rules relating to the city's architecture: mirror glass is out, and so is neon. Las Colinas certainly isn't garish or tacky, but it also seems lifeless and cold.

I walked down the steps to the Mandalay Canal, reminiscent of San Antonio's Paseo del Rio. This brief stretch of water, with walkways and buildings on both sides, serviced by mahogany water taxis that don't go anywhere you can't walk to in five minutes, is welcome but curiously pointless. On one side rises a massive Spanish mission belfry, of all things, capped with a turquoise tile roof. Further along stands a low range of Spanish-style houses with elaborate wrought-iron balconies, shutters, and carved wooden doors. I pushed open one of the doors and found myself peering into a multi-storey car park. The trouble with false façades is that they dangerously introduce the element of sham, of architecture as frill that disguises function. That things are not what they seem is a theme for carnival, for the slyness of baroque, a deception justified by the drama of the reality concealed. But a car park? No, a disguised car park is even more banal than a blatant one.

The opposite bank is embellished with an attractive arcade of shops. The McDonald's is deprived of its yellow arches – in Carpenter's town you follow his rules – but not of what the publicity brochure calls the 'traditional McDonald's menu'. Nearby is the Sample House (baskets, candles), Le Coteau (French country antiques), Little Rebels (children's wear), Kitchenworks (Olde English tea room), and Dear John (stationery). A TexMex restaurant offers blue enchiladas. At Las Colinas it's easier to buy a chiffonier than a loaf of bread.

When they get round to colonizing the moon, it's going to look like Las Colinas, I imagine: spacious, impeccably planned, crammed with amenities, a technologically sophisticated oasis of pseudo-civilization, searching purposefully but uselessly for its own style, unwilling or unable to blend corporate reality with urban fantasy. Cities grow and breathe, flexing muscles, gaining strength in one part while another atrophies. Las Colinas is growing, to be sure, but only in prescribed ways. If it never comes to life in any organic sense, it will be because the model is depressingly conventional: that of downtown flanked by mini-suburbs, with the country club and recreational land thrown in for good measure. Progressive cities, such as Austin and San Antonio, are reverting to mixed use, encouraging the commercial and residential and recreational to rub shoulders. At Las Colinas, the visionary project will come to fruition and offer a style of urban living that may well be outmoded by the time the last unit is sold.

*

When I'd arranged to meet Sherwood Blount, I'd imagined him to be a typical grey-locked oligarch. I'd been waiting for all of five minutes in the reception area of his offices near Addison in far north Dallas, when a sleek, well-groomed man of roughly my own age came bounding through a door with his hand outstretched. Not until I saw him heading straight for me did it occur to me that this burly, almost cocky young man was Blount.

'Will you still talk to a guy that's kept you waiting?' he said, a delicately disarming way to open our meeting. He swept me into his office, rang for some coffee, and seated himself behind a horseshoe-shaped desk. I didn't ask for the story of his life but he gave it to me anyway, as if it were an exemplary tale.

'I was born in Dallas on September 25, 1949, and I haven't

left since.' He grew up in East Dallas and went to SMU on a football scholarship – 'I was very fortunate, played on some great football and baseball teams in high school' – and then enrolled in the graduate school in 1972. Became bored, 'so I got out on the street, spent the next two months, just solid, talking to people in the real estate industry. People like Crow.' In 1976, after working for another company, he started his own brokerage business.

'In the last years I have built a very good – again, this is opinion – very good brokerage company. We've sold, will sell or lease, over a quarter billion dollars' worth of land and improved buildings this year. I've sold in my career over a billion dollars' worth of properties and have met some of the nicest and finest people you could ever hope to meet in the process, which has really been a reward.'

'Is there much competition?'

'Terrific competition.' He nodded slowly.

'Do they all know what they're doing?'

'No.' He paused and a smile began to creep up on his features. 'Thank God.'

Blount was laying it on a bit thick – poor boy comes up the hard way and makes good, but is still a modest easy-going guy for all his success – but I enjoyed his openness. Nothing reticent about the man; his vanity was so transparent that it became endearing. This smooth-cheeked, fresh-faced, lightly jowled millionaire was a tenacious and canny businessman, but too thrilled with his own success to be pompous about it.

'Our business is a glamour business. People pick up the Sunday newspaper and they see a guy like Sherwood Blount and other guys doing a big deal, and they say, hey, that's a glamorous business, I want to get in that business. Here' – and he pointed to a bulging file – 'this will blow your socks off – or blow your dress up, as we say in East Dallas – those are resumés of people that just in the last six months want to go work for us. But the reason we've all been so successful – and don't let anybody tell you different – the reason I'm successful is not because I'm the smartest guy in the world or work harder than anybody else, the reason I'm successful is that I'm smart, I work hard, and I've done it in Dallas, Texas. I would not have had the same level of success had I tried to do the same thing in Pittsburg or Cleveland. You know the reason for a bad joke?

Timing. Timing's the reason a bunch of us has been very very successful, and I'm the first to admit it and give God thanks for it too.

'Recently, the airport has helped. I don't think anyone recognised – oh, the dreamers did, the guys that have always had the visions – the tremendous impact that 17,000-acre airport would have on our city. We're the largest city in the country without a water port. But we're also halfway between New York and Los Angeles. We're a state that has no corporate income tax, no personal state income tax, basically corruption-free. You have no Mafia, no gangsters, and this state and this city have been built by God-fearing people. From the early days of the republic when that band of two hundred soldiers fought Santa Anna at the Alamo, and then ambushed them at San Jacinto, to the great stories you've heard over the past 150 years about Texans who've settled the land, farmed it, cultivated it, raised cattle – people here, they don't figure out a way not to do something, they figure out a way to do something.'

There, in pure undiluted form, was the myth of Texas. From the fervour of men like Sherwood Blount and the many others who'd enunciated the same tale to me as I travelled around Texas, it's clear that the epic foundations of the state still prop up and inspire those who inhabit it. Nothing, they believe, is impossible. But not all can succeed.

Blount carried on down Texas's favourite road, Free Enterprise Way. 'If you will let the real forces of the market place work – now if you go in and you arbitrarily set rental standards, put stops on the increases, do this and do that, put stops on construction, and so forth, where you indicate the supply or you dictate the demand, then we're not free to flow, as we learned early on with Adam Smith. Because ultimately somebody has to use the land.'

The last remark was significant: those fields between Don's house and Plano will someday be built over, so it's only reasonable, in their own eyes, for men like Blount to do all in their power to control that coveted property. We went on to talk about the way that most of the downtown skyscrapers had been built not by Dallasites but by outsiders from Canada and Europe. Blount agreed that some years ago, when those buildings started to go up, Dallas businessmen had underestimated the commercial possibilities of their own city. All that had changed. Some of the foreign interests were getting out of Dallas.

'Many of these guys will never do another deal in downtown Dallas. Why? 'Cause the local boys like Trammell Crow and others have hammered them over the head. I tip my hat to some of those Canadian outfits, but they've learnt that you'd better have the best community interests in mind and at heart if you're going to be successful in this town, because although the Metroplex has three million people, the real estate circle and the business circle is very very small. You learn to put everything right here on the table or you don't do business. And you get a reputation, and your reputation precedes you.'

'Are you insulted if I say there's something stuffy about Dallas?'

'No sir. I will agree that for the most part people here are very, very conservative. These are God-fearing people here, they're in church on Sunday, they're with the family during the day, and sure they'll take time out to watch the Dallas Cowboys, but it's a conservative style of life. But I don't know that's really a stuffy city. I know this. I can get on the elevator with Bunker Hunt' – he who tried to collar the world's silver, all of it, a few years ago, and nearly succeeded – 'as I have many times, or with Herbert Hunt, and they don't want to talk business, they want to talk football. They're just downright ordinary people when it comes to being people.' It was OK for a self-made man like Blount to be one of the boys because so too, despite their billions, were the richest men in Texas. 'I've grown up outside of the social circle, but I know many people who are involved within the social circle, some of the most delightful people you'd ever want to know.'

Was Blount intending to stay in this business all his life?

'You know, I'm in a real crossroads in my life. I've been to the mountaintop in my profession, like you have in yours, and like you, I'm sure, I've been in the valleys too. I love what I do. I can truthfully say to you, and to anyone else, I've never worked a day in my life in the real estate industry. Work to me was growing up in East Dallas having to cut yards, throw newspapers, working my way through college in the summers – that was work. But the only way out of that was a good education, and darned if it didn't work out the way I hoped and prayed it would. To answer your question: I love what I do, I love being associated with these thirteen guys and gals that are associated with me, I interact with each of my people every day, I love the people you come in contact with on a daily basis, and every buyer and seller is different, every deal is different. But I don't know that I want to be fifty-seven years old and out here on the street every day, selling, working at the same pace that I'm working now.'

'Do you feel you're more than a man who pushes paper about, transferring property and collecting commission? Do you make a contribution to Dallas in any way?'

'Sure. We've sold a lot of land in this town that now has buildings, shopping centres all over it. It gives me great pride to drive through Plano and to think we've sold as much if not more land than anyone out there. We sold that land seven or eight years ago, that land was cut up into single family divisions, houses were built upon it, families are now occupying those homes, and I can remember when I drove up those dusty roads, cotton growing all over the place, and you say to yourself – you know, I've done something for mankind. I hope that family there enjoys living where they live, and not for a second am I thinking: Boy, if they knew who I was – because we get paid well for what we do, we don't need any gold medals or blue ribbons, we're well compensated.'

Dreams of More

Conversation need never flag in Texas. You can always talk about the Dallas Cowboys. You don't need too much information, just the latest scores and snatches of gossip about the quarterbacks, and a deferential word for the legendary coach Tom Landry. Devotion to the team, and to the sport, is intense. As a fan once remarked to me, 'Son, in Texas we tape our ankles just to watch the game on TV.' Sherwood Blount, more solemnly, had spoken of football as glue that binds all sections of the community, black and white, rich and poor – sport as the great leveller.

When I arrived in Texas the Cowboys were on a winning streak; they couldn't put a foot wrong. With military precision they dug traps for their opponents, who unfailingly tripped into them; effortlessly the Dallas team piled victory upon victory. The calm of Tom Landry, whose unflappable dignity has always been in stark contrast to the demented rantings of most other coaches as they urge on their teams, seemed entirely justified as he quietly paced up and down the sidelines, nattily dressed in jacket and tie – no sports shirt tumbling over a beer gut for Landry – and a soft hat on his balding head. On TV ads Landry assured us that his love for Jesus was even greater than his love of football, and the deity had certainly been on his side through most of November.

Then his luck changed; the Cowboys stumbled. They started to lose games, and their devoted Texan supporters reacted not with sorrow but with rage and a sense of betrayal. The Cowboys have restored Dallas's good name. Say 'Dallas' to a Californian these days and he won't think assassination or Sue Ellen; he'll think Roger Staubach or Tony Dorsett or Butch Johnson. When the Cowboys falter, the image of their home town slips too.

I was at Joe Miller's bar in Dallas. In a brilliant article in *Texas Monthly* Jim Atkinson had declared it one of the best in the state. Atkinson had dismissed from consideration 'fern bars, bistro bars, singles bars, jazz bars, disco bars', et cetera. He was only interested in 'bar bars, which can best be described as places where you can go and engage in the sacred rite of public drinking and *not be there*. The principle is summed up in Atkinson's First Rule of Drinking: If someone knows where you are, you aren't in a bar bar.' This is all a trifle metaphysical for a simple-minded drinker such as myself, but he wrote with such authority that I knew I could trust him absolutely, and so found myself in a dark and very popular room where tipplers could lean against the bar or sink into comfortable chairs around tables, and above all, drink generous slugs of whisky and beer and talk.

I found myself talking to a heavy young man who, like me, was in communion with Jim Beam. How did he feel about the Cowboys' performance last Sunday? Well, he felt terrible, real sore, just couldn't believe how badly they'd played. Was Landry doing a good job? He wasn't so sure, he was going to have to rethink that one, see how the Cowboys did against the Redskins. We compared notes on wide receivers, tight ends, and how well a linebacker had red-dogged in a game against the Dolphins; and we pondered Landry's disciplinary methods with the rowdier Cowboys.

'Ain't so much a question of rowdy behaviour. If you ever seen Butch Johnson score a touchdown, you'll have seen him do this little jig just after. Landry don't like that one bit, and told Butch if he ever saw him doin' that dance of his again he'd fine him a few hundred bucks. Well, the other day Butch scored a touchdown, and sure enough he did his little jig. Landry fined him, but Butch said he didn't care, he didn't mind payin' the fine just so long as he could jump up and down a bit when he scored.'

Landry's austerity wins him respect but not much affection. His lack of expression is as legendary as his tailored wardrobe. At moments of high emotion, field glasses are trained on Landry's waxy features to see if he'll venture a smile, but he grins as infrequently as the computer that helps him train his troops, work out his game plans, and even select new recruits. I'd seen him smile when talking about Jesus, but coaching the Cowboys is no laughing matter.

'Good for Butch,' I said. 'I don't think Landry's exactly my cup of tea.'

My neighbour looked at me in disbelief. 'Christ, you English guys talk weird.'

'I know, I know, we do, it's quite true. Same again?'

'Thank you, I will.'

I was relieved that Sam hadn't brought his co-worshipper Landry back to the house for a grapefruit juice after church. What could I possibly have to say to a man whose idea of a statement to the press is: 'We haven't really restructured the flex because most of the blitzing comes from the 4–0 (passing) defense.'

'Is it true,' I asked my new acquaintance as the barman slid two ice-filled tumblers towards us, 'that the Cowboys are known as America's team?'

'Yup. Only a few years ago there were rumours that some guys on the team were involved with drugs, so people started calling the Cowboys South America's team.'

When, the next day, I 'phoned Cowboy Stadium in Irving to inquire about tours, all lines were busy, and I was put on hold. Instead of anaemic music, I heard down the earpiece a selection of recorded replays – great moments in Cowboys history.

Opened in 1971 and holding 65,000 spectators, the stadium cost $35 million to build. Some of the money was raised by issuing bonds, and anyone who bought $50,000 worth was given a private box, one of 177 glass-fronted rooms ovalling round the stadium on two levels. Each box seats twelve, plus bartender. In addition each box owner must purchase season tickets to the tune of $1500 a year. Some of the boxes have been lavishly decorated by their proprietors; one, said to belong to an Englishwoman – though it can't be true – is lit by an exceptionally valuable antique chandelier.

Down in the locker room, the holy of holies, small boys went bananas as they found the lockers of their favourite players, identified by their names on blackboards, because when the players had had individual nameplates, they proved, like sign-posts to Luckenbach, irresistible to souvenir hunters. Excited little girls scrawled graffiti over them while their horrible little brothers stood under the blackboard naming their idol and had their photograph taken.

*

Bill invited me to lunch for the simple and sufficient reason that Don Earney had asked me to get in touch with him. Being a friend of Don's was all the identification he required.

At a shopping mall off the North Central Expressway is a

restaurant called Le Louvre, where I sat waiting for Bill. Noon, he'd said, but forty minutes later he still hadn't shown up, and I was growing nervous. In the empty restaurant I nursed a glass of white wine, wondering whether I'd come on the wrong day. Eventually I got the nod from the maître d', who seemed to know my host well, and a moment later a burly man of about sixty pounded down the short flight of steps into the dining room. I'd worn a pinstripe suit, assuming that a Dallas oil millionaire would in his way be formally dressed. I was wrong. Bill wore a soft flannelly shirt and slacks.

'Ugo, get me an old-fashioned, willya,' he ordered, and the maître d' scurried off. The decor was not to my taste: the colour scheme, fawn chairs on a red-brown carpet, made the room look musty, and the artificial flowers, Muzak, and elaborate electrified chandeliers gave it formality without elegance. Complex murals made visual reference to the Mona Lisa and the Venus de Milo. Le Louvre! Of course!

Bill watched my eyes travelling around the room. 'Like the place?'

'Mmm.'

'Yeh, it's kinda elegant. In fact, I used to own it, and my wife did the decor.' No wonder four waiters were hovering about us like flies over meat. We ordered our meal.

'Will you have salad or vegetables, sir?' inquired a waiter.

'Neither. I'll drink my vegetables. Bring me another old-fashioned. That white wine you've got there,' he was turning to me, 'I bet it's terrible.'

'It wouldn't win prizes.'

'OK. Bring my guest a glass of red wine. That OK with you?'

'Fine.'

'I can't drink white wine. Never did like it. Good French red wine, that's another ball game. Back at the house I've got a dozen vintages of Lafite. Now that's a wine!'

Back came the waiter with a glass of red jug wine.

Bill was, he told me, one of 1100 oil millionaires in the Metroplex, but he had diversified his operations: he owned mines in New Mexico, businesses in California, oil wells in Oklahoma, and refineries in Louisiana, and bars and restaurants.

'I got into the oil business by acting as an intermediary for some guy I knew. He needed oil, a particular kind of oil, and he needed it in a hurry, and he asked me if I knew where to get it. So I made a couple of 'phone calls, found the right oil at the right price, and we made the deal.'

'How come your friend couldn't make the 'phone calls himself? He could have saved himself a lot of money.'

'He was from out of state, didn't know who to call. Anyhow, I reckoned that was a pretty easy way to earn money fast, and so I thought I'd stay with oil and went into the refinery business. That was easy money too. I could make myself a nice profit and the oil companies even paid for the transportation. Then about ten years ago I started drilling.'

'Any luck?'

'No. A dry hole. Then I struck oil with the next fourteen.'

'Has the slump affected you?'

'Sure. But it's bottoming out, and we're a year to a year and a half from honkin' and blowin' again.' We'd finished our steaks and Bill called over the waitress, then looked at me. 'How about a cognac? OK. Well, honey, bring me another old-fashioned, and a Remy Marteen for my guest. Now what were you saying?'

'About the slump and the recovery . . .'

'Well, as I say, it's bottomed out. Hard times makes people change the way they operate. This past year I've seen drilling contractors prepared to drill for nothing and take a percentage if they find oil. It's a risky business, always has been. I'm a high roller. I gamble. You have to.'

The waitress returned with an old-fashioned, his fourth, for Bill, and a glass of red wine for me.

'Honey, I asked for Remy Marteen, not red wine . . .'

The waitress flailed and dithered.

'Honey, do you know what Remy Marteen is? It's cognac, not wine. Now take this glass away, sweetheart, and bring back a balloon glass with some Remy Marteen in it. Now what were we talking about?'

'Risks . . .'

'Oh yes. I'm onto a sure thing now. I've developed a mileage extender. I'm not marketing the product myself but I've developed it and I get a royalty on every barrel that's sold anywhere in the world. Give me your address, I'll send you a case to London.'

'I don't have a car.'

He shrugged. 'Then I guess I won't. I don't know how good

you are at math, but I figure that my royalty on millions of barrels each year is going to add up mighty fast.'

The waitress returned with my cognac. Bill, a little woozy after his ingestion of bourbon, leaned back in his chair. 'How long you going to be in Dallas?'

'Another couple of days, though I may come back for a day if I can find a way to get to the Cowboys game against the Redskins.'

'It's gonna be the big one.'

'I know, but a friend is trying to get me a ticket through some contacts, though he doesn't hold out much hope.'

'I may be able to help you.'

'Really? How?'

'I own three boxes at the stadium.'

'Three? Nobody owns three.'

'I do. I use one, lease the other two. I'll tell you what I'll do. I've put an ad in the Washington paper offering to lease one of them for $7500. I don't know if I'm going to get an offer, and if I don't you can be my guest.'

He dismissed my surprised protest. 'It'll be my pleasure. Don Earney helped me out years ago. When no one else would back me, he listened to me and then decided by the seat of his pants to help me. So I'm always happy to help any friend of his.' (Bill found some Washingtonians prepared to pay $625 each for a seat, so I never got to the game. The Cowboys lost.)

Bill checked his watch. He had to get back.

'Can I ask you something impertinent? You live like a millionaire. But are you one?'

'I've been a millionaire three times.'

'You mean you've lost it and made it back again.'

'Uh huh.'

'You a millionaire now?'

'If I stay on course, in a couple of years I'll be a billionaire.'

*

I kept stumbling over the ultra-rich that day. I took Sam and Carmen to dinner at Ceret, a French restaurant, vaguely nouvelle cuisine in style, that had just opened in a converted warehouse. After a good meal, Carmen said she wanted to show me The Mansion at Turtle Creek. Formerly a private house, it had been converted into a sumptuous hotel with one of the best

French restaurants in town. The setting, in the splendid house crammed with antiques, was indeed magnificent. Carmen wanted me to see her city at its most elegant. She persuaded Sam to drive by. He had no desire to make a lightning tour of the public rooms and stayed in the car while I rampaged through the Mansion with Carmen, who looked ravishing in full-length mink. Just as we passed the entrance to the restaurant she froze.

'Why, Lenny!' she exclaimed in her rich throttled tones, unable to conceal her surprise as we almost collided with a demure, silver-haired man with a gently lined face.

'Carmen! Great to see you! This is Sally.' And we exchanged nods and smiles with an attractive, well turned-out woman of about thirty.

'This is our friend from England,' Carmen rapidly explained. 'He's been staying with us for a few days. Sam's in the car outside. He didn't want to come in.' Carmen had suddenly realised her own presence at the Mansion with a strange Englishman could prompt the same kind of speculation that was now rambunctuously coursing through her mind. After a brief uneasy conversation with Lenny and his girl, we moved on. Carmen clutched my arm and uttered an expletive that would have earned her a hefty fine from Tom Landry. The excitement had been too much. To have spotted Lenny, whose marriage, it was widely known, would soon be dismantled by costly lawyers, leaving the Mansion with another woman – well! As Carmen said, 'He might as well put an ad in the paper.'

Back at the car Sam looked ready to uproot trees with his bare hands, but after she'd breathlessly reported the news, he too became enthralled. She told him to drive past Lenny's house. All gossip or information from Carmen had to be instantly provided with a visual analogue.

'Slow down, Sam! I want Stephen to see. That's the house there. Lenny's is the only house in Highland Park with a four-car garage.'

Ah Dallas! What a town, where the citizens live in a state of perpetual envy. As soon as a family hauls itself onto a higher social plateau, there in the distance it sees the land rising again, and so it trudges on to the next escarpment, the swisher car, the more exclusive country club, the more costly mink. These Texans, living luxuriously inside their fully fitted custom homes, were by any standard rich, yet they couldn't perceive their own wealth. At night they would dream of More. Europeans are not without ambition and greed, but, less restless, they pause to fashion their own style from what their resources will provide. In Dallas there was no question of style, not because nobody had any, but because everybody had the same. Money was desperately coveted, and once acquired the uses to which it could be put were strictly laid down. The rules of display were prescribed – 'I have nine partners in my business ventures,' Hank told me, 'and eight of us drive German cars' – and so were the rules of consumption. The rules of acquisition were more loosely applied – Clay had his dozen cars, some had Impressionists or porcelain, many had acreage. At the dizziest height of worldly success, none of it seemed to matter much anymore. Trammell Crow was still a good ole boy, and the late H. L. Hunt took his lunch to the office in a brown paper bag; nor are his burly heirs, Bunker, Herbert, and Lamar, known for ostentation. I'd read a good deal about the Hunts, and they possessed not even a modicum of charm or style; they lived for money because they had been trained to no other purpose. It was their names that Sherwood Blount had dropped obsequiously, and their names that Carmen had mentioned with humorous envy.

Glumly I took my intrigued boredom with Dallas to a New Yorker who had lived there for some years, hoping he would corroborate my impressions with some sharp-edged Yankee spite. But no, he regretted that he couldn't.

'Dallas is a better place to live than it was five years ago when I first arrived. It's changing and for the better. It's more sophisticated – I can think of many expensive New York restaurants infinitely more vulgar than the Mansion, which even you admit is elegant – and even the architecture is improving. In the old days it was shitty, for the simple reason that the city fathers just handed out the jobs to their pals. That's stopped.

'I know it's hard to excuse the political organization of the city, but it actually works reasonably well. Dallas is a great argument against democracy. Under the reformed system the old moneyed interests aren't as powerful as they used to be. Newer entrepreneurs have been co-opted into the system, so the make-up of the power structure has changed. But the ideology's essentially the same. There's no real opposition to the oligarchy in this town.

'The press here isn't much good either. Two daily papers, both establishment-oriented. The *Morning News* is the leading offender, ass-licking like crazy, running endless profiles of eminent citizens, and admiring articles about rich kids from North Dallas who've taken up bracelet designing and become even richer. Dallas is more status-conscious than any other place I know. To fail here must be truly crushing. There's a bank here that runs an ad that goes: "In business, if you're not on the way up, you're on the way down."

'Every objection you can possibly raise about Dallas I will probably agree with. Its values are terrible. Yet the traffic moves, it's not hard to get a nice apartment or a decent house, taxes are low, you can make your mark quickly if you're any good, and you're not having continually to fight your environment. A reporter once said to me that living here is like living in a Dutch tulip garden. He spends his working days looking for corruption, chemical poisoning, graft, and so forth, but there's hardly any around. It's almost frightening how easy it is to get on in Dallas. Let me put it this way: Dallas is a terrible place to visit but a great place to live.'

Double Bass

Fort Worth, outdazzled by its flashy partner to the east, is regarded by Dallasites as a dinghy trailed behind a yacht, linked yet separate and scarcely significant. Dallas constantly sings its own praises, pointing puff-chested at its own achievements, while by comparison Fort Worth is shy and self-effacing, blushing behind its tag of Cowtown. Not that it's ashamed of that tag; the city is still a livestock and agribusiness centre. Its citizens, however, are undemonstrative, reticent; no soap opera is ever likely to focus on their adulteries and betrayals. Yet the burghers of Fort Worth are far from being low-voltage hicks more interested in the dimensions of their steers than the shapeliness of their women. Whether through accident or lightly concealed design, Fort Worth has a cultural life that eclipses that of boastful Dallas. It's a rich town – oilmen Sid Richardson, T. Cullen Davis (tried for murder in 1976 and acquitted), and Eddie Chiles were all based there – and some of its grandees chose to found museums as their memorials.

On every block I seemed to stumble over one of them with elegant white concrete arches loping over well-watered lawns. Amon Carter, whose pride in his native city and complementary loathing of Dallas informed everything he did, founded a superb Museum of Western Art, which Philip Johnson designed in 1961. Lurid paintings of cowboys, shootouts, and Indian scouts, vivid in their sense of movement, melodramatic in their colour, leave me cold, but if you want to see the genre at its best, this is where you'll find it. Well no, wait a minute, you might prefer to stay downtown and look in at the Sid Richardson Collection of Western Art on Main Street, with its dozens of Remingtons and Russells.

Kay Kimbell founded the city's most international museum: the Kimbell Art Museum, almost as famous for the placid, beautifully lit Louis Kahn building that houses it as for the contents. The collection is not especially large, but most of the Great Names are represented, prompting the thought that the collection relies on the principle that when you've seen one Velazquez you've seen them all. Philip Johnson also designed another of Amon Carter's legacies to his city, the beautiful

Water Gardens, which dramatically group fountains, pools, and cascades.

Let's face it, though, nobody travels to Texas in search of High Culture. The McNay and the Kimbell are jewels of their kind, but they can't compete with the big guns of New York and the Northeast. The trouble with Art is that most of it has already been identified and cornered, and the good stuff that's left is pricey. British museums hesitantly fork out for their annual Claude or Goya, and only the Getty Museum can afford to fill its shopping bag every time it goes to market.

Fort Worth's museums wouldn't have come into being had it not been for oil and for the snorting, chomping, richly scented passage of livestock through its stockyards, now moribund, so much so that they're undergoing restoration. Some cattle sales still take place here and cattlemen such as Chip have come here to set up shop. Chip is typical of many new cattlemen in that he rarely sees a cow; instead he advises on investment in livestock as a tax shelter. He isn't even a Texan – he comes from Alabama – but his wife Rhonda is from Lubbock, and you can't get much more Texan than that.

Not that she looks typically Texan. She's slender and quick, her lovely face kept constantly vivacious by an easily ignited grin and dark eyes hedged by tiny wrinkles that add piquancy to features that might otherwise seem over-charming. For Rhonda, teasing was a principal means of communication, and as her darts hit home she would smile as though dazzled by the pleasure she was giving herself, and then crease with the hilarity of it all. I envied her access to such deep pools of exhilaration.

I'd met Chip and Rhonda in a lift in San Antonio, yet another instance of Texan serendipity. I'd walked into the lift to descend to a hotel lobby and emerged from it seconds later with another name and address scribbled in a notebook and the parting words: 'Be sure to give us a call when you're in Fort Worth.' Since I accept all invitations as a matter of principle, I now found myself sitting in their new townhouse on the eastern edge of town talking about the cattle business with Chip, a slim youthful man with a wary smile and a spectacular pair of ostrich boots, until Rhonda put a stop to our serious conversation about percentages and yields, and then we set off for town.

Fort Worth, like every other American city with a building constructed before 1920, has a conservation area downtown, where old commercial buildings have been smartened up and new uses found for their antiquated spaces. The district's called Sundance Square, in tribute to Butch Cassidy's sidekick, patron of the city's best-known brothel in the days when Fort Worth really was a rough brawling Cowtown. Some buildings have been hollowed out to form a small shopping mall called Sundance Court, with art galleries full of Western bronzes, costly Navaho rugs, duck decoys, pueblo pots, and other mass-crafted bric-à-brac. Another shop features Teddy Bears, and next door are restaurants and ice cream parlours smelling of strawberry topping. A small band, dominated by the granitic sound of a tuba, entertained passers-by. It's a curious juxtaposition, gleaming glass towers and low-slung concrete convention halls rising without a thought for their neighbours, and the older structures, rarely more than three storeys high, belatedly reasserting themselves, with their scrubbed brickwork and Victorian detail fancifully mocking the glass and concrete all around them.

On the roof of a new $5-million restaurant/theatre/jazz club complex called the Caravan of Dreams is a bar set in a curious grotto; rising behind it is a geodesic dome that warms a terrarium filled with three hundred varieties of cactus. Seated here under the shade of palm trees, I had a good view of the Sundance area crouched below the tall irregular black lozenges of the two Bass towers. The Bass brothers, Sid Richardson's nephews, built these huge office blocks and, it's said, paid for them in cash. At a stroke they provided Tarrant County, of which Fort Worth is the seat, with over ten per cent of its office space. They miscalculated: many of the offices have not yet been leased.

'But the Basses aren't too bothered,' said Chip. Since one of their other enterprises was building the ski resort of Vail, Colorado, I dare say that's true.

'They're a bit overpowering next to this dinky little arts complex we're sitting on top of,' I observed. 'Who built this Caravan?'

'One of the Bass brothers,' shrugged Rhonda, astonished at the naiveté of the question.

The only thing wrong with the swish Caravan is that hardly

anybody has climbed aboard. In Dallas it might succeed, but tranquil Fort Worth, so peacefully rich, doesn't seem to have much call for the avant garde, and has been reluctant to inflict modern jazz on itself as further proof of its cultivation. But the rooftop bar is a treat.

'You look nice,' said Rhonda sweetly, and I knew there had to be a qualification crawling along her tongue, 'but there's something missing.' She pondered and then pounced. 'You need some boots, not those funny brown shoes you're wearing!'

'They're handmade!'

'So? You need some boots. Not those awful ostrich boots like Chip's wearing. We'll go to Luskey's and find you some good Texan boots. Finish your beer.'

Chip defiantly recommended his ostrich boots. 'You'd be amazed how comfortable they are.'

'But ugly!'

I had to agree. The surface of the hide was studded with the stumps of the quills that had been plucked out. At Luskey's Western Wear shop I was more taken with the anteater boots, but discouraged by the price ($700). I was tempted too by the sheen of eel and the meticulousness of lizard. Chip then steered me to the hat department. The choice was excessive: Stetsons and Resistols of different finishes and colour – silver belly, puma, chestnut – and different heights and brims – it was all too much. And once you've selected a hat, you must instruct a Luskeyite on how you'd like the brim rolled, and choose from among fourteen creases, which are then hand-steamed onto the crown. Chip selected a hat for me that was already creased and I tried it on. I looked like a mushroom.

On emerging from the shop we all noticed that the temperature had dropped sharply. Perhaps a norther was blowing in.

'Could be bad tonight,' speculated Chip. 'We'll have to take the plants in.' He thought for a moment, then added darkly: 'Hey, Rhonda, that means you get to sleep in the house tonight.'

The stockyards are a mile or two away from downtown. Nobody wants pungent farmyard whiffs wafting into their offices. At the indoor arena the Texas Police Rodeo was feebly under way; the calf-roping contest we briefly observed was sparsely attended. The rough-edged prisoners of Huntsville put on a far better display of skill and showmanship than did their captors. There was a choice moment when a rider successfully flung his rope round the calf, leapt with a dash from his moving horse, and sprinted over to the writhing animal to complete the operation by tieing its legs together. On coming nose to nose with the calf, the cop realised he'd left the tieing rope on his horse, which by that time had cantered over to the other side of the arena. Oh ignominy!

'I've had enough of this,' said Chip. 'Let's go eat some calf fries.' We walked into the Saddle & Sirloin, one of many Western-style restaurants in the stockyards area. Its interior was got up as a rickety street from the Old West, and the door to the lavatories was marked Marshall's Office. Here in the stockyards was a genuine, if no longer thriving Western ambience, yet the local restaurateurs felt obliged to fake it, to invent a phoney style as if hoping to better the authentic faded style of the actual streets outside.

'What are you ordering?'

'Calf fries. Just as an appetizer. A local specialty. You'll love them.'

'But what are they?'

'That's kinda hard to explain. You'll see. They're very popular. Even French restaurants serve them in Fort Worth.'

The fries resembled large oysters and had a delicate if nondescript flavour.

'Like 'em?'

'Quite nice.' My teeth sank all too easily through the bland pulpy texture. 'So what are they? Polyp?'

Rhonda took a deep breath. 'Well, you know what happens when you turn a calf into a steer?'

Ah. Got it. Scrumptious testicles.

Chip forked the last of the fries into his mouth. 'We used to cook 'em on hot rocks when we were branding cattle . . .'

Was he having me on? I didn't get a chance to ask, as Rhonda, scrabbling through her handbag, cried 'Good news!' She was brandishing a small pillbox. 'I have just three Tylenol left – that makes one each!'

In the souvenir shops, and there were many, I found among the usual racks of T-shirts and comic bumper stickers, innumerable variations on the standard local joke: a Texas housefly (nine inches long in black plastic), a foot-long Texas eraser, and an equally exaggerated pocket comb. More compact were the Texas passport and playing cards with photographs of leggy Cowboys cheerleaders on the back.

After dining at a Mexican restaurant we returned to the stockyards to enrich Billy Bob's, the largest honkytonk in the world. It was more like a county fair than a night spot; the immense shed enclosed not just a dance floor, but a number of restaurants, an oyster bar, concession stands and souvenir shops, a shooting gallery, pool tables like fallow green fields stretching into the murky distance, and even a small rodeo ring. The noise was deafening. I saw Rhonda scribbling a note, which she handed to the MC.

'Folks,' I heard him say over the loudspeakers, and I knew a familiar ritual was about to unfold, 'we've got a fella here from England. He's travelling all over Texas and I guess we oughta give him a good welcome. I want all you folks from out of state now to say hi.' Loud cheer. 'And now I want all true Texans to –' Great roar. 'Now I want everybody to do it.' About 3000 voices were raised, and I felt I ought to be stepping forward to accept the nomination.

We didn't stay long. Rhonda was tiring ('My shoes kinda ouch too'), so we returned to the house for a nightcap. Reflecting on the fullness of our day, she placed her hands on her hips and with loud satisfaction declared: 'We did good.'

*

I don't know whether Kelly is a typical Fort Worthian, but there was nothing brash or vulgar about his luxurious and elegant house on a guarded estate. His main recreation is big game hunting, but tall, spare, and donnish in manner, Kelly didn't look like Hemingway or Teddy Roosevelt. His months spent in the forests of Ecuador or the Congo, his recent return from the wine auctions at Beaune, and his expertise at preparing advanced cocktails, testified to a dual dedication to the dangerous life and the good life. I sat by a fireplace fronted by a screen of foliage and fern. To the left a stuffed lion paced through the greenery, and to the right crouched a leopard; while from above the fireplace the mournful jowly head of a water buffalo – 'from the Amazon estuary' – peered down. It was not so much Kelly's old-fashioned hobbies that intrigued me, but his almost scholarly urbanity, not a quality I'd encountered much in Dallas. He not only visited the capitals of Europe and his remote jungles for many months of the year; he also gave the impression that he felt perfectly at home in them.

That was what was peculiar about Fort Worth, this bizarre presence of cultivated sensibilities amid the boisterousness of Cowtown. Kelly wasn't sure why this should be so, but he suggested that whereas in Dallas money was made within the city from insurance or property, in Fort Worth fortunes had been made outside it, from oil, gas, or ranching. There was less bustle, less commercial frenzy, in Fort Worth; the city was quiet and unassertive, even complacent. 'We don't brag about our city the way Dallas people do. The last thing we want is to be invaded by thousands of folks from Dallas.'

Late that afternoon I drove back to Dallas. Along the highway a billboard advertised the Carlsbad Caverns in New Mexico. Beneath the ad was the useful information: GO BACK 462 MILES. Not as ludicrous as it appears, this humorous injunction, at least not in a state where you must drive 800 miles to get from one corner to the other. Entering the city I thought I saw a UFO landing to the north, as a lurid egg-yolk glow pulsated low in the air so blindingly that it was impossible to discern its outlines. Turning up towards North Dallas I gradually realised that it was the setting sun reflected in the golden glass skin of some of the new office towers. The sun, so often represented as golden though it rarely is to the eye, was here transformed, in literally reflected glory, into a dazzling manifestation of its emblematic self, casting an inappropriately beneficent light over a city too bland to deserve it. Dallas flourishes not through the richness of its site or resources but through the energy and determination of its severe citizens, the Elect of the business world. The result is a city that's oddly admirable yet characterless, a city that's pleasing to be in, yet it neither draws one to it nor inspires so much as a wisp of regret on leaving it.

*

And leave it I did, making my way southeast towards Houston. As I approached the city from the Big Thicket, the air became clammy and torpid. Drizzle slicked the surface of the highway with damp brown grease which was then chucked up onto my window by the churning tyres of immense trucks roaring past. An even greater hazard literally lay on the shoulders of the highway and occasionally in the middle of it, in the form of jagged strips of metal – bumpers that had dropped off pickups? chrome flashing? freezer doors? – and plumbous lumps of rubber torn from blown-out tyres. I'd spotted no motels along the highways from the north, so in downtown Houston I consulted a garage owner. He directed me to South Main Street, which runs from the centre past Rice University and the Medical Center to the Astrodome. One side of the broad avenue was lined with motels, none especially inviting.

I checked into the Astro, intending to stay one night only before moving to somewhere more central. The room, with two double beds, was large and clean. It would serve. I showered and rested, then went out to dinner. I drove round the livelier parts of the city before returning to the motel late that night.

It was still hot. Taking the ice bucket from my room I strolled along the pathway to the ice machine. A young black woman with a dour expression stood in an open doorway talking to a more handsome tall woman in a red singlet. They gave me a perfunctory glance as I walked back past them carrying the clinking ice. I let myself back into the room and poured myself a drink. As I flopped onto my bed I noticed that the other one had been moved slightly and the cover was rumpled. Then a chill far frostier than the ice in my glass fell through me as I suddenly realised that my luggage, all of it, had gone.

A Hitch

To be exact: all my clothes, my typewriter, my passport and driving licence, my diaries, notebooks, address book, house keys, a few hundred photographs and negatives, and a large amount of cash. Even my razor and toothbrush had gone, and the book I'd left lying open on the bed when I'd gone out. All that remained were the few items I kept in the car, and my credit cards which I was carrying with me. Since I hadn't unpacked much, it must have been a joy to rob me, and I could picture the thieves scarcely able to believe their luck as they simply picked up my bulging cases and carried them away. It couldn't have taken them more than a minute to wipe me out.

I strode towards the motel office. Again I passed the loitering girls but this time I didn't so much as glance at them. They were silent, motionless. It seemed obvious to me that they knew what had happened. The office was locked – it was after midnight – but my hammering roused the night clerk. I indulged in some therapeutic yelling and ordered him to call the police. Then I marched back to my empty room, where I tried to calm myself. Two feelings were paramount: the sense of outrage, violation, that anyone who has been robbed experiences, and a sickening desolation at the thought that almost a month's notes had been stashed in one of the stolen cases. It seemed distinctly possible that with no notes, no money, no photographs, and no clothes, I would have to abandon the journey.

Checking the room once more, I spotted two items that the thieves had missed. Indeed, they were of no value, except to me. One was the notebook from which I'd typed up the stolen notes. That meant that I could in theory reconstruct much of what had been lost. Secondly, a blue folder in which I'd thrown the addresses and 'phone numbers of every single contact I'd made or would be making in Texas. It dawned on me that if I could rewrite my notes, get my hands on some more money, and replace some clothes, I could continue after all.

There was a flashing light outside my door, then a knock. Not the police, but a security man employed by the hotel. I told him what had occurred; he was sympathetic, until I pointed out that his visit and his concern came rather late in the day. The motel, I opined, had some cheek sending round their security man, since my room, situated on the ground floor and facing the main forecourt, had not been broken into but had been entered with a key. It was therefore painfully evident that the motel had no security to speak of. He went away.

Another fifteen minutes went by. Just to sit in that room depressed me, so I went out and paced up and down the forecourt. Even at such a late hour the place was humming, and it didn't take long to realise that the motel fulfilled a very different function at night from that of resthouse for the road-weary. Large battered sedans swooped in and out. Pairs of men sat quietly in darkened cars, talking, watching. The tall woman in the singlet spoke to some of them on her way to visit her dour friend again. One of those cars, bumping on spongy springs towards the Main Street exit, could well have my property stowed in its boot. The thought was intolerable, so the next time I saw a car making for the exit, I stepped out and flagged it down.

'Excuse me,' I said politely as the driver, bemused, lowered his window, 'but I've just been robbed at this motel and am anxious to recover my possessions. Now I've no right to ask this, but I'd like to inspect your car. It's not that I suspect you, it's just that I suspect everybody. You're perfectly at liberty to refuse, but I should tell you that I've noted your licence number and if you refuse to let me look inside your car, I shall pass it on to the police.'

To which pretty speech the driver replied: 'Hey man, you're crazy. You think I got your stuff? That's crazy, man. I don't want you givin' no number to the police. I ain't got your stuff but this car – well, I just don't want you giving out no number.'

'I promise you I won't if you open the trunk.'

Shaking his head in disbelief, the youth got out of his car and opened the boot. Tyres, toolbox, comic books. No suitcases. I apologised for troubling him and, muttering, he drove off.

The next motorist I stopped was less co-operative. He refused absolutely to let me search his car. I didn't argue. He was with a girl, and it was unlikely he'd back down in front of her. Off he went, and I jotted down the number. It began to occur to me I wasn't getting anywhere.

As an alternative way of passing the time, I approached the

dour whore. Had she seen anything suspicious going on near my room?

'Ain't seen nothin'.'

After half an hour the police arrived. I explained what had happened. They nodded, made notes; they'd heard similar stories too often before.

'It's real tough, something like this happening your first night in the city, but can I ask you something?'

'Of course.'

'What are you doing staying in a whorehouse?'

'How was I to know this is a whorehouse? It's obvious now, but when I checked in this afternoon in broad daylight it looked like any other cheap motel. How could I tell?'

'Because every motel on Main Street is a whorehouse.'

'I didn't know that. They don't tell you that in the brochures your tourist offices hand out.'

The Astro had, on its signboard, not only advertised its proximity to the Medical Center but offered a shuttle bus service to its hospitals. Like most of the other establishments on the street, it looked minimally respectable. How wrong I'd been. Whores who make regular use of a room almost certainly have a duplicate key. How easy it must have been for a whore, observing my departure at dinnertime, to let someone know that the sucker in Room 102 had just driven off.

'Think I'll get my stuff back?' I plaintively asked the police.

'You'll never see it again. Maybe they'll throw your papers and those notes you're so anxious about into a dump truck or a pile of trash near the road. You could check 'em in the morning. But my guess is you won't see your clothes again unless you check out every flea market in Houston.'

'I did try searching some cars that were leaving the motel.'

'You what?'

I explained how I'd flagged down vehicles and attempted to search them.

'That was not smart,' said the horrified cop. 'If you'd stopped the guy who had your stuff, he'd probably have shot your face off. They shoot first round here.'

'Mmm, that hadn't occurred to me. Look, I can't search this place, but can't you?'

'No sir. It's possible that your luggage is sitting in some other room in this motel – either that or it's on the other side of

Houston by now. But we can't just go into people's rooms and search them.'

'Of course not. All you can do is pat my shoulder and tell me I'll never see my things again.'

'Just count yourself lucky you were out when it happened. Listen. We're gonna take a statement from you, and then after we've gone my advice to you is to have a word with those whores out there. If it's just those papers you're worried about, they just may be able to get through to some guy who had something to do with it and he may agree to dump your stuff somewhere. You could give it a try.'

I did. The dour whore was sullen, said she knew nothing about it, but I made sure she understood my message. I woke the night clerk again and screamed at him till he gave me the room number of the tall tart. I gave her a call.

'Yeh?' It was a man's voice.

I explained who I was and why I was 'phoning, but he interrupted me. 'Hey man, will you quit botherin' me and my ole lady?'

'Look, this is terribly important. I know you have nothing to do with what happened, but –'

'It's two in the morning. Will you leave us alone? She don't want to talk to you. It's too bad some guy ripped you off, but it ain't nothin' to do with me or my ole lady.'

'It's my papers, you see – I don't care about the clothes. They can keep all that – all I want . . .' It was hopeless. I was talking to a pimp in the middle of the night, and could I really expect him to work up much interest in some sheets of paper? If the police had no intention of investigating the robbery, why should a pimp put himself out? In the ice bucket sat what was left of a bottle of 1980 Chateau St Jean Gewurtztraminer (Frank Johnson Vineyard), a stunning wine I'd picked up quarter-price in Lubbock. At least some pleasures were left to me. I carried it to bed and drank myself to sleep in style.

I woke two hours later, got up early to begin an exciting day that consisted mostly of searching rubbish dumps and checking pawn shops. I bought myself a razor so I could at least shave, and moved to another motel. I returned to Astro later in the afternoon, when I'd been told the manager would be there. To my astonishment Mr Khan had not yet been informed that one of his guests had been relieved of his worldly goods during the night. In my presence he called in a clerk and reprimanded him, but I wasn't fooled for a second. I informed Mr Khan that I had no intention of paying my bill.

'I must remind you, Mr Brook,' said the glacial Mr Khan, 'that this motel is not liable for your losses.'

'I dare say, but if you think I'm going to pay you thirty dollars for the privilege of having been robbed here, you're mistaken.'

After a further exchange of courtesies, he agreed to tear up the bill. I probably could have sued him, especially in litigation-crazed Texas, but from across the Atlantic there would have been little point. Instead, I had the grim satisfaction of warning some travellers about to check into the motel that they would be better advised to go elsewhere.

It was a miserable weekend. On Sunday evening an acquaintance came by with her boyfriend to take me out for the evening. 'I'm so shocked that something like this should have happened to you in Houston,' said Regina, and to show she meant it she tried to thrust a hundred dollars into my hand, thinking I might be short of cash. I successfully resisted, as I had enough to get by until fresh supplies arrived from London. But her thoughtfulness to a near stranger struck me as remarkably generous. After dinner we went to a protest meeting about the treatment of Soviet Jewry, and there I met Republican Congressman Bill Archer. We talked about grapefruit.

The weekend was punctuated by frequent 'phone calls to the Astro and to the police just in case any of my belongings had been handed in. No, nothing. As my hopes gradually sank, my determination to recoup rose. I borrowed a typewriter from the sculptress Gertrude Barnstone and began to rewrite the notes that had perished.

On Monday I went to the British Consulate to apply for a new passport. The staff there were efficient and impersonal and postponed payment of the fee until the passport would be ready for collection a fortnight later. They also gave not the slightest indication of regret or concern. Oh, I know, British subjects are murdered, raped, mugged, and robbed all the time in Houston – why should I expect special treatment? Yet it was disheartening to this innocent abroad that my consulate didn't so much as inquire whether I might need anything, while strangers were pressing money into my hands.

Despite the kindness of strangers, I didn't want to lean too heavily on their goodwill. I recognised that my morale needed a major overhaul. My labours at Gertrude's typewriter in the air-conditioned gloom of my motel room were dogged but dispiriting. I needed rest, even pampering. I had another reason for wanting to leave Houston. I was, to my shame, developing mild paranoia around black people. The whores and pimps at the Astro were all black, and I assumed that whoever robbed me probably was black too, though I had no proof. When a pair of black men would walk towards me on the street, I would tense with fear and anger. It might have been them, was the unreasonable thought that invaded my mind. If a black laughed anywhere near me, I immediately suspected he was laughing at me. This, I recognised, was preposterous. Not that a small measure of paranoia comes amiss in Houston, where there was public rejoicing because there hadn't been a murder for two whole days. If the trend continued, the murder rate for the city would drop that year from over 700 to a mere 550. 'Houston,' someone later explained to me, 'lulls people into a false sense of security. They come down from New York or Chicago, and find a city that's open and tolerant. The weather's hot and balmy. So they walk the street late at night under the palm trees. Next thing they know five kids from Baytown are leaping out of a pickup that's arrived from nowhere and you're being beaten to a pulp. To pass the time. This is a dangerous city.'

I decided to take refuge with Christopher and Ann in Austin, and 'phoned to warn them of my imminent reappearance in downcast condition. Four hours later I was there.

'You're in luck,' said Christopher. 'Ann's been trying out some recipes for her book. And we've chilled a bottle of something good in the hope of cheering you up.'

So we sat down to a dinner of redfish with scallions and ginger, stuffed pompano, salmon with raspberries, and trout bourguignon, and drank a bottle of 1973 champagne. For that hour at least I felt I was happily back in a corner of sweet, intense, cosy, much missed Europe.

'That was wonderful,' I murmured, replete and even content. 'I must get robbed more often.'

*

I used those days in Austin to sleep, write, buy clothes, recuperate. At the end of the week the money which had been cabled to me had arrived and I presented myself at the bank to collect it.

'Yes sir, the money is here. We can let you have it as soon as you tell us the codeword.'

'Codeword? What codeword?'

'That's what we need to know from you, sir.'

I'd known it wouldn't be easy to obtain that money without any identification, but this was the first I'd heard of a codeword. I frantically pulled strings and five minutes before the bank closed for the weekend the cash was in my hands.

I planned to return to Houston on the Monday, immediately after renewing the rental agreement for my car, which had to be done each month in Austin. The day before my departure I went to a lunch party where I met a friendly woman called Jane. Where was I staying in Houston? she asked.

'I don't know yet. Not at the Astro.'

'You can't stay in another motel. Listen, I have some friends in Houston. They'd love to have you stay. Call me tonight. By then I'll have talked to them.'

'But they don't know me.'

'So? They know me.'

I 'phoned Jane that evening. She was apologetic. 'My friends are in town, but their kids are back for the vacation and the house is full. They're really sorry.'

'That's quite all right. It's most kind of you to have asked. I'm sure I'll find somewhere safe to stay tomorrow.'

'Oh, but I've found you a place. 'Phone this number and ask for Barbara or Jonathan. They say they'd like for you to stay with them.'

'Who are they?'

'I've no idea. But they're friends of my friends, and it's all arranged.'

The morning of my departure I drove to Budget to renew the car.

'Can we see your credit card, sir?' Certainly.

'Can we see your driver's licence, sir?'

'I'm afraid not. It was stolen.'

'We do need to see it if you want to rent the car again.'

I pointed out that the licence number was on the previous

months' contracts, and that the Houston police could confirm that number.

'We don't doubt that you had a valid licence last month,' they patiently explained, 'but we need proof that it's still valid.'

'It's valid into the next century!' Astounding but true.

'But we need to see it, so we can be sure.'

Panic rose, and I stomped it down and tried to think. 'Look, we'll solve it this way. Forget you've seen me this morning, and I'll return the car late in a couple of weeks.'

They slowly shook their heads, and as they were also jingling the keys, I didn't pursue that line. I called for the manager, who confirmed what his staff had said. This time the panic could not be so easily repressed. Without wheels my travels would definitely be over. Eyeless in Gaza is nothing compared to being carless in Texas.

'We don't doubt your word,' said the manager, 'but if you have an accident and the insurance people find that your licence has expired and that we hadn't checked it, they could close us down. Is there anyone who could confirm that your licence is valid?'

'Only the Ministry of Transport.'

'Where are they?'

'Swansea. In Wales. Near England.'

'Can we call them?'

Oh, inspired manager! I checked my watch. It would be just after four in the afternoon in Swansea. Directory inquiries gave me the number; then I dialled Wales. Two minutes later the much maligned DVLC in Swansea had confirmed the validity of my licence. And five minutes after that I was driving away in my familiar little Toyota, though I soon had to pull over for a few minutes until the trembling ceased. All those brushes with ruin were scraping at my nerves.

I was passing through barbecue country once again, so I couldn't resist a pause for nourishment in Bastrop. Approaching La Grange, I was surprised to find no Chamber of Commerce billboards celebrating the town's internationally famous (former) attraction: the Chicken Ranch, the best little whorehouse in Texas until it was run out of business. But not a word: there seemed to be a conspiracy of silence, and I was unable to find the site and raise my hat. Country roads eventually led to Interstate 10 which took me directly into

Houston. A placard over Charlie's hamburger stand proclaimed: OVER 2 DOZEN SOLD.

An hour later I was back in Houston.

Guzzle

At the Contemporary Arts Museum, which was packed with contemporary artists who'd flocked to the Christmas party, with romping children and adults drinking, a painter was complaining to me that the slump in oil prices had also meant that corporations were buying less art. Houston was no longer a lucrative market for a large crop of artists.

'Do corporations know a great deal about modern art?'

'Zilch. See that guy over there? He's an art consultant. He tells them what to buy.'

'Does he know a great deal about art?'

'You gotta be kidding. And you'll find a lot of us resent that people like him are determining what gets bought and what doesn't.'

After an hour Gertrude Barnstone, who'd invited me, retrieved me and took me off to another party, at the Art League. We soon located the room with smoked salmon and cornered a table. With my mind dulled by the easy-going blandness of Dallas, to meet someone like Gertrude was refreshing. She was a feminist and quite radical in her politics. I wasn't used to that in Texas. The previous evening I'd dined with a prosperous lawyer, and he'd drawn an embarrassed smile from the ladies present by referring to Senator Alan Cranston as a 'bald-headed fart' and to the *New York Times* and *Washington Post* as 'rags', which, I suppose, compared to the journalistic splendours of the *Houston Chronicle*, is fair comment. All over Texas I'd either had to keep my head down or explain myself. With Gertrude I could relax, as it became obvious that many ideas and values were shared and did not have to be either tactfully suppressed or strenuously established. She was puzzled by my surprise at this, not knowing – how could she? – that endless conversations about property prices and skiing trips had begun to anaesthetize my brain.

She did, moreover, recognise that her native Texas was not the centre of the universe. As another woman, not a native, but confined to Houston by her children's schooling, put it to me with some bitterness: 'Texas is like a great big fraternity.

Texans seem hardly aware that there's a world out there that has nothing to do with Texas.'

We were joined at our table by a tall bearded man called Ed, a former arts administrator. For some reason he felt sure we had come there specifically to listen to his life story, which he proceeded to narrate with practised fluency. A former 'sixties radical, he'd become part of the establishment, he told us, and was now searching anew for the radical commitment he'd once abandoned. Gertrude stifled a yawn as her bright green eyes began to dim. I interrupted the monologue by offering to fetch some drinks, but Ed ostentatiously refused. He used, he explained, to drink heavily. Now he was a teetotaler, and explained why. Many paragraphs later he learnt why I was in Houston and offered to show me round. 'Just give me a call in the morning and I'll be happy to give you a tour.'

*

The Houston art world is dominated by Dominique de Menil, who inherited so much money that she can afford to give much of it away and still remain ludicrously rich. In the faintly raffish Montrose district, an old section of the city, an immense hole in the ground will soon, at the cost of $30 million, be filled by a long low shed in architectural harmony with the modest houses that surround it. It will be the permanent home of the Menil Collection. In the meantime her best known gift to Houston is the Rothko Chapel, an octagonal brick building, also in Montrose, with interior walls covered with fourteen large monochromatic paintings by Mark Rothko.

The chapel is, in accordance with contemporary custom, nondenominational, which is why it fails. The powerful rectangles of dark paint, murky browns, thick purples, and black blacks, boom out like a ground bass that will match any harmonies superimposed by whatever religious activity has been scheduled for a particular day. The chapel exudes an all-purpose religiosity that makes it an equally fitting setting for eucharists, Hanukah ceremonies, and whirlings of visiting dervishes. Rothko's canvases, brooding on the walls, speak, allegedly, to all mankind. Given their poverty of expression, that may be true. But hush, for Houstonians are inordinately proud of this bleak little chamber.

It's not only the visual arts that flourish in Houston. The

Houston Ballet has been directed for some years by a petulant Englishman, Ben Stevenson. It hadn't been easy to track him down. 'It'll have to wait,' an aide had explained, 'as we're opening our *Nutcracker in Orange* on Wednesday.'

Since both the Houston Ballet and the Houston Grand Opera receive minimal subsidies, aggressive fundraising is essential to their survival. The Opera has a 'development staff' of five solely to raise money – and a dependence on corporate generosity means that programming must to some extent conform to the safe tastes of the sponsors, though neither company finds that it has been too hampered by corporate conservatism. Stevenson had little difficulty persuading foundations and corporations to support new work – the glamour of a new production meant good publicity. But it was harder to find corporations willing to fork out when the roof needed an overhaul.

For the first time in years the Grand Opera was thinking of cutting some new productions. Rich Houstonians had been sending cheques to the Wortham Center, a proposed $70 million arts complex downtown, and by the time the Grand Opera got to them, their resources were depleted. Despite the pinch, the company mounts an ambitious season and attracts the greatest singers. The Ballet too has an international reputation. In the great rivalry between the two largest cities of Texas, Houston, which also has a splendid Museum of Fine Arts, a symphony orchestra, and the well-known Alley Theater (which, while I was there, was performing plays by such local talent as Michael Frayn and Caryl Churchill), is laps ahead of Dallas in terms of the arts.

*

Houston, like many American cities, is ringed by a highway. Although the city has expanded for many miles beyond the ring road, almost everything of interest lies inside the loop. Running west from downtown is the city's best known street, Westheimer. At the downtown end are a few thoroughly nasty blocks of old frame houses, almost every one of which is an Oriental Massage Parlour. Moving west, heterosexual sleaze blends with gay sleaze, and then follows a stretch of cafés, restaurants, nightclubs, and boutiques that stay busy day and night. A couple of miles on, Westheimer ducks under the loop and crosses Post Oak Boulevard. All around are shopping malls and office blocks; it's like a downtown that isn't downtown. There's more office space at this intersection than in all of Cleveland. Cars pour in all day long, since this is also the site of the best-known shopping centre in Texas, the Galleria, and some of the most expensive restaurants and real estate in Houston. The skyscrapers gleam with newness.

South of Westheimer, at the downtown end of the street, are the graceful houses of the residential districts of Montrose and West University Place and Southampton. During the suburban expansion of the 1950s these older neighbourhoods began to fray, but with the energy crisis of the 1970s many people returned to these quiet oak-shaded streets around Rice University.

A few blocks north of Westheimer lies the enclave of River Oaks, a copybook example of the opulent suburb. Here enormous mansions seem to have been dropped, fully fitted, from the clouds onto their neatly fenced lots. Standard Colonial is the most common style, red brick with white porticoes, shutters optional, service wings and garages attached. (Just such a home with a pool and tennis courts but with a paltry five bedrooms was offered for sale that autumn at $4.5 million.) The cross streets meander in deference to notions of the picturesque, since Houston is flat and there are no hills or natural impediments, other than the occasional bayou, to keep developers from the straight and broad. Here even more luxurious houses – haciendas with pantile roofs, a château and a Tudor palace, and a very stylish adobe house the size of a supermarket – lie half concealed behind walls and gates and a screen of vegetation. River Oaks derives its tight-assed charm from trim thickets of flowering shrubs and a proliferation of dignified trees, but it proclaims its exclusivity too loudly. Exclusivity, after all, excludes; it's more like a club than a suburb. Immaculate lawns and crisply maintained flower beds surround many of the mansions, yet there is always a sense – and it's present all over Houston – that a paludine fecundity has to be kept in check. Creepers, shrubs, and weeds, mosses and ferns crawling up from the bayous – there's wet greenery all around, and its unruliness seems to infect the city.

The centrepiece of the enclave is the Country Club, a magisterial building that blocks the end of River Oaks

Boulevard. Flags flap heavily in the sodden air over the high roof, while pastel-shaded Cadillacs and Lincolns glide through the gates and up the ramp to the porte-cochère. Houston doesn't share Dallas's obsession with German cars, and it's socially acceptable to drive an American model here, as long as you can't coax more than 10 mpg from it. When I first glimpsed the clubhouse, I took it for an official residence; in a capital city it could have been an embassy. Driving closer I realised my mistake. Then, watching the comings and goings, it occurred to me that my uninformed instinct hadn't been so mistaken after all. It was an embassy, to which rich men, in their absurd Madras slacks and sports coats, and their rich wives in their hairdos and furs, came to present their credentials to society. Dallas has what it likes to think of as society – balls and debs and women who devise elaborate entertainments for good causes – but Houstonians will laugh derisively if you speak to them of Dallas society. For true Texas society, they insist, is based in Houston. There's even a baron, Ricky di Portanova, a grandson of oilman Hugh Roy Cullen. There's old money, and there's new, and, as elsewhere, old is better. Why, in Houston there are even families who made their fortunes in the last century. That's society for you.

*

Ed asked me to meet him at the Boulevard Café in Montrose. When I arrived he asked me to excuse him for a few minutes while he put the finishing touches to the design of his personal Christmas card. An hour and a half later he finished it, and said: 'Well, I guess you're ready for our tour. Do you think you'll be able to drive and look around at the same time?'

'No, I'm quite sure I won't. Don't you have a car?'

'Yes, that big Buick outside. It's a tremendous gas guzzler, but that's the kind of car I like.'

'It's all the same to me.'

'It's a tremendous gas guzzler, and I wouldn't usually take it all over the city. But we can take it if you don't mind paying for the gas.'

I paid for our breakfast and we set off. I liked Montrose, unpretentious, a bit scruffy, with a few mansions left as reminders of its more fashionable past. The large homosexual population (the free gay paper the *Montrose Voice* has a circulation of 11,000 in Houston, twice as many as the *Dallas Gay News* in Dallas) encourages a proliferation of cafés and galleries and clothes shops, jumbled together in the Houston fashion.

For Houston is notorious for its lack of zoning. In theory you can build whatever you like wherever you like. In some places this is exactly what happens. It's not unusual to find a fashionable restaurant on Westheimer squeezed between a garage forecourt and a porn shop. However, Houstonians have devised ways of keeping such chaos at bay; there are, for instance, no shops or factories in River Oaks, though there are no zoning ordinances to forbid it. Instead there are covenants in property contracts that designate the use to which that property may be put, and these covenants are transmitted to a new owner whenever the property is sold. There are time limits on these contractual restrictions. Around Chimney Rock, not far from the valuable Galleria, the covenants will shortly become void. As the expiration date approaches, the value of these houses grows substantially. Developers can't wait to get their hands on that land; the homeowners, meanwhile, sit tight, happily adding noughts to the valuation of their nondescript houses as the years drift by. Fortunes are about to be made.

Ed drove west to the Galleria, an enclosed mall loosely modelled on its famous namesake in Milan. The skylit interior is a many-storeyed atrium; above the two levels of shops rise seven floors of offices, each with a balcony overlooking the shoppers and ice skaters below. As you emerge from Laura Ashley or Crabtree & Evelyn, look up and you'll enjoy an excellent view of the sweaty legs and contorted faces of executives pounding round the running track that hugs the glass roof. On a good day you may even spot a jogger crumpling into cardiac arrest.

'When you're flying north from Caracas or Bogota, the first big American city you come to is Houston,' Ed explained. 'At certain times at least half the people shopping here are South Americans. They fly in one evening, eat at Tony's, shop all the next morning in the Galleria, then fly home that afternoon.'

Ed bought himself a rum truffle for a dollar. At Royal Indian Jewelers I wandered into a back room and came across the manager with a handkerchief over his head, lighting joss sticks and placing them in front of a small idol over the door.

Somehow nothing seems odd in Houston. Dallas is landlocked, enclosed, but Houston is a major port, and populations drift in and out, forming unassimilated enclaves that preserve cultural traditions. In this city you can find an Afghan community, a British pub (there are 10,000 Britons here), a Czech ballroom, a replica of a Hindu temple, and substantial numbers of Koreans, Thais, and Vietnamese.

But not in City Post Oak, which is where executives have gone in search of *Lebensraum*. Philip Johnson is not my favourite architect. I dislike the AT&T Building in New York, and I like even less the absurd ziggurat of his recently completed pink granite Republic Bank Building in downtown Houston, with its preposterous grey cones sitting like candle snuffs on the peak of every gable. But the office blocks he designed near the Galleria, especially the Transco Building, are superb; the tallest American skyscraper not in a downtown area, the tower is spectacularly good, with its elegant black glass projections set against the dark grey glass of the curtain walls.

We drove downtown. The pavements weren't crowded, but that was because labyrinthine passageways, lined with shops, burrow beneath and connect the buildings. In summer especially, when the humidity is overwhelming, office workers can drive into subterranean car parks from their homes, do their lunchtime shopping and eating underground, and then return home in their air-conditioned cars. They can complete the operation, door to door, without ever having to breathe the swampy air; Houstonians can, if they wish, live troglodytically all summer long in a succession of air-conditioned caves. South of downtown we crossed a district I was to revisit a few times. They call it Nam Town, and this is now home to 80,000 Vietnamese immigrants. The neighbourhood is full of restaurants with excellent food, though ordering can be hit or miss if, like me, your command of the language extends to no more than a list of dead politicians.

Northeast Houston, the Fifth Ward, is black, and we drove along the usual rutted streets past car repair shops, soul food restaurants, and wooden shacks from which the paint had long ago flaked off. We were crossing this rundown section of the city on our way to the Ship Channel, the source of Houston's prosperity before oil enriched it further. The city was founded in 1837 by the Allen brothers, who bought up 6000 acres of unpromising swampland in the purest spirit of land speculation; they named their marshy lots after the heroic Sam Houston and the new city took root. In those days Houston was not a seaport; it was just about possible to get there from the coast by barge on a wet day. Galveston, fifty miles south on the Gulf, was a far more important and sophisticated town, one of North America's leading ports. Its site, however, was unfortunate, and hurricanes, gathering speed as they zoomed over the Gulf, soon made a habit of calling on Galveston. In 1900 a hurricane, and the ensuing tidal wave, killed 6000 people and wrecked the stately old town. This disaster demoralised the port, which failed to make a serious attempt to revive its fortunes. Houston took the initiative, and with the help of federal money, built the Ship Channel, which opened in 1914. In terms of tonnage Houston has become the largest American port, though the value of goods that pass through the port of New York is still greater. We found the Turning Basin at the head of the Channel and stood on the observation deck and watched the ships slowly making their way round the basin and back out to sea. Cranes angled up over the endless docks, and the horizon was crenellated by the funnels and flags of motionless freighters.

Further east we came to Pasadena, as beguiling as a sump. From here to Baytown and Texas City on the coast is a fifty-mile stretch of oil refineries and electrochemical plants, oppressive by day and haunting by night, when the cracking towers and oil drums glitter with tiny lights, while great spotlights whiten, presumably for security reasons, large tracts within refinery compounds, and high in the air flares, like perpetual flames, burn off waste gases. Refinery work is skilled and dangerous. Cracking towers seethe with toxic gases that hover at different levels; miscalculate and you're either dead or covered with chemical burns. The smell was sulphurous and awful.

To view this grim industrial landscape, we ascended the San Jacinto Monument, a 570-foot column erected on the edge of the battlefield where Sam Houston won his famous victory. The triumphant Texans, typically, wanted to build a column even taller than the Washington Monument, but Congress said no. Wily as well as proud, the Texans kept the column lower than the Washington Monument, but added a Lone Star that made it a couple of feet taller. Curiously, given that the heavily polluted Ship Channel passes the battleground, which is encircled by chemical plants, the marshes around the Monument teem with wildlife: crabs and shrimp, herons and egrets, and even the occasional alligator slinks by.

Another feature of the landscape is much more worrying: it's sinking at the rate of two inches a year. So much water has been extracted by the conurbation over the decades that the land has subsided. On the coast the subsidence is so marked that some refineries are now below sea level, and the coastal road from Galveston to Port Arthur is impassable. Much of the land near the Monument is now under water; landfill has been hauled in to raise the land level, while along the coast threatened refineries are now protected by dikes. In Houston itself it's not uncommon for the bayous to overflow and flood whole districts.

I'd left my car at the Boulevard Café, and Ed drove me back there. I paid him the twelve dollars he was, exorbitantly, charging me and thanked him for the tour he'd so generously offered. 'What's important in Houston,' the lawyer had told me at dinner, 'is not who are you but what you have to offer.' Having been taken for a ride by Ed, I began to see what he meant.

When I returned to England a copy of the Christmas card Ed had been laboriously composing was waiting for me. Laid out as a poem was the following text: 'There might be a Big Chill in the air this time of year, but never, never, ever in my heart, for you, and your loved ones and their loved ones and their loved ones' loved ones and their's and . . . Be confident, not only this time of year but year round. Peace on Earth in our lifetimes *is* at hand, even when it appears otherwise.'

Thanks, Ed, for your thoughts on this matter.

The Oil Well That Ends Well

The days when a wildcatter would sell his furniture to get his hands on a promising oil lease and then auction his children to obtain an old drilling rig that might tap a previously unknown field of oil that would gush millions of barrels for decades to come – those days are probably over. Many men who began in this way and ended up as multimillionaires were just plain lucky; on a hunch or a good guess they might drill successfully in patches which the major companies, with their teams of geologists, had written off. Many Texan families with fortunes derived from oil never drilled in their lives; they were lucky enough to be sitting on land that happened to cap a sea of oil, and royalties alone would keep the coffers filled.

Those fantastical days of oil exploration, when good ole boys became millionaires overnight, were not, however, that long ago. The first great discovery at Spindletop, near Beaumont, Texas, a field that within a year was producing as much oil as all other American wells combined, was made in 1901. The East Texas fields, the largest pool of oil ever found in the United States, were first tapped in 1930, and later that decade the huge reserves of the Permian Basin in West Texas were discovered. Nowadays much exploration is offshore, an enterprise so costly that only the major producers, or a consortium of many independents, can afford to undertake it. The best-known wildcatter in Texas, Michel Halbouty, is no redneck, but a skilled geologist and the author of many learned articles; a building at Texas A & M University is named after him. 'I'm a real wildcatter,' he insisted to me, adding: 'But I'm an educated wildcatter.'

It was no longer likely that a lone prospector would make a swift discovery that would lead to a local oil boom such as the one that occurred in Borger, north of Amarillo, in January 1926. That winter a wildcatter brought in a gusher, and within weeks the population of the small farming community had risen to 40,000. Overnight the streets had filled with wheeler dealers, fighting over leases and cornering every rig for miles around, double-crossing each other at every opportunity. And with them came the roustabouts and truck drivers, the saloon operators and the prostitutes, the land speculators, the lawyers to draw up, or forge, documents and contracts, and the gamblers ready to relieve the roughnecks of their pay packets.

There are many in Texas today who participated in those hectic dangerous times, and one of them, to my surprise, turned out to be Gertrude's mother, Gisella Levy. Mrs Levy is ninety and had the translucence that sometimes comes with great age. She was tiny and very frail, though in no discernible way did she appear infirm. She wore white: a V-neck pullover tucked into loose trousers tied with a draw-string, a woollen shawl around her shoulders, and on her head a knitted cap – all white, as if defying the convention that impels many old people to flirt with the approach of death by wearing black. Delicate but spirited, with eyes reddened by cataracts but still lively and swift, she pushed some books and papers off the sofa and motioned me to sit beside her.

She'd been studying for her doctorate at Columbia University when the First World War put a stop to that aspiration; her husband was in the regular army. The war ended, and they heard that an oil company was offering free passage to Houston, and free return passage after ninety days if the would-be roughnecks weren't happy with what they found. So Arthur and Gisella Levy set sail from New York to New Orleans.

They almost didn't make it. A storm pummelled the ship so violently that the radio operator went berserk and raced around the decks screaming 'We're lost! We're lost!' The passengers were confined to their cabins until, eventually, the ship docked. When they saw the newspaper headlines – 'CREOLE' SAFE – the passengers realised the ship had been assumed lost. They travelled on to Houston, a small town of 90,000 in those days, and then forty miles south to West Columbia. They arrived to find all the reserved housing taken, so the Levys' first home in Texas was a tent, pegged insecurely into thick clay mud kept slick and deep by the incessant rain. Out by the rigs the fields had to be covered with boards so that the mule wagons could get through. A while later they found a house and Gisella was able to unpack her trunk full of books in fine bindings, not a common sight on the oil patch. Although the presence of a highly educated New York couple must have puzzled the other citizens of West Columbia, the neighbours were friendly and helpful, bringing freshly baked cakes over to the Levy house.

Many of them were farmers who'd been tricked out of their land by rapacious banks; ruined, they'd come down to the oilfield to start a new life.

So had the Ku Klux Klan. Their presence was pervasive. When they heard that a man with nowhere to stay was boarding with a couple, Klansmen took this as an affront to the dignity of family life. One night they came for him, tarred and feathered him. Two weeks later he died. One afternoon Mrs Levy had run down the street to avoid an imminent downpour. That night there was a knock at the door. Arthur Levy went to see who was there, while Gisella stayed in bed with one hand on the Colt they kept by their side – not that she knew how to use it. There were two Klansmen at the door. They'd seen Mrs Levy rushing home and concluded that she was running in terror from a coloured boy who was standing nearby. They'd taken the boy ('nigger' in Klanspeak, of course) and were about to string him up 'for insulting a white woman'. Gisella Levy explained that she'd only been running because of the rain. 'Thank you, ma'm,' they'd said, and released the boy.

'Did you ever miss New York?' I asked her.

'Miss it? No. I used to go back there every year for a visit. And I did have the *New York Times* sent down to me every day.' She leaned back and laughed as she caught my eye. 'Well, I guess I must have missed it after all.'

*

Nobody would call Michel Halbouty retiring. His skills as an engineer and geologist haven't smoothed the edges of a pugnacity that's made him a conspicuously successful oilman, and he claims to have more oil wells than any other independent producer. 'My discovery rate is pretty high,' he told me. 'Thirty-seven, thirty-eight per cent. The average is around ten.' In his offices are copies of his standard book on *Salt Domes*, photographs of his plane, photographs of Halbouty with Reagan and Bush, and dozens of gold medals and awards. He's a dapper man in his early seventies, short, sprightly, silver-whiskered and moustached, beautifully groomed, and with a high gruff voice frayed by excitability. Like many successful men, he was resolutely optimistic, quite convinced that the slump in oil prices was little more than a hiccough, 'provided that our so-called recovery, economic recovery in the world, continues. The mini-depression we've had all over the world has caused a lot of factories to shut down, and therefore less productivity, and whenever you have little productivity you use very little energy. So consequently with all these plants going back to work, and unemployment now being eliminated somewhat, and your productivity increasing, you're using more energy, and if we use more energy that means more oil and gas is being used.' So simple, so simple.

He was sitting close to me at a conference table in his office, his fingers rat-tatting the teak surface. He rightly felt it was a poor use of his time to explain such elementary economics to me. I decided to throw him some raw-meat.

'Somebody told me the other day that what's good for Texas is bad for the United States. Do you think that's true?'

Halbouty, who is one of President Reagan's advisers on energy policy, straightened up and tilted his head in puzzlement. 'What's good for Texas is bad for the United States? I've never heard that before in my life. He must be nuts.'

'I'll tell him so.'

'What's good for Texas is good for the country!'

'That's exactly what he wasn't saying.'

'Then I don't understand his view. I don't know what he's talking about.'

'I think he meant that Texas prospers from high energy costs which are hurtful to other parts of the country.'

'I don't agree with that at all. If Texas prospers, the country prospers. Let me tell you this, this fellow who's been talking to you, he's categorically wrong!'

No doubt about his views on that question, so I asked him instead how he viewed the seemingly endless growth of Houston, which he, like Gisella Levy, must have known as a fairly small town.

'Houston's just as flat as this table and has the room to grow. This area will be in my opinion the true megapopolis, one of the true megapopolises of the world. It will consist of Houston, Galveston, Beaumont, Orange, and Liberty.'

'Are you looking forward to the day when there's a continuously built up area from Beaumont to Houston?'

'I'm looking forward to it. Why not?'

'Because the city may not be able to service such an area.'

'It won't be one city. It'll be a megapopolis, a group of cities that combine because of their communication and transportation system.'

'But transportation's already a serious problem in Houston.'

'Why? Not more than any other city in the world. In London the traffic's awful.'

'Terrible. No, I was comparing it to Dallas.'

'Dallas? Dallas is worse than Houston. That same guy's been talking to you.'

'Are you proud of being a Texan?'

'Yes. I'm a native Texan, born in Beaumont. Having been in Texas all my life and seen it grow, those who were here to really make Texas grow were the natives. We had very few influxes of people from out of state until people saw the economic picture here was bright. Some native Texans feel like they're being encroached on by people who are not Texans and they don't want them to adopt the Texas ways and traditions, but people like me, I don't feel that way. I feel that the more people that come in, the more cosmopolitan the city becomes, the better off we are, with new knowledge, new culture, new art, new ideas – but there's no question, in the rural parts of the state they resent anybody that's a so-called foreigner. Even if you're from out of state they consider you a foreigner. But I think most of the people involved in the growth of Texas and Houston welcome people from the outside. That keeps us from becoming stagnated.'

The intercom crackled. His car was waiting. Halbouty jumped to his feet, vigorously shook my hand and propelled me towards the door of his office. He hadn't responded adequately to my admittedly uncertain postulations about the future of his industry. He was either being deliberately evasive, or he truly believed in his sublimely simple analysis. His job, after all, was to produce the stuff; he had scarcely any control over the price it would fetch. Yet it seemed obvious to me that it was in the interests of Texans to keep consumption of oil and gas as high as possible. Price was not the only factor involved. Detroit is under pressure to produce cars that are more energy-efficient; houses are better insulated. Though most Americans still believe it's their God-given right to consume as much energy as they're prepared to pay for, there are others on whom the warnings and pleas of conservationists have had some effect. These factors, of course, had to be balanced against the gradual economic recovery that would inevitably give the energy industries a boost. No Texans seemed remotely despondent about the long-term prospects for those industries.

*

Jonathan suggested I might like to visit a refinery. He could fix up something through his law firm, as he had many clients in the oil business. A few days later I found myself back under the shadow of the San Jacinto Monument, and drove into the Battleground Plant of the Diamond Shamrock Corporation. One of the foremen, a midwesterner called Gary, took me round. We drove past colour-coded overhead pipes and drums and tanks of various sizes. A few workers in hardhats strode about and waved at us as we slowly passed by.

'OK,' said Gary. 'The basic feedstock is brine. It's purified of minerals, then filtered to get the calcium out. We add salt to saturate it, and then it's acidized with hydrochloric. This is all a continuous process. It's passed into three strings of two hundred cells each.' What was he talking about? Gary must have thought I was a visiting engineer, and I thought it best not to disillusion him. I hummed and nodded and jotted down salient points. 'A current's passed through the cells to give chlorine, caustic, and hydrogen gas. We don't want the hydrogen, so we burn it or sell it. OK?'

'Yes, fine, thank you.'

'The chlorine's then sent through a cooler, which knocks the water out. Water, as you probably know, makes it corrosive, so we have to "dry" the chlorine. A suction chiller removes impurities. Right now we're running 45 PSIG.'

'Oh really?'

'A centrifugal compressor compresses the gas, and this liquefies most of the chlorine, which goes into storage tanks. We use a snift recovery system, which takes the unliquefied gas and pipes it to other plants, where it's made into PVC.'

Very interesting, of course, but it did all seem beside the point. 'And the oil?'

'Oil? There's no oil here,' said Gary, equally puzzled now. 'This is a chlorine plant.'

*

About a hundred times a year, worldwide, there'll be blowouts on oil rigs. Pressures from deep in the earth will send rocks shooting up into the air, and should a splinter spark against the derrick or shatter a light bulb, the result can be a fierce oil well fire. Red Adair has made a fortune, and acquired a legendary reputation, by extinguishing oil well fires, but there are two other companies that specialise in this awesomely dangerous work. I first ran into Joe Bowden in Leakey, when I parked my car next to a black Cadillac with the words WILD WELL CONTROL on the door. Joe has a ranch in Rio Frio but his offices and workshops are in Houston. Like so many men in the oil business he started out as a roughneck, though he picked up a geology degree along the way.

I'd been expecting to find a man in the Red Adair mould, powerful and brawny, someone who could quell a gas blowout just by sitting on the well, but Joe proved to be a kind and mild-mannered man, friendly and slightly sorrowful. As he showed me the equipment his workshops manufacture specifically for this specialised but crucial work, I wondered whether the job was as perilous as it appears.

'The danger isn't so much from the fire itself – we know how to deal with that. Where it gets risky is when the well is blowing but there's no fire – it's the danger of explosion that's the problem. We never quite know how difficult the job's going to be. We fly all over the world, even to China. If the well's in arid country we have to haul in water, dig pits. Some jobs take days, others take months. The first thing we do is clear the site, just move all the rig support equipment right away. Then we drop explosives into the well. The explosives detonate, burn up the oxygen, and that kills the fire. But every job's different. It's like women – no two are alike.'

'It must be difficult to get men to work for you.'

He shook his head. 'I get hundreds of applications. The men think it's glamorous. The money's good, and when it's quiet they can go out to the ranch and hunt and fish.'

'You gonna be back at the house for lunch, Joe?' We were interrupted by a young woman leaving a workshop.

'Yeh. About twelve. That's my daughter-in-law, lovely girl. This is family business, real close.'

'Does your son work for you?'

'He did. He flew out to a fire last year and two men were killed. He was one of them.'

Surgical Spirits

'This is it? It all happens in this tiny room?'

'Yes.'

As Apollo made its spidery descent onto the surface of the moon, or as Skylab spun lazily around the Earth, I'd assumed that the operations would be controlled from a vast complex of computer terminals and backup systems attended by teams of bespectacled scientists and calm shirt-sleeved technicians wearing headphones, while excitable assistants collided into one another as they rushed about carrying vital charts under their arms. Not a bit of it. Mission Control Center at the National Aeronautics and Space Administration some twenty-five miles south of Houston is the size of a small lecture hall. Four rows of consoles, twenty-two in all, face six large screens that fill an entire wall; during a mission the two outer screens on either side relay data, while the two middle screens usually display a map. At the rear is a glassed-off VIP gallery, which during tense moments on space missions is packed with politicians and their molls. The technological achievement of going to the moon and back should, one feels, be rooted in a ground support and communications system more outwardly elaborate than this modest bank of gibbering consoles. It was somehow mildly alarming as well as awesome that the greatest adventures of our century should be so discreetly monitored.

All of NASA's Johnson Space Center, the President's most munificent gift to his native state, is laid out on this unassuming scale. Most of the buildings are no more than two or three storeys high, dotted over lawns and reflected in pools. A stranger stumbling across it might think it was a high school, not the command centre for an enterprise that, after all, is described in quasi-religious terms as a mission. Visitors are free to stroll through half a dozen buildings; there is no obsession with security, though I daresay an unauthorised foray into the wrong building without an identification badge could result in swift zapping. From a visitor's viewpoint, NASA is well run, and mockups and old modules retired from active service are laid out for close inspection. I was especially enthralled by the dental kits and the equipment required to rehydrate astronautical 'food'; it was these details that brought home to me the heroism of space travel more than photographs of astronauts floating through nothingness. Cramped hours inside a command module no larger than a his-and-hers coffin, constant monitoring not just of scientific procedures but of body responses to the fierce jostlings of space travel, manipulation of devices with such splendidly blunt names as Thumper Geophone Assembly, and above all, not being able to take a piss without a bank of instruments giving a complete analysis to the wizards in Houston – it adds up to a peculiar form of bravery.

I was filled with admiration but not with awe. I wanted some awe. I eventually found it at Rocket Park, an open-air museum on the edge of the NASA compound. Here, lying on its side, is the Saturn V rocket, which was used from 1968 to 1973 to propel Apollo and Skylab into space. It is 363 feet high, and if it were set upright inside St Paul's Cathedral, there would be only two feet to spare under the dome. A few feet away from Saturn V is the vertical form of the Mercury-Redstone rocket that took Alan Shepard on his fifteen-minute flight in 1961. It's no taller, and not even wider, than an average oak or beech, and I wasn't sure which alarmed me more: the power of the huge Saturn rocket, or the frailty of this pencil that launched the first American into space.

I drove back into Houston on the busy highway, unable to resist the modish reflection that while NASA is effectively building a space shuttle to provide rapid transit from here to nowhere, the city which conceived it hasn't managed to devise an adequate transportation system for its three million residents. After town planners and administrators and politicians emerged from a decade-long huddle, the best they could come up with was the idea of special bus lanes, which, in fact, already exist in Houston. Drive towards the airport in the rush hour and you'll see buses hurtling towards you down one of the contraflow lanes. Terrifying until you get used to it.

*

Driving around large American cities can be strangely pleasurable. Cruising at a steady speed up broad highways with as many lanes as most people have fingers, the pace is oddly relaxing. I'd roll down all the windows, turn up the radio, tan an elbow on the sill, and sling my other arm along the unoccupied passenger seat beside me. I might whistle or sing, and idly look about me, though outside the central areas there's little to observe from the elevated highways – just tract housing and shopping malls and warehousing and light industrial plants and hospitals, barely distinguishable from each other. The view will be the same whether you are twenty miles north of downtown Houston or twenty miles south. Only the names change: the shopping precincts will be called Cottonwood Plaza or Heritage Oaks Mall or Spring Valley Center, each with its K-Mart and Safeway and Sears Auto Center, liquor stores and gun shops, late-night Seven Elevens and a battery of fast food huts.

Culturally this endlessly repetitive urban landscape ought to be deeply depressing, yet I've always found it soothing, and in part it's the satisfaction of knowing I don't live in it. At a dollar a gallon, driving aimlessly is cheap entertainment, and at the first sign of fatigue I can revive myself by dipping off the highway and onto empty side streets, where I could be sure of remaining lost for half an hour. Driving into Houston one day on I-10, a narrow brute of a highway, I felt a yawn flowering in my mouth and I decisively headed for the nearest exit ramp and drove south. I found myself in a small incorporated township, one of many embedded within greater Houston, called Hunters Creek Village. The main road crossing the suburb is Memorial Drive, a pleasant parkway that meanders westwards from Memorial Park through a number of choice communities. From time to time I'd turn off Memorial and crawl up dead-end lanes lined with houses that in many cases were still unfinished.

They were, most of them, white brick boxes embellished with grand architectural features. Here was a mansard roof to give height to a building easily a hundred feet long and filling one whole side of its acre lot; the house opposite was embraced by a portico that was extended into an arcade that ran around all visible sides of the structure. Yet in all these cases the architects never had the courage of their pretensions. The grand purpose-less arcade – for no family would ever sit out on this porch shelling peas or spooning in the hammock – was supported on spindly columns with what in a kind mood I'd call Doric capitals, though the builders' merchant probably describes them as square flat tops. The front door of this monstrous house was a full two storeys high, panelled with clear glass, so that the envious passerby could gaze into a hall that also rises to the full height of the house.

It was approached by a semi-circular drive that curved round a saucer of newly laid turf and a few spindly saplings. That nasty term *nouveau riche* – with its snobbish implication that money that's been earned is somehow less wholesome and honourable than money inherited – made some sense to me at Hunters Creek. These swaggering houses are priced at between half a million and a million, but the money would not be purchasing style or privacy or beauty or splendid grounds. It was buying a gesture, a proclamation to the community that you, very obviously and conspicuously, had made it. The scale of the houses was, I suspected, deliberately at odds with the size of the lots; the over-insistent ostentation of those sprawling fronts resulted in a terraced row of mansions.

There was no sign of life in this street. A Rolls Royce dozed beneath a two-storey Venetian window, but there wasn't even a cat on a lawn, let alone a human being in sight. I pictured the executive, newly promoted to vice president (marketing), who had just moved from a cosy eight-room house in Braeswood or Houston Heights into one of these twenty-room chateaux. The children were at college, the live-in Guatemalan couple were in the servants' wing watching game shows on TV, the executive was in his office high in a downtown tower working, as usual, a twelve-hour day so as to be able to meet the enormous new mortgage payments, and his wife would have returned from her aerobics class and was now alone in her frilly pink dressing room twisting the cap off the vodka bottle.

*

There are hundreds of such streets in suburban Houston, and there must be thousands of people who both want, and can afford, to buy these hypertrophied houses. As Hank the Dallasite unkindly observed: 'Houston's an example of what happens when you let unimpeded greed run its course. Houstonians are like kids in a candy store who eat everything in sight and then can't figure out why they're sick.'

When Houstonians do get sick, there's never any doubt about what action to take. They go straight to the Texas Medical Center, which is more than just a large hospital. Let me dazzle you, as they dazzled me, with statistics. There are 29 institutions here, both public and private, employing 30,000 people. In 1982 2 million outpatients paid visits, while 168,000 patients were admitted to beds. While the institutions are independent of each other, they do share libraries, laundries, and parking facilities. To be part of the Center, hospitals may not restrict their activity to patient care; laudably, they must also be involved in teaching and research.

It's not just the size of the Center that makes it peculiarly Texan. This is the home of free enterprise surgery. When Dr Michael DeBakey pioneered open heart surgery at one of the hospitals, a rival surgeon, the equally celebrated Dr Denton Cooley, broke away and established his own base at the Texas Heart Institute. Those readers contemplating being opened up by one of these two doctors might like to know that at Dr DeBakey's Methodist Hospital, the luxury suites serve food specially catered by Jamail's, Houston's best-known delicatessen. Whoever makes the incision, the operation is going to cost you $25,000 or more. At the M.D. Anderson Hospital, which specialises in cancer treatment, in-patients pay up to $700 a night for a bed. Not all the hospitals are private. The Ben Taub Hospital, which is also the Baylor University teaching hospital, has special rates for the 'indigent and needy', and the Shriners Hospital for Crippled Children is free. Women about to give birth should give serious attention to the merits of Hermann Hospital, at which happy new mothers, on returning to home and husband, are treated, courtesy of Hermann, to 'a gourmet candlelight dinner'.

I lunched one day on the terrace of the Café Moustache on Westheimer with an acquaintance who runs a scanning unit at one of the hospitals. Only the breeze saved us from asphyxiation under a surf of exhaust fumes. As I tucked into a seafood salad she echoed Ed by telling me that the Center, like the Galleria, was swamped by South Americans. Like ailing Arabs in London, they stumble off the plane, check into a classy hospital, and then, if they survive, settle the account in cash.

'That's all very well for obscure dictators who can rob the peasantry to earn their living, but most of us aren't in that league,' I protested. 'What happens if you're at death's door but just can't afford tens of thousands of dollars for your operation?'

She shrugged. 'Guess you die.'

*

'This is Doctor Red Duke of the Texas Medical Center.' There it was, three times a week on the evening news, this tall thin surgeon with the auburn hair and bushy moustache, swallowing his consonants and masticating his vowels as he instructs Texans on the rudiments on health care. When Jonathan suggested I might like to spend some time with Red Duke, I reminded him of his earlier good idea, but he and Barbara assured me, and later proved it by turning on the television, that Red was indeed a surgeon at the Center and not a local Ford dealer.

I communicated with him through the Hermann Hospital paging system, and after a few rounds of bleeping I did wind up in his cluttered little office at the nearby UT Medical School. On the walls were photographs of grateful patients and sheep.

'You interested in bighorn sheep?' he wondered.

'Do I look as if I would be?'

'Guess not.' But that didn't deter him from playing me a video tape of a publicity stunt in which he'd starred in order to raise money for sheep conservation in West Texas. On the screen I watched the famous doctor, in jeans and boots, being arrested on a charge of pulling a knife; he was thrown into the Van Horn jail for a night, tried by Judge Roy Bean, and then hanged, despite the scaffold-side pleas of a frenzied woman in scarlet. What all this had to do with sheep conservation I never gathered.

Dr James Duke Jr., for that's the name that appears on the framed diplomas, was far from being the hick he affected to be; he had spent some time in a seminary before becoming a doctor, and did research at Columbia University for a few years.

'Howdee, Red. How's it going?' A tall burly man, about thirty, wearing a startling yellow PVC jacket, put his head around the door. His accent was even thicker than Red's, treacly and hostile to consonants.

'Hey, Mike! Come on in.'

'Been away, Red? I been looking for you.'

'Yeh, I just got back from Austin. Willie's mother died. I've been out at the hospital.'

'She died? How old?'

'Eighty. Willie's on tour and he decided not to cancel. It's tough.'

'Yeh.'

'Son of a gun. This is Willie right now.' Sure enough, from the radio that was permanently on in his office came the rasp of Willie Nelson's unmistakable voice. Red introduced me to his visitor, who turned out to be his godson. 'Mike's a damn good cowboy, but a questionable doctor.'

'Where you from?' Mike asked me gruffly.

'London.'

Mike scratched his head and turned to Red. 'London, London . . .' he murmured, knowing that name sounded familiar. Then he jabbed a finger in the air. 'Isn't London that town between Mason and Junction?'

'That's right, Mike, that's right. You're smart. Coming to lunch?'

'Nah. Got some patients coming to see me. See y'all later.'

It was hard to talk to Red as we walked down endless hospital corridors on our way to the doctors' dining room, as he would either greet or be greeted by every doctor and nurse that passed by. For such a skinny man he had a loud voice that boomed and reverberated. One 'How ya doin'?' was enough to turn every head from one end of the corridor to the other.

At lunch we were joined by a sleek man in a suit. His identification badge read Associate Executive Director.

'He's a goddam administrator,' explained Red genially. 'He controls the money here – most important man in the hospital.'

Two young doctors sat at the neighbouring table and Red saw me glancing at them. 'They're orthopaedic surgeons. You can always tell an orthopaedic surgeon, 'cos they dress real nice. Say, Jack, those are real fancy boots you're wearing.'

Hermann Hospital is famous for its trauma unit, which I particularly wanted to see. Red pointed out that although most people live in constant dread of heart disease and cancer, if you're young you are more likely to be killed in a car accident or shot or knifed. If you're merely maimed and not eradicated, they'll probably bring you here. Sometimes the hospital will go to you: on the roof three helicopters are parked in a state of readiness; a complete medical unit can be flown out just minutes after an emergency call is received. Trauma units, which require machines and staff to be on constant standby, are expensive to run, but Red is convinced it's worthwhile. I said I hoped there wouldn't be too much blood on the floor.

'Don't worry,' said Red. 'They clean up real fast. This is Dr

Li,' introducing me to the head of the unit. 'He looks terrible because he's been up all night. Haven't you?'

Dr Li nodded. 'We had sixteen, seventeen admissions last night.'

Red looked at his watch. 'I've got to get to the studio, do some voice-overs. Why don't you come along?'

At the hospital studio we sat down with the producer while Red, consulting the back of an envelope, reeled off some ideas he'd jotted down for a new series aimed at children. 'Playgrounds. Playgrounds is good. You've got swings, monkey bars.' He looked earnestly at the producer. 'I seen some good injuries from monkey bars.' He peered at his list again. 'Then there's swimming. Currents, tides, sand.'

'Sand?'

'Sure. I've seen the little shits bury each other in the sand.'

The recording over, we walked a half mile or so down corridors and through double swing doors. I saw the administrator we'd lunched with approaching. As he passed he said to me loudly: 'If he tells you any more lies, just check with me.'

A very portly doctor stopped Red to ask him something. Red answered his question, then poked him in the paunch. 'Morris, some time round New Year's we're gonna have to do a C-section and deliver that baby of yours.'

*

The Texas Medical Center was, it seemed, the only major group of buildings in the state that Jack Rains's company 3D/International hadn't designed: the Galleria, the Johnson Space Center, half a dozen hotels, the Bass towers of Fort Worth, the Johnson Library – not to mention a couple of new cities and palaces in Saudi Arabia. Rains describes his company as 'a supermarket' that oversees a project from start to finish: from feasibility studies to the master planning stage to architectural and engineering design. They'll take care of purchasing, construction, and all interior design.

3D/I is as corporate in its structure as many of its august clients. Rains himself is no architect, but an administrator who identifies with an entrepreneurial spirit that is quintessentially Texan. The desire to make money is universal, but in Texas it's exalted into an ideology in which prosperity and the good life are more likely to come into being if free enterprise is encouraged to flourish without restraint. I also suspected Rains was typically Texan in his bragging, but I did him an injustice. When I said I thought I. M. Pei was the architect of the Texas Commerce Tower, he replied: 'We're associated architects with Pei. We did the engineering, the interior architecture. Mr Pei is responsible for the aesthetic sculpturing, but our design team worked very closely with him. It's common for a developer to bring in a design consultant – someone like Pei or Philip Johnson – while the local boys really execute the project. It's good marketing.'

From the top of 3D/I's 22-storey tower, we looked out over the loop to the area just inside it. Rains, burly but impeccably groomed, from the cut of his hair to the shine on his shoes, gestured out over the landscape. 'Houston is a construction site, an unfinished symphony. There's a saying here that the national bird of Texas is the building crane. See over there? In a few years that will all be high rise. The land price is now $100 a square foot, and that dictates that all those low apartment blocks you see will eventually come out. They're just warehousing the land. Come back in the year 2000 and it'll be much more interesting to look at.

'These developments are all private initiative. That's what distinguishes Texas. We rely on the marketplace, free enterprise. People will say to you, "Look how little money Texas puts into the arts – it's forty-ninth out of all the states." That's very true. We don't do it through taxes, but there's more money spent on the arts here per capita than most places in the world, with the possible exception of New York City, which has a lot of tax-funded art and endowments. In time we'll have those endowments here too. But we don't believe that taxpayers should subsidize cultural stamps, like food stamps for the rich. It's just a different philosophy and a different approach. We're more individual and self-reliant. And that carries over into the way we run our cities, our state, our institutions. We believe that the private sector creates jobs. Our low taxes attract business here, and we think that's the way to help people rather than to tax everyone and redistribute income.'

I hadn't asked for this crystalline exposition of the trickle-down theory but it was clearly something Rains wanted me to appreciate. Yet surely, I argued, private initiative could create wealth but not determine how, indeed whether, it could be used to benefit those in need. Or, for that matter, to deal with such banal yet pressing problems as the immobilized traffic on the loop two hundred feet below where we stood.

Rains was untroubled. 'When a problem gets bad, you develop a political concensus. Public pressure's built so that we've got to do something about the freeways. The state will double gasoline tax, which will still keep us very low, but that'll create a billion dollars annually for road improvements. And much of the city's growth is user paid for. A developer goes out, he creates a water district, he sells his own bonds, he paves his own streets, and then the people who buy the lots have to pay for it. Then one day the city gets out there and annexes it, but it's the users who've paid for it.'

It's a peculiarity of Texas law that cities can vote to annex neighbouring areas, except where other cities already exist. Houston can't annex Galveston, but it can, and did, annex the land around the Johnson Space Center. In, for example, Boston, the suburbs are all separate townships; as inner-city residents moved out to the suburbs, the city was unable to recoup the taxes they had formerly contributed. In Houston, on the other hand, annexation expands the tax base, and this in turn helps the city to provide services.

Houston, with thirty-five per cent of its economy dependent on the energy industry, had, its citizens repeatedly told me, suffered more than most other Texan cities in recent years. But was it as bad as all that? A prominent attorney claimed that native Texans hadn't suffered too badly. He pointed out that 'overpaid union workers' had flooded into the city a few years ago, but as soon as the recession hit, 'most of those people turned around and went back to Michigan'. Judge Tom Phillips didn't agree with the overpaid lawyer: 'I can get a good indication of how hard times are from the number of bankruptcy cases that come through my court.'

Jack Rains had no doubts about his assessment. 'The city has the resources to overcome its problems. We're not recession-proof. We were hit by our export business here, by the strong dollar. Mexico went absolutely on its back, and that was our major trading partner, the oil industry went down at exactly the same time, and agriculture did not have an outstanding year. You combine all those things and we still created new jobs and grew.'

Sun and Sand

Houstonians, secure in their triumph over Galveston, have simply dismissed it from their minds. Their will to succeed has little patience with the will to failure that Galveston, in their view, exemplifies. Not that Galveston is entirely moribund. A large medical centre and a burgeoning tourist industry have revived its fortunes, but for the most part it survives by exploiting its glorious past rather than by asserting a role for itself in the future.

Galveston is the Miss Havisham of Texas: faded, decaying, yet still splendid in a batty way. Its commercial inertia since the devastating hurricane of 1900 has kept the island settlement small and manageable; the population of 65,000 hasn't altered much in fifty years except to age. Young people see little future in this beautiful but stagnant town, and have moved to Houston or Dallas, abandoning Galveston to the old and infirm. Although the tourist offices will direct visitors to such grand and hideous Victorian mansions as the Bishop's Palace, the glory of Galveston lies in street after street of more modest but exquisitely proportioned and detailed wooden houses, many with spacious verandahs and gingerbread or Gothick ornamentation. It's the scale that makes these streets so lovely: the white friendly decorative houses shaded by oaks and palms on trim lots, communal yet discrete, stylistically matched without being uniform. Strolling down one of these quiet residential streets I saw pedalling slowly towards me a very old lady on a tricycle, a sight inconceivable in Houston, where she'd be dead in a minute if she ventured onto the streets on such a contraption, yet sadly fitting in this dowager city.

Hurricane damage and an indifference to zoning have inflicted great damage on old Galveston, and it's remarkable that so much of the nineteenth century town has survived. Indolence probably contributed as much to its preservation as to its commercial stagnation. In recent years the town, urged on by its more energetic and philanthropic citizens, has made vigorous efforts to restore its beautiful buildings and streets, and the old commercial district called the Strand has been brought back to life. Like downtown Port Arthur today, the Strand used to be an area of bars and flophouses, seedy by day and dangerous by night. Now its streets are filled with portly couples in shorts and sticky-fingered children emerging from ice cream parlours and confectionery shops. The Strand has not become twee because the architecture won't countenance it. The row buildings are made of severe brick and costly stone, at best austere and practical, pompous and over-ornate at worst.

It was exactly a hundred years ago that Colonel Gresham, a lawyer and railway tycoon, spent $250,000 building a mansion that is now the Bishop's Palace of the Galveston-Houston diocese. It is more remarkable for its lavishness than for its beauty. Damask wallpapers were shipped in from London and marble sinks and fireplaces came from Italy; obscure American hardwoods were used to doleful effect throughout the house, which is unalterably gloomy. The guide, plump-breasted and manic-eyed, drew my attention to the 'layumps' of Italian manufacture and to the dismal 'frescas' that Mrs Gresham insisted on painting of her children as winged angels. The hand of the carver is everywhere. The surfaces, both the wooden interior and the frenziedly eclectic exterior of multicoloured stone, are furiously decorated as though there were some moral relation between excess and virtue. The Palace is a most alarming house. The guide wants you to believe it's beautiful. But on the contrary, it's relentlessly, hypnotically hideous.

Along the south side of the island runs the five-mile seawall that guards Galveston against a repetition of the disaster of 1900. At the same time that the wall was built, sludge was pumped onto the island, raising its ground level by seven feet. A hurricane had blown in three months earlier and along the front the damage was still evident. Some motels and restaurants facing the Gulf had been scalped by the storm; others had been reduced to jagged piles of timber as the fist of the wind thumped down on them. On the broad beach were the remains of a trailer park, resembling an overturned pencil box, with caravans slung in all directions and one or two, lifted by the hurricane and hurled across the beach, still lying on their sides. To the east the seawall gives way to rocks that round the tip of the island, from which there is a lively view of the strait known as the Bolivar Roads. Through these waters, tankers and pleasure craft move in and out of the Galveston Ship Channel, reminding one that although Galveston is much diminished, shipping is still a major occupation.

I crossed the Roads on the free ferry to the mainland, and drove along the Bolivar Peninsula that shelters Galveston Bay for about twenty miles. To the right were long empty beaches, and here and there were feeble attempts at resort-making. Beach houses were raised fifteen feet off the ground on stilts, offering an immediate explanation for the failure of these sandy expanses to attract hordes of holiday makers. Hurricanes and floods between them are common enough to deter most tourists from choosing this stretch of shore as a playground. I turned down sandy tracks that led to the shore past a dozen or so of these wooden houses that didn't look as if they'd withstand a gentle sea breeze, let alone a muscular Gulf hurricane. All deserted.

Thirty miles further on I came to barricades. The road, which eventually leads to Port Arthur after fifty miles, was closed: it was, quite simply, sinking into the sea. I drove back through the drab coastal prairie, in some places forested with pump jacks and drilling rigs. Cattle grazed indifferently among the ironware. In pools and creeks herons and pelicans stood motionless. They were, I suppose, keeping a watch for succulent fish, but to me they appeared frozen by the same inertia that grips so much of this wretched coastline as it totters into the sea.

*

The winter Texans – northerners who flock southwards to avoid the ice and snow for a few months – were to be cruelly disappointed this particular winter. An Arctic freeze, lumbering down from the Canadian tundra, had sunk its claws into the American Midwest. As it moved down the continent, record after record was broken as the mercury in thermometers contracted into its tightest spaces and refused to measure. In the wastes of North Dakota and Minnesota, residents were advised to stay indoors; mere exposure to such gelidity would be dangerous to health. Each day brought news of fresh tragedies, frozen bodies in drift-bound cars, hypothermia-stricken grannies, teenage girls dead on doorsteps because they'd lost their house keys.

Usually Texans can afford to chuckle lightly over such

northern misfortunes. Yes, snow has been seen on occasion in southern Texas, a brief sprinkling that vanishes the instant it touches the ground. But not this year. The front was crawling into the South. While I was in Houston the frigid air hit Dallas, and how we laughed as the TV news showed us motorists, unaccustomed to sheet ice, slithering at all conceivable angles over the frozen surface of the North Central Expressway. During one morning rush hour there were two thousand accidents, enough to keep insurance companies busy for weeks. A few days later we stopped laughing. The temperature in balmy Houston, where British diplomats used to be paid danger money to compensate for the unbearably humid climate, dropped into the thirties. As I drove down the Gulf Coast from Galveston I realised that the globules troubling my windscreen wipers consisted of freezing rain. Signs outside pet shops advised: TIME TO WINTERIZE YOUR DOG. BUY YOUR SWEATERS HERE.

I stopped at Palacios, a lazy little fishing town looking out onto the leisurely sweep of Matagorda Bay. I'd intended to stay for a couple of days at the Luther Hotel, the very picture of Southern indolence, its white frame structure sprawled over a wide palm-lined lawn. But in freezing rain? So I pressed on, past Port Lavaca, over Big Chocolate Bayou, and into the resort town of Fulton, with its succession of trailer parks and holiday houses, and condominium developments that have overwhelmed the attractiveness of its port and fishing fleet. Groves of live oaks and pines along the coastline reeled backwards from too many punches on the jaw by the powerful winds that, even in better weather, come pounding in from the Gulf. It was disorienting: the sight of a mile-long stretch of leaning trees made me wonder whether the trees or the shore were out of kilter.

Fulton and neighbouring Rockport are popular with winter Texans. Along the quite remarkably ugly coastal highway were small shacks offering seashells or fireworks for sale, large billboards pointing arrows towards local alligator parks, even a mobile tattoo van parked under a bridge. In between settlements the scrub prairie was dotted with the neat installations that monitor natural gas fields; pipelines torpedoed the horizon. Even allowing for the nastiness of the weather, I didn't care for these resort communities. I pressed on to Port Aransas, a village at the top of Mustang Island only accessible by ferry from Aransas Pass. I hoped it would have some of the lazy scatty charm of Palacios. From the ferry I looked back at the immense Brown & Root plant at Aransas Pass. No political history of Texas is complete without a close look at the affairs of this powerful construction firm, which, like so many defense contractors, prospered nicely from the care it took of its favourite politicians. Brown & Root is still very much in business and the plant had just completed the largest offshore rig ever built, a megastructure 1300 feet high, with a three-acre platform servicing 48 wells. For months its huge metal skeleton had loomed awesomely over the town.

Port Aransas would have been a pretty place were planning not a dirty word in Texas. Just the modicum of control would have saved the little port from looking tawdry and ramshackle. I put up for the night at the old Tarpon Inn, and from my dingy room had a fine view of a fifteen-foot-high image of the Marlboro Man, thoughtfully spotlit at night, ads for real estate brokers trying to dispose of the empty lots opposite the inn, and a radio mast. In spring and summer, 100,000 people pack Port Aransas to enjoy its beaches and the deep-sea fishing, but on this bleak December evening I appeared to be the only visitor in town. At a pleasant fish restaurant – all the fish I could swallow for six dollars – the only other occupied table was the scene of a small birthday party. As I was finishing my meal, the waitress came over with a slice of cake – the revellers hadn't wanted me to feel left out.

In the morning I went down to the beach. I struck out across the unobstructed sands and eventually spotted the waves licking the shore. I gazed at the white salty fringes of the ocean, at the icy drizzle smearing my glasses, and at the thick fog just twenty yards from my nose. So much for the ocean, and so much for my vision of a few lazy days supine on South Padre Island, a long narrow leg of sand and scrub that follows the coast for almost a hundred miles, from Corpus Christi down to the Mexican border. Much of the island is 'national seashore' and free from obtrusive building. Elsewhere developers have not been reticent, and down a long stretch of the island runs a string of condominium developments all with predictable clumsy names: the Windjammer, the Dolphins, Sandpiper, Lost Colony (now, evidently, found again). Only partially completed was the 1100-acre La Concha Beach Club, which offers one and a half miles of shore, recreational health facilities (every American over thirty being convinced that he or she is on the brink of cardiac arrest), a boardwalk with shops, and a housing development which will be called Admirals Row. Atlantic City and Miami Beach have come to Texas. I took an access road down to a private beach, but no security guards troubled me. I was quite alone as I strolled through the fog, and the only sounds above the noise of the sea were the cries of the gulls and the grunts of the bulldozers.

*

Corpus Christi has the reputation of being the windiest city in the United States, outclassing even Chicago in the virility of its gusts. When I arrived Corpus had borrowed a trick or two from its rowdy competitor in Illinois, and to the usual coat-flapping gale it had added sleet and icy blasts that clipped the edges of my ears. I drove the length of Ocean Drive and came to the handsome museum designed by the ubiquitous P. Johnson. Dozens of children, their mittened hands clasping those of their parents, were swarming up the steps. I'd known Corpus was famous for its beaches, but I hadn't been aware of it as a cultural centre. Pleasantly surprised that a minority pursuit in southern Texas had such an enthusiastic and youthful following here, I followed the infant procession into the art museum. The entire interior had been converted into a Christmas Tree Forest, to which different schools from all along the coast had contributed decorated trees. Lifting toddlers out of my way as I rapidly traversed the forest, I looked about me for signs of the permanent collection. I couldn't find it. I opened doors that led to broom cupboards. No art anywhere, not even a token Remington or a Norman Rockwell print.

In the museum shop a young woman was filing her nails behind the counter. I inquired as to the whereabouts of the permanent collection.

'We don't have one to speak of,' she informed me, 'though we periodically have exhibits on display. But the folks who came to see the trees were offended by them, so this year we decided to do without any.'

I lunched at Kingsville, a few miles from the 825,000-acre King Ranch, the largest in Texas. 2700 oil wells – it would be intolerably bad luck to own such a vast slice of Texas and fail to find oil beneath it – and horse-breeding, not to mention possession of a further few million acres in Australia, have helped to keep the operation prosperous. The ranch, which supports 85,000 cattle, is still owned by descendants of the King and Kleberg families, to whom the locality pays repeated tribute. In the ranch town there's a King Boulevard and a Kleberg Boulevard, and the Kleberg National Bank. Hungry, I successfully applied the old trick of looking for the sheriff's car. Two of them were parked outside Allen's Steak Place, and there I wolfed down a few enchiladas. The sheriffs, both as massive as steers, were refuelling their paunches in the company of their wives, who both, as befits sheriffs' wives, sported beehive hairstyles. I began to understand why this part of Texas dispenses with museums. The items that might otherwise be on display – automobiles, varieties of barbed wire, plaid shirts, weaponry, hairstyles – are out on the streets.

It was a long drive south to Port Isabel, just across from the southern tip of South Padre Island, which seeks to replicate Miami Beach. Port Isabel itself is a somewhat bedraggled little yachting and resort town; in clement weather it might have been quite charming. Finding the Yacht Club Hotel, which looked as dignified as its name led me to imagine, well beyond my means, I pressed on through a dusk made more tenebrous by unrelieved cloud to Brownsville on the border.

Tex Mex Trex

Ice storms? I rose in the morning to find my car sheeted in a layer of ice that had to be hacked at like a crème brûlée. The elevated highway that whisks traffic to the bridge over the Rio Grande into Mexico had been closed. Cars and trucks shuffled into town along the parallel service roads. The wind howled and the palms flapped. The weather was the sole topic of conversation at gas stations, hotel reception desks, coffee houses, not only because of the novelty of temperatures about fifty degrees below the seasonal average but because the economy of the region was threatened by the freeze. The towns of the Valley, as this stretch along the Rio Grande is known, were all centres of the citrus fruit industry in Texas. Congressman Archer had been quite serious when in Houston he'd restricted our brief chat to a paean of praise for the Texan grapefruit, which many consider superior to its California or Florida brethren. Oranges too grow plump along the Upper Valley, but with temperatures already in the mid-twenties (and worse to follow) the entire crop was endangered. Some growers were placing smudge pots in the groves at night, raising the temperature by about five degrees, but it was already too cold for such measures to prevent serious damage. Some of the crop had been picked before the freeze, but the remaining seventy per cent would be left to rot on the trees. This was disastrous not only for the growers, who put their losses at $70 million, but for the thousands of Mexican workers who would no longer be needed.

Brownsville is an overwhelmingly Mexican town. In restaurants and shops English was often not spoken. A century ago Brownsville must have resembled a European farmers' conference. In the elaborate old cemetery, tombs are engraved with epitaphs in German and French as well as English and Spanish, and those who ended their lives at this most southerly point in Texas had begun them in places as diverse as Brunswick, Dundee, Toledo, Cork, and the Pyrenees.

In spite of the (usually) semi-tropical climate along the whole Valley and its intricate multi-cultural history, its settlements are astonishingly unattractive. McAllen, Pharr, Harlingen, and Brownsville are ramshackle ragouts of uncontrolled urban sprawl. At Brownsville there was some attempt to exploit its most attractive natural feature, the profusion of resacas, the ponds and lagoons, often stuffed with green lily pads and bordered by ferns and palms and bougainvillea, that were scattered throughout the town. The streets of Rio Viejo, a luxurious suburb of Spanish-style houses, curled prettily around some of these curious but welcome patches of water.

The centre of town shows Brownsville's age. Brick commercial buildings, now marred by garish shopfronts, often date from the 1850s, while dotted between them are equally old, and mostly dilapidated, frame houses with verandahs and shutters. The shopping streets breathed recession. The ruined citrus crop was only the latest disaster to strike Brownsville, which had already been severely hit by the devaluation of the peso. No longer did Mexicans cross the border in droves to shop on the American side, though the rich, eager to transfer some of their wealth out of Mexico, had invested heavily in Rio Viejo and the flashy condominium complexes of South Padre Island.

Further south, not far from the river, are rutted streets intersected to form blocks clustered with unpainted shacks, though the luminous colours of the flowering shrubs help to gloss over the poverty of these crowded little houses. The grandest structure in the neighbourhood is the church, where I met Father Sal de George. His parishioners are almost all Mexican, many of them workers who commute over the border. Now that the recession had made the labourers less welcome, the border partrols were more likely to round them up and deport them. It's a system that the priest considered fundamentally cruel, and a futile way to prevent illegal immigration.

'If the government really wanted to prevent it, all they'd have to do is impose a $20,000 fine on any employer who uses illegal labour, and it would soon come to an end. But so would many of the industries in the Valley. It's so easy to cross the river that it's impossible to stop the illegal traffic anyway.' He recommended me to take a drive past Fort Brown to the golf course that follows the bend of the river. I did so, and spotted the large plastic bags he said I'd find discarded along the levee. Mexicans who swim across at night bring their dry clothes in these plastic bags, which they then throw away. Count the bags each morning at dawn and you'll get a fair idea of the number of wetbacks who made it over the Rio Grande the night before.

'You've got to consider that to many people Brownsville and Matamoros are one town that happens to be divided by a river. Whichever side you live on, it's likely you'll have relatives who live on the other. Citizenship to them is just paperwork. Their allegiance is dual – they take what they can from both cultures.' Many of those who work in the clothing plants in Brownsville live in Matamoros and cross legally every day. They'll even send their children to school on the American side so that they'll learn to speak fluent English – or Texan. All they have to do is give the school authorities the address of relatives who live in Brownsville and there's no problem. Others use Brownsville as a resting place on their way north. They'll stay a while with friends or relatives before going off in search of jobs.

Father de George observed that however bad the economy might be in Brownsville, it was even worse in Mexico. 'Still, there's a lot of poverty in this town, as you can see. Unemployment's high, families are large, there've been cuts in welfare services. But they're adaptable people. If a family earns two hundred dollars one week, fine, they'll spend it. If they only have fifty the next, OK, they adjust and make do.

'It's not much of a life, though. Brownsville could have been a jewel, but it's a mess. People from outside have bled this whole region.'

*

I hadn't been to Mexico for ten years, and now that I was literally yards from the border, I was keen to cross. My new passport, however, lacked an American visa. I anticipated no difficulty in leaving the United States, but re-entering without a visa would be impossible. So it was imperative for me to obtain a new visa from the nearest consulate, which happened to be in Matamoros. I 'phoned the consul, who foresaw no problem. I should simply come to the consulate the next morning. I walked over the bridge and presented my passport to the Mexican immigration official. He looked unhappy.

'Visa? American visa?'

'Haven't got one. That's why I have to go to Matamoros for a few hours.'

He shook his head and shrugged his shoulders. He didn't

understand English and neither, astonishingly, did any other Mexican official on duty. My own Spanish was inadequate for protracted argument, and my protestations were having no effect other than to keep my passport in circulation among various officials. One with more gold braid than the others seemed to be admonishing me for my lack of an American visa, which struck me as an unlikely obligatory document for entry into Mexico, and then gave my passport to a chubby man in a green coat. He put it in his pocket and motioned with his finger for me to follow him. Moments later I found myself walking back across the bridge.

'Where are we going?'

'United States.'

Exasperation turned to alarm. If the nakedness of my new passport had caused consternation among Mexican officials, it would have more troubling results at American Immigration. Before me loomed the possibility that, refused admission to both countries, I would have to spend the rest of my life pacing this windy bridge, a life that would be mercifully shortened by the noxious fumes emitted by a sluggish queue of Mexican vehicles waiting to be searched for contraband at the border. I thought of offering a bribe. Twenty years ago, when I first crossed into Mexico from Laredo, the Mexican customs official had refused to return my luggage to me until I'd given him a 'teep'. But here I had to deal with a whole squad of officials, and the middle of the international bridge was not the best place to open negotiations. I decided to yield to the lunacy of the situation. To my relief the American officials not only understood English but were able to convey in Spanish to the dutiful Mexican why it was essential for me to enter Matamoros. So for the third time in ten minutes I crossed the bridge, and returned two hours later with a US visa issued to an Englishman in Matamoros, a collector's item that will, I'm sure, be cherished by the next hoodlum who steals my passport.

To celebrate my return I ate a huge lunch at a café called Maria's. I was the only Anglo there and had to place my order by pointing at other people's plates, a method of ordering I have since employed even in restaurants where the language is known to me. Leaving Brownsville, I took the river road, past ruined orange groves divided by avenues of palm trees as tall as poplars, and then headed north to San Juan on the outskirts of

McAllen. A few blocks from the main road rises the campanile of the shrine of Our Lady of San Juan de Valle, which is visited by 15,000 pilgrims each week. This particular devotion to Our Lady – or Their Lady, to be more precise – began in 1623 in Mexico, after a fatally injured acrobat had been miraculously resuscitated. A sub-shrine had been built here in the Valley in 1920, and so popular did it become, mainly with migrant workers, that a new church was built here in 1954 to accommodate them all. This was the occasion for a further wonder. A local evangelist went berserk and took off in his plane vowing to crash into the tallest spire he could find. This happened to be San Juan, and the apocalyptic preacher kamikaze'd into the roof just as fifty priests were celebrating Mass. Within minutes the church was in flames, but not a single priest was hurt.

'This was seen as another miracle,' explained Father Brian Wallace, the syntax dissociating him gently from the interpretation of luck as divine intervention. 'Naturally that only increased the celebrity of the shrine, but round here we feel that the real miracle is that the place exists at all. You've got to admit, San Juan isn't the most obvious site for one of the most popular shrines in America.'

But not if one thinks of it, as one must think of much of the Valley, as an extension of Mexico. Nearly all the pilgrims are Mexicans, many of them hoping for a booster injection from Our Lady before making the journey north in search of work and a new life; other worshippers are only in the Valley to visit relatives and friends, a visit that would be incomplete without lighting a candle at San Juan. Indeed, on one side of the shrine a room with a large table is filled with slowly burning candles. When there is no longer any room for candles in front of the altar, they are moved to this candle room until they burn out. 'Sometimes,' said Father Wallace, 'even the candle room gets filled up, so we have to stack them in a garage.'

I drove on up the Valley and when it grew dark I stopped at Rio Grande City, which is neither grand nor a city. But I was able to find a room for the night that was equipped with a working heater, and I ate a good dinner at Caro's. Shortly after I sat down a family group came in, leading a white-haired man who spoke with that slow-paced loudness peculiar to the deaf.

His daughter explained to the waitress: 'Pa's ninety-five. That's a fact, ninety-five. He's real excited 'cos tomorrow he gets to go huntin' with my husband. Pa don't shoot no more, but he still likes to go out with the boys in huntin' season. Don't you, Pa?'

'That's right Lucy! That's right!' And the old gentleman sank his gums into his *carne asada*.

*

In Bracketville, near Del Rio, is a replica of a nineteenth century Western town called Alamo Village, which was built as a movie set for *The Alamo*. How odd to build replicas when the real thing is dotted all over this landscape, as the makers of *Viva Zapata* realised when they chose Roma, just up the road from Rio Grande City, for their location shots. Authenticity, however, didn't bring prosperity, and Roma is as delapidated as most of the other towns along the Valley. Empty brick buildings, many of them with shuttered French windows leading onto balconies fronted with charming ironwork brought from New Orleans, cast a hard shadow over the unpaved streets. There's a prettily terraced plaza – entirely European in conception – with a view of the church spire up the slope, though the flowering bougainvillea looked miserable in the twenty-five-degree weather. One Heinrich Portscheller was the man who built most of Roma, and he designed with a flourish. The cornices over the houses are of brick in relief, giving a lively motion to the line of the street, and some of the doorways are topped by fanlights, a Georgian touch that is slightly dotty in this harsh desert country.

Roma seemed deserted, but it was the strong wind as well as the bizarre cold that was keeping its few inhabitants indoors. A few of them probably crept out at night to the local cinema, where *I Spit on Your Grave* was the attraction for that week. On the main street a sign read ROMA POLICE ON DUTY. DRIVE SLOW, with its charming suggestion that the rest of the time, when they're not on duty, you can do as you please. This must be welcome news to the drug smugglers who have, I was told, a tendresse for Roma.

Citrus groves had long been left behind. The trek north along the river from Rio Grande City past Roma to Laredo took me through dry empty brush country which was frequently over-run with mesquite and prickly pear. The arid hills were welcome after the flatness of the Valley. In the afternoon I arrived in Laredo. It was Christmas Eve. I gave in to the weather and hibernated, emerging only briefly for meals and exploratory drives. The rest of the time I spent in my hotel bed watching a succession of second-rate films on television.

In the evenings I would drive down to the pretty San Agustín Plaza, park the car, and walk over the bridge to Nuevo Laredo. Like Brownsville, Laredo is overshadowed by its bigger Mexican brother. While Laredo is shabby and dispersed, Nuevo Laredo is shabby and concentrated, and, with an eye on the tourist trade, many of the shops and restaurants are within a ten-minute walk of the bridge. Unlike the American side, the Mexican town was bustling. Cars, interminably snarled in the narrow streets, wailed their horns as irate drivers leaned out of windows to yell enviously at anything that was moving. A car parked on Guerrero had a loudspeaker attached to the roof, blaring out political slogans interspersed with popular music. The beggar women, *las marias*, who used not to be seen in northern Mexico, sat pitifully in doorways, a baby or two cringing under their shawls, an unmoving hand outstretched towards a large indifferent crowd of shoppers, who were peering into windows crammed with ceramic junk, glass animals, records, clothes. Americans were wisely stocking up with extremely cheap tequila and mescal.

At night Nuevo Laredo lost some of its allure. The liquor shops stayed open late, but most tourists had vanished, and Mexicans stood massed along the pavements waiting for buses to take them home to more distant parts of the city. Returning from a hearty dinner of cabrito, I slid on gnawed corn husks and debris from the market as I made my way down poorly lit streets. Solid unmarked doors would suddenly open and I'd hear loud harsh voices competing against the Mexican songs blaring from a jukebox, as a shaft of jaundiced light from the seedy cantina slapped onto the pavement. Sniffing danger, I didn't linger, let alone enter. I passed the famous Cadillac Bar, source of the Ramos Gin Fizz, but white-coated waiters outnumbered customers and I gave it a miss and walked back over the bridge, bracing myself against the bitter wind. At the old church in San Agustín Plaza, Mass was being said – in Spanish, of course. As in all the border towns, the Anglos were outnumbered.

Not so over on the other side of the county, in Freer. There were plenty of Mexicans in this drab little town, but they ran the Chick-Inn restaurant, where I stopped for a buffet lunch (there was fried chicken on offer as well as standard Mexican dishes), and the Muy Grande Village supermarket. They were there to serve the community, which in its turn served the big ranches such as Clinton Manges' enormous spread just outside town. Freer offered garages and auto supply shops, the Brush Country Bank, the Guinn Well Service, a mobile home dealer, the Club 44 Bar, the usual selection of churches, and a gun shop. The owner of the latter must have been doing good business, as most of the talk at the Chick-Inn was hunting chat. Four men in camouflage outfits compared notes: one had bagged four deer in a single morning, he boasted, and another had wiped out a dozen quail.

The hunters turned to a topic that was absorbing all Texas that week. Oil leases on Clinton Manges' ranch had been sold to Mobil Oil over fifty years ago. Manges, a deeply litigious man, had claimed that the oil company had failed to renew the leases when they expired, and that he was owed considerable compensation. Manges took Mobil to court. What's more, he was joined there by none other than Texas Attorney General Jim Mattox, who realised that the Lone Star State also stood to benefit if Manges were successful, and that a victory would bolster his own reputation as a populist battling against the major oil companies – though it was hard to claim that the very rich Manges was your ordinary man in the street. A few days earlier, the court had ruled in Manges' favour. He, and Texas, cleaned up to the tune of about $100 million. Not a bad day's work, and here in his ranch town the victory was spoken of with awe.

It's a peculiarly Texan form of populism that roots for the ultra-rich individual in his struggle against an ultra-rich company. A distrust of organization and bureaucracy – reflected in Gil's disdain for the salaried executive – led to an exaggerated admiration for the free-wheeling maverick entrepreneur. No rules! cries the Texan – except in dry counties. Or, in the words of the bumper sticker on the battered Chevy I trailed most of the way to Austin: DEREGULATE EVERYTHING.

Gimme That Honkytonk Gelato

Up the steps marched the Longhorn Band, tooting around the plaza in front of the administration building, which was ringed by a crowd cheering and stomping its feet as the parading musicians in their unbecoming orange-brown and white uniforms came into view. Brown and white? The scheme reminded me of something. Of course, a Hereford! Here in Austin, the richest university in the world had chosen bovine colours to represent it. Longhorn is not only the name of a Texan breed of cattle but of the UT band and football team. The UT cheer, moreover, pays tribute to cattle. As the band played, the crowd – which included bald professors as well as nymphs in jeans, skiing jackets, and sun visors – would clap three times, raise one arm in the air with forefinger and little finger projecting in a representation of antler-like growth, and cry with one voice, 'Hook 'em horns!' – the battlecry of the UT football team. Even the august Board of Regents, standing on the dais in dark suits, jabbed their hands in the air and yelled the motto. (Not only land and livestock but oil too has kept the university's bank balance frothing at the brim, and UT have paid tribute to this by re-erecting Santa Rita No. 1, the pump jack that pulled up the first oil ever found on UT's two million acres, on the edge of campus.)

I was crossing the campus with a senior professor when we came across this noisy little ceremony, which marked the end of UT's official centenary celebrations. The professor felt he couldn't walk on now that we'd stumbled upon the gathering; both staff and students might take it as haughtiness on his part. I couldn't help remarking on the extraordinary sight of grown men and women performing the 'Hook 'em horns!' ritual. The professor nodded. 'Never underestimate the fantastic loyalty students and alumni feel for this place. For the rest of their lives their devotion will be unswerving.' As the Board of Regents took their places on the dais, he whispered to me: 'Forget the governorship. The most coveted office in the state is being chairman of the Board of Regents.'

'Why?'

'With an endowment of two billion and campuses and

medical centres throughout the state, UT's influence is enormous.'

The university has changed over the last twenty years. Abandoning provincialism, UT made a deliberate decision to earn academic distinction comparable to that of the more august institutions of the Northeast and West. Fat salaries lured academics from all over the world. Some of them earned almost as much as the football coaches. The Humanities Research Center, with its vast and ever expanding archival collections documenting modern literature, film, and photography, draws visiting scholars by the thousands. Its law and business schools and observatory are first-rate. Christopher Middleton was typical of many other scholars and teachers who had been drawn here over the past twenty years by good salaries, a delicious climate, stirring scenery, and lively colleagues – in short, the good life – and had stayed.

Since it was the Christmas season, it was party time every evening in Austin, and he and Ann would drag me unprotesting to a different celebration every night. One evening I'd be sipping wine with Russian translators, a Czech anthropologist, a New York doctor, and an Italian opera scholar, and the next I'd be wolfing down *feijoada* with a crowd of Brazilian students. Dancing with a girl I'd only heard speaking Portuguese, I asked her if she too was from Brazil.

'No, I'm from North Carolina.'

'Amazing. What's it like being a North Carolinan in Texas?'

'Weird. It makes me feel like a Yankee.'

I'm not adept at opening gambits, but when after I asked another girl where she was from, she replied, 'Corpus Christi', I was delighted. I tried to get her to talk about her home town, which I'd visited not long before, but she simply wasn't interested. What did she do? I asked.

'I'm in data analysis,' she replied, and I offered a lame pleasantry about how it had superceded Freudian analysis. I was getting nowhere. In the car on the way back I complained bitterly to Christoper about my inability to engage the interest of these irresistible women. 'How many people would come all the way from England and end up in Corpus Christi? Surely that's worth two minutes' polite conversation and a night of bliss?'

'Why should she want to talk to you about Corpus Christi?'

replied Christopher unsympathetically. He had a point. Who would ever want to talk about Corpus Christi?

*

Austin has more to offer than days of learning and nights of dancing to the music of Fafá de Belém. As the state capital it possesses a state capitol. Just as the San Jacinto Monument added a lone star so that its height would exceed that of the Washington Monument, so the Texas Capitol is seven feet taller than the Washington Capitol. This is the kind of information that gets Texans excited. Beneath the stately leisure dome the duties of the legislature are far from exacting. The House of Representatives only meets for 142 days every two years; its principal obligations are to protect special interests and resist any attempts to raise taxes. When the legislators stumble back into Austin from the boondocks, Austinites can be heard to mutter that the circus is back in town. In the House chamber are brass chandeliers which, when lit, spell out the word TEXAS. Our guide loved this toy, and demonstrated it repeatedly for the benefit of the six of us on the tour; he flicked on the lights and yelled 'Go Texas!'

He hummed with pride as he showed us the governor's reception room. It was the usual thing: panelled walls, thick carpets, flags behind a broad desk.

'Neat room,' said the informative young man. 'Neat curtains.'

The political inertia of Texas has now become *de rigeur* in cabinets on both sides of the Atlantic, where the belief that the best government is the least government is heartily endorsed. Social legislation and welfare programmes are not high on the agenda – when there is an agenda. A new governor can come storming into office with golden promises, but the constitution leaves him almost powerless to fulfil them. Governors have power of patronage and veto, but in Texas it's the lieutenant governor who presides over the Senate, and exercises considerable control over the budget and over appointments to crucial committees. Texans' legendary independence, the frontier spirit, the Calvinist yeast bubbling amidst their doughy Baptist faith, their distrust of collective action, their firm belief that God helps those who help themselves – none of this was ever likely to lead to liberalism in local government.

The Texas constitution of 1875, which imposed strict limitations on executive power in the state, was a direct reaction against the rule of the Carpetbaggers forced on ex-Confederate Texas in 1869. Under that regime, sustained in office with the help of electoral fraud, the governor had dictatorial powers; Texas in the early 1870s was in many respects a police state. Ever since, Texans, with their long memories, have been justifiably wary of big government that imposes policies without reference to local wishes and interests. The backlash represented by the 1875 constitution required that as many state offices as possible be elective rather than subject to executive appointment. That was also true of judgeships. According to Judge Phillips of Houston: 'It's an excess of democracy. It was fine when there was one judge per town and you knew who you were voting for. But Houston alone has a hundred judges and no one pretends they're voting for individuals. People just vote the party ticket.'

There's an extremely funny play – more a collection of skits – called *Greater Tuna*, which portrays and satirizes the mores of fictional Tuna, 'Texas's third smallest town'. One morning on the radio the two authors, who also perform in the show, assumed the voices and mannerisms of two of their creations, Thurston and Arles, and answered questions on a 'phone-in programme.

'I've been trying to call Tuna for some time now,' said a caller, 'but Southwest Bell tell me they don't have an area code for Tuna. So I'd just like to ask you gentlemen what the Tuna area code is.'

'Way-ell,' drawled Thurston, 'we don't have no area coe-edd in Tuna. Fact, folks in Tuna regard area coe-edds as gurvermen innerference in ahr lahves.'

A joke, of course, but only just. Jack Rains' lauding of private initiative and private charity represents the more sophisticated version of this philosophy. Don Earney, who doubtless would go along with it, nevertheless observed that Texans were probably not quite as conservative as they liked to think. Certainly the current occupants of high elected office at state level were far from being diehard reactionaries. Sissy Farenthold almost won the governorship some years ago, and Barbara Jordan had not only been a successful woman politician, but black to boot. The present state treasurer is an unstuffy but shrewd woman called Ann Richards. Like the governor, Mark White, she is on the moderate wing of the Democratic Party, but ideological deportment is relatively unimportant. Her job is to invest the state's money, not decide how to spend it. It's those who spend the money, those who set the state budget every two years, who are more likely to get involved in political squabbles. Even those rows tend to be pragmatic rather than philosophical.

As she poured me some coffee, I asked her why she'd chosen to run for treasurer. We were sitting in the living room of the airy house she'd just moved into, and around us in terracotta tubs languished once healthy plants that had been killed or severely wounded while being moved. (The temperatures had continued to drop after Christmas, and we were looking back on the twenty-five-degree days as balmy compared to the eight or ten degrees being recorded now.)

'Because I thought I could win it. My predecessors hadn't done much with the post for forty years, and I thought I could make something of it. One of my predecessors was called Jesse James, and I thought of changing my name to Bonnie Parker.'

Her campaign had cost over a million dollars, but that was a handful of peanuts compared to the spending of the gubernatorial candidates. Bill Clements had spent $16 million and Mark White only slightly less. In Texas the only efficient way to cover the state is by plane, and that's expensive. Smaller states may have one or two TV systems on which to advertise; Texas has thirteen. Ann Richards estimates it would take two years to pay off her campaign debts.

She'd won and moved into her State House office down the hall from a legislature still dominated by rural interests with little concern for pressing urban problems. A new coalition, however, including women and minorities and allied to growing urban representation, would slowly be changing all that. Even so, the nub of the problem was persuading the legislature to vote for new taxes to pay for new programmes. Even organized labour was often hostile to taxation, sharing the fears of conservative businessmen that new taxes could ice over the 'hot' economic climate and dissuade companies from continuing to invest in Texas.

This lucid and entertaining politician sitting across from me like an exotic dandelion with her bushy white hair and lurid purple raffia slippers, was clearly as canny as any baccy-chewing farmer from the Panhandle. She avoids public disputes whenever possible. 'Part of my job is to figure out what makes the political machinery move, and then I have to figure out why an individual should want it to move – I have to discover *his* reason for going along with an idea, not mine. If there's deep disagreement, I'll express it, but I'd only go public with it as a last resort. I'm not going to take on an issue unless I can win it, and if I can persuade whoever it is that I can win it, that opponent is likely to back down anyway.'

To my surprise, Ann Richards was not unhappy about the rise of the previously invisible Republican Party in Texas. 'As the Republicans gain strength, they drain away the conservative Democrats and allow the Democratic Party here to represent more moderate opinion. In the old days the primary was the battle, not the November elections. But it makes for more honest politics to have a two-party philosophical contest at election time.'

After our talk I went to have lunch at the Texas Chili Parlor. Its rusticated interior – beer ads, ranch signs, antlers – was clearly modelled on that of the Texas Lone Star Saloon on Gloucester Road. The chili came in three strengths: X, XX, and XXX. If you ordered XXX, the jokey management insisted that you sign a formal document releasing them from liability.

*

Austin is also a hi-tech city, and that, more than its status as a university and government town, is responsible for its swift growth in recent years. During the previous twelve months Austin, it was estimated, had gained 21,000 new residents, making it the fastest growing city in Texas. Further expansion is likely. Recent legislation enabled computer companies to form a consortium and pool resources in order to develop 'fifth generation computers'. A national search was undertaken to find a home for the new Microelectronic and Computer Technology Corporation, a consortium of six companies. They chose Austin, Jack Rains explained, 'because we said we'd raise $23 million in Texas. UT and Texas A & M offered research facilities and training programmes. In the past this kind of project would have gone to MIT or Silicon Valley, but Texas landed it. The energy industry is crucial to Texas but, quite frankly, that's not where job creation's going to lie in the future. High technology, that's where the future lies, and here in Texas we're ready for it. So what happened? Well, the Governor called Ben Love, the banker, and said, "Ben, you're raising $23 million." Then Ben calls a bunch of us and we all went to have lunch with the Governor. I got out light. I only have to raise $2.7 million.'

A young businessman from an old Austin family had mixed feelings about MCT's arrival, fearing the impact of these new industries on the life of the city. With relief, he pointed out that any expansion would be to the north and south, because the highways run that way. The rich Austinites who live to the west have deliberately kept their roads modest to deter new settlers; while to the east live the blacks and Mexicans, and poor whites, mostly former hill dwellers despised as 'cedar choppers'.

Hank, the Dallas restaurateur, was in Austin getting ready to open a new downtown restaurant, and, even though he didn't live in Austin, he expressed a passionate contempt for the executives flooding into north Austin and for the rapacious entrepreneurs lying in wait for them. 'In five years' time there'll be complete paralysis up there, and all because of greed. When that land was developed it hadn't been annexed by the city, so the developers had a free hand and didn't bother to plan properly. Soon they're gonna find that nobody wants to live in their tacky apartment complexes because it's too much of a hassle to drive into the city. The developers will get burnt, but Austin natives don't care. North Austin is alien territory to them.'

One morning I went to a lunch party in furthest north Austin, a part of town so new it was blank on the map. The houses in this street were mostly incomplete wooden frames on shallow foundations – no walls yet. Back gardens were communal, patches of grass separated from neighbours' by spindly oaks. Our hosts had come from Warsaw the year before. After protracted negotiations with the Polish government, and with the aid of a Texas senator, they eventually made a deal by which their small daughter was allowed to join them. This was their first party as a reunited family in their new country. The brand-new house felt empty. There were carpets and furniture, but no pictures, no books, no ornaments. The money they earned was paying for the house and for retraining. Their eagerness to please was touching, and we were painfully aware of the efforts they were making for their guests' benefit. In their way, this determined yet still hesitant couple, so far from their native country to which they could never return, were pioneers just as other settlers had been a century before. To them north Austin, so sunny, so friendly, so suburban, so fresh, was a paradise. As we were leaving I saw little Katina charging down the street on her bicycle in pursuit of the other children on the block. Her parents would probably feel a constant wonder at their replanting in Texas, but not Katina – she was already a Texan.

Outsiders might be despised by Texans with pretensions to ancestry, but just about everybody in Texas is an outsider, whether the poor whites who trekked east from the Old South, or the farmers from Bohemia and Bavaria, or the Mexicans from south of the border, or the academics from Princeton and Oxford. Although secure, rich, populous, and sunbelted, Texas still needed new blood. When it came to oil exploration or a complex property deal, there was little that outsiders could teach the Texans, but when it was a matter of designing a prestigious new skyscraper or running a ballet company, then Texans looked beyond their borders for help, not just because they lacked sufficient talent nurtured on their own soil but because they needed to have their worth validated by the costly importation of qualities and abilities they sensed as lacking in themselves. Yet all this was changing as Texas, increasingly the object of envy more than disdain, began to shed its cultural shyness.

*

At night, students and other sybaritic Austinites descend on 6th Street, one of the downtown streets that, after years of neglect and dilapidation, has been fixed up and made fashionable. One or two old cafés and shops remain, but the Truly Tasteless bar and the Gelato Grazie ice cream parlour are more typical of the street's offerings.

The trendiness hasn't stopped Austin from remaining a centre for country music, and every week the boys with their guitars still step off the bus from the Panhandle. Kenneth Threadgill used to run a gas station and in 1933 he was granted

273

the first beer licence in Austin after the end of Prohibition. Every Wednesday evening Kenneth and his mates occupy a corner of his cheap and cheerful restaurant, pick up their guitars and fiddles, and play and sing country music. Old Threadgill, white-haired now and using a stick to hobble about, still sings and yodels. Jake's, one of the old downtown bars, also hasn't changed much since the 'thirties. The two rows of booths are separated by a long shuffleboard table. Ask for a beer and you'll be handed a can; ask for fried oysters and you'll be given a gulf full.

Hank took me to Jake's as part of his unnecessary campaign to convince me of the virtues of Austin. 'Austin's a real city, the only one in Texas apart from San Antonio. Its centre is alive, people walk the streets after dark. Dallas and Houston will be dead before their inner cities are rejuvenated. Austin's happy with itself, but Houston and Dallas are always eyeing the outside world, seeing how they stand in relation to each other, or to San Francisco or New York.

'And you can have a decent conversation in Austin. In Dallas, when rich men get together, they talk about duck shooting and football. It's the women who bring the culture to Texas. All those museums you've been admiring here – they're made with men's money but the women were the driving force behind them. In Dallas it's hard to be a good ole boy and go to the opera. Making your intelligence or love of art too obvious would be threatening to the average Texan. But it's OK to be educated in Austin. You can sit on your own in a restaurant and read a book and nobody's going to look at you funny.'

Christopher also acknowledged the attractions of Austin's intellectual openness and its unashamed enjoyment of food and drink and the pleasures of the boulevard. But to him these were not the city's most striking features.

'It's the planetary quality of this town that always astonishes me. It's a booming hi-tech city, lively and sophisticated, but drive out of it just ten miles and you're in the middle of wild country that doesn't seem to have experienced any human intervention at all.'

At the Summit

'When I die,' they sang, 'I may not go to heaven . . . just let me go to Texas, 'cos Texas is as close as I have been . . .' Season fierce local pride with a dash of sentimentality, and you have Texas country music. Over the months I grew steadily more addicted to the stuff. How better to end my travels than by attending Willie Nelson's New Year's Eve concert at the vast Summit auditorium in Houston. Red Duke had offered to get me a ticket, and he not only got me into the crowded concert, but deposited me in the fourth row with a few of his friends.

Willie Nelson is an unlikely object for the adulation of millions young and old. Now a grandfather in his early fifties, his life has been dogged by personal tragedies as well as artistic success. A man of no obvious glamour, he looks in performance as though he'd just walked in off the farm. His hair is gathered back into a now unfashionable pigtail, a red bandana is loosely tied around his neck, and his lined face shows his age, though his eyes are bright and warm. After a particularly rough year – of which the highlights were one of his divorces and a few car crashes – he wrote one of his finest songs, 'What Can You Do to Me Now?' Plenty more, was the answer, as the next day his house in Nashville burnt to the ground. In retrospect that disaster was welcome, as it brought Willie back to his native Texas in 1970 and he's been there ever since.

Before Willie came on stage we were warmed up by an old-fashioned group called the Geezinslaw Brothers. (It does sound unlikely, I agree, but that's what I was told.) 'Your Daddy don't live in heaven,' they sang, 'he's in Houston.' It's the strength of country music that its sense of place, its terms of reference, are shared by performers and audience. Then too the themes of the songs are both particularised and matched to the probable experiences of the audience. The songs are not only about love, loyalty and betrayal, but about drinking ('The beer I had for breakfast wasn't bad so I had one more for dessert'), drugs ('Stay away from the cocaine train' and 'Take back the weed, take back the cocaine, baby'), work ('Take this job and shove it, I ain't workin' here no more'). The locale is specific and familiar, as in 'Luckenbach, Texas' or the Gatlin Brothers'

275

'Houston Means That I'm One Day Closer to You'. The Geezinslaws' songs and patter were peppered with references to Willie and Waylon and Merle and Hank, and there was no need to identify further Messrs Nelson, Jennings, Haggard, and Williams. Waylon Jennings' 'A Long Time Ago' refers to 'me and ole Willie' – and the audience needs no footnotes. The band also told Aggie jokes. Texans don't need to tell Polish or Irish jokes. They can amuse themselves for hours with anecdotes illustrating the stupidity of students at Texas A & M University. A typical offering: 'A girl asked an Aggie to kiss her where it's hot and damp – so he took her to Beaumont.' You get the idea.

At 10.30 the Geezinslaws vanished into the wings, and Willie Nelson came out. In honour of New Year's Eve he had dressed up. He was wearing jeans of course, but also a white shirt, bow-tie and tails, and a black top hat. The effort of performance soon led him to discard the coat and tie, but the hat stayed on. As he walked on, a huge Lone Star flag fluttered down to form a backdrop across the entire stage. Willie Nelson's voice is no more lovely than his face. It has a nasal quality, and a good range up to a high, almost whiny register. Although not a voice of great power or lustre, and although it lacks the mellifluous virility of Johnny Cash or Waylon Jennings, it's immensely expressive and its timbre is unmistakable. It was his authority that was most striking. In the vast spaces of the Summit – used for sports more than for concerts – there was utter silence as this slight figure in the black top hat picked at his guitar and sang 'Funny How Time Slips Away' and 'Hello Walls'. These, like many of his famous songs, and he's written hundreds, are intensely sad, telling of loneliness and isolation and loss. And then the mood would change as the band would launch into more raucous numbers, 'Whiskey River' or 'If You've Got the Money, I've Got the Time'.

He was a generous performer, keeping the chat to a minimum and singing without a break for two hours. The only significant interruption came at midnight. Friends and admirers – including Kris Kristofferson, Earl Campbell, and, yes, Red Duke in full Western attire – came onto the stage from the wings as thousands of balloons dropped from the roof. There was kissing, there was hugging, there was pandemonium. Up in the galleries beer cans popped and whisky glugged down scrawny throats. Girls with I LOVE WILLIE T-shirts rushed up the gangways to get a good view of their hero, and in front of me a girl with a Willie patch on her bum climbed onto her chair and jumped up and down calling his name over and over.

That wasn't the end of the evening. The music continued. Willie tired of his top hat and replaced it with a stylish Stetson that someone had thrown on stage. Twenty minutes later he tired of that one too, and sent the hat zipping through the air. Quite casually I raised my arm in the air, and the brim floated into my palm. How appropriate that during my last hours in Texas Willie Nelson himself should send a cowboy hat into my outstretched hand. It fit me too. Unfortunately the rightful owner was soon signalling to me, and I graciously though reluctantly returned it. Willie's head was next covered by the grey hat worn by the girl with the Willie patch on her bum. When, many songs later, that one was sent flying back into the crowd, it overshot and landed many rows behind her. The man who'd caught it did not seem anxious to return it. The girl was standing for no nonsense and tore down the aisle to where her hat, now sanctified by contact with Willie's locks, could be seen on an alien head. She launched herself in a superb rugger tackle, knocking down an entire row of chairs, and after some rapid poundings with her eager little fists, retrieved her headgear. As a tigerish brawler she was second to none, a real Texan, and we cheered as she stalked back to her seat.

The concert ended at about one in the morning. Many in the audience were too drunk or too stoned to leave their seats. Half an hour later I was sipping champagne with Red and the rest of his party. I told Red how much I'd enjoyed the evening, and that I couldn't imagine a better note on which to be leaving Texas.

'Yeh,' nodded Red, 'Willie's an old wheel whose treads have seen more than you ever will. Or me neither.'

*

ON THE EIGHTH DAY GOD CREATED TEXAS, says a popular postcard with typical Lone Star braggadocio. Still, Texas is gloriously special, separate in style and panache from anywhere else in the United States. It has a culture that's forthright and unmistakable. Its rich brew of cattle, oil, chili, country music, TexMex food, Stetsons, cookoffs, beauty pageants, rattlesnake round-ups, ostentation, pickup trucks, silver belt buckles, machismo, and chauvinism inspire as much loathing as affection. But no one can deny that Texas has a vibrant character of its own, and a determined optimism that makes most Europeans look world-weary and effete in comparison. Nothing is impossible, say the Texans. And they mean it.

There is one omission from my list of ingredients essential to Texan culture: sentimentality. Let it be the last note to sound, borrowed from a song Waylon Jennings sings:

'Ain't no easy way of saying goodbye,
So be sure and tell them all down in Texas
I said Hi.'

Index

Hugo Williams
No Particular Place to Go £1.95

Hugo Williams went looking for the America he'd been dreaming of most
of his life – B-movie, back-lot, rock 'n' roll America. He found it in bars and
Greyhound buses, clubs, beds, record stores and mean streets. With the
excuse of a poetry-reading tour, he zigzagged across the country, missing
nothing with his watchful poet's eye, and coming back with a freight of
strange, hilarious, unforgettable impressions.

'Rich scraps of lunacy which seem to promise some imminent insight into
the much plundered American psyche but, in the meantime, are simply very
funny' TIME OUT

'Martian picture-postcards'
BLAKE MORRISON, THE TIMES LITERARY SUPPLEMENT

Colin Wilson
The Outsider £3.50

The classic study of alienation, creativity and the mind of modern man . . .
In a new introductory essay – written specially for this Picador edition –
Wilson says of the book: 'It still produces in me the same feeling of
excitement and impatience that I experienced as I sketched the outline plan
on that Christmas Day of 1954 . . . a feeling like leaving harbour.' This
famous bestseller for the thinking man surveys the iconoclasts, from
Barbusse to Camus, looking back to Dostoevsky and Tolstoy, to Blake and
Nietzsche . . .

'Astonishing' EDITH SITWELL

'Extraordinary' CYRIL CONNOLLY

'Staggeringly erudite . . . a brilliant and unusual analysis of the pessimistic
tradition in civilized thought' TIME MAGAZINE

Eric Newby
Slowly Down the Ganges £3.50

The story of the 1200-mile journey made by Eric Newby and his wife from
Hardwar, where India's holy river enters the great plain, down to where the
waters of the Hooghly flow into the Bay of Bengal. Travelling in a variety
of boats and by rail, bus and bullock cart, they met an engaging assortment
of characters and the dusty enchantment of India, all evocatively described
with Newby's brilliant talent.

'Vintage Newby' GUARDIAN

'No journey into an unmapped interior to carry the word or find a lost
explorer was more obstinately seen through to its end than this do-it-
yourself pleasure trip' THE TIMES LITERARY SUPPLEMENT

'Any book by Eric Newby is an event' LEN DEIGHTON

Love and War in the Apennines £2.95

After the Italian Armistice of 1943, Eric Newby left the prison camp in
which he'd been held and evaded the advancing Germans by going to
ground high in the mountains and forests south of the river Po. He was
sheltered and protected for over three months by Italian peasants, and his
account of these idiosyncratic and selfless people and of their bleak lifestyle
is interwoven with a tale of dangerous, funny and bizarre incident and of
his hopes of the local girl who was to become his wife.

'The men, women and children, weather and woodsmoke are as fresh as
yesterday' OBSERVER

'An exciting story, superbly told' PUNCH

'Italian village life, full of notable characters . . . and the reactions of one
sensitive man to being out of the war in the middle of one'
DAILY TELEGRAPH

Eric Newby
A Traveller's Life £3.50

Eric Newby's life of travel began with strange adventures in prams, forays into the lush jungles of Harrods with his mother and into the perilous slums of darkest Hammersmith on his way to school. Such beginnings aroused his curiosity about more outlandish places, a wanderlust satisfied equally by travels through the London sewers, by bicycle to Italy and through wildest New York. His book chronicles the whole range of situations into which he has thrown himself with characteristic verve and optimism, and his perception of the incongruous is as sharp when travelling abroad in search of high fashion as buyer to a chain of department stores, as it is when recalling his reluctant participation in a tiger shoot in India.

'Eric Newby writes as lightly as he travels. *A Traveller's Life* is a tonic and a pleasure' GUARDIAN

Jan Harold Brunvand
The Vanishing Hitchhiker £1.95
urban legends and their meanings

The take-away chicken that was really a batter-fried rat . . . the carnivorous spider hidden underneath a well-lacquered hairdo, busily eating away at the scalp – these are the stories that always happened to a friend of a relative of the man in the pub. But as Jan Harold Brunvand demonstrates in this entertaining book, they're a great deal more. These tales form the folklore of modern man, some gaining enough credibility to appear regularly as genuine news-stories. So sit back and enjoy the myth and legend of the fast-food joint and the parking lot, the executive lifestyle and the urban jungle, the alligator in the sewer and the madman and the babysitter.

'A string of legends . . . inherently unlikely, even if they did happen to your best friend's best friend' SUNDAY TIMES

Oliver Statler
Japanese Inn £3.95

The beguiling story of the Minaguchi-ya, an ancient inn on the Tokaido
Road, founded on the eve of the establishment of the Tokugawa
shogunate. Travellers and guests flow into and past the inn – warriors on
the march, lovers fleeing to a new life, pilgrims on their merry expeditions,
great men going to and from the capital. The story of the Minaguchi-ya is a
social history of Japan through 400 years, a ringside seat to some of the
most stirring events of the stirring period.

'Statler has created a strangely beautiful book that succeeds in conveying
intact not only a great deal of its history but the mood of that land. The
result is sheer delight . . . the stories unfold as one narrative, as beautifully
and memorably as the unrolling of a long Japanese scroll.' CURT GENTRY

Japanese Pilgrimage £3.50

Revered as a saint, a deity, a miracle worker, he lived from 774 to 835 AD
and is best known as Kobo Daishi. Born on the island of Shikoku, he came
back to its mountains, struggling to find the right spiritual path. In China,
he inherited the mantle of master, before returning to preach the
inwardness of the Buddha-consciousness. The holy men of the flamboyant
medieval era transformed him into a saviour, and their faith gave rise to the
pilgrimage. This book tells the story of that pilgrimage encircling the saint's
home island. A demanding and rugged route, it takes two months to walk.
Statler tells not only the story of the saint and the journey, but shares his
own experiences along the thousand-mile route, revealing a Japan
outsiders seldom see.

'Oliver Statler knows more about Japan than any other living American'
JAMES MICHENER

Peter Matthiessen
The Snow Leopard £3.50

Winner of the US National Book Award.

In autumn 1973 Peter Matthiessen and biologist George Schaller made the dangerous 250 mile trek from Katmandu to the Crystal Mountain in Tibet, one of the holiest places in Buddhism. While Schaller studied the Himalayan blue sheep, Matthiessen sought a glimpse of the near-mythical snow leopard, seen by only two westerners in a quarter-century. And as a student of Zen, he wanted to consult the revered Lama of Shey Gompa, who had been in seclusion for years. This is both an exciting epic of wilderness travel, and an inspiring account of a 'journey of the heart'.

A beautiful book' PAUL THEROUX

'A masterpiece' JOHN HILLABY

The Tree where Man was Born £2.95

'On the great East African plain it is the human who feels himself the intruder. Here, and perhaps only here, the world is that of the animals. This evokes a feeling of being privileged to observe ancient forms, settings and behaviour that have survived intact from, prehistory. This is *the* Africa book par excellence' JOHN BARKHAM

'Skilfully blends history and anthropology with precise observations of animals and landscapes' NEWSWEEK

'A splendid book written with love and understanding. It transported me back to the Africa of my youth' ELSPETH HUXLEY

'Matthiessen talks about the animals, the changing environment, the complex and confusing histories of tribes, the effect of modern politics, the timeless and spare grandeur of the region' FRIENDS OF THE EARTH

Maxine Hong Kingston
The Woman Warrior £2.95

memoirs of a girlhood among ghosts

In the six years since it was first published and won the US National Book Critics Circle Award, *The Woman Warrior* has become a modern classic.

'Tells more than I ever imagined about the strangeness of being Chinese and a woman' NEW SOCIETY

'An investigation of soul, not landscape, its sources are dream and memory, myth and desire; its crises are the crises of heart in exile from roots that bind and terrorise it . . . as fierce as a warrior's voice, and as eloquent as any artist's' NEW YORK TIMES BOOK REVIEW

'Dizzying, elemental, a poem turned into a sword . . . reimagining the past with such dark beauty, such precision that you feel you have saddled the Tao dragon' NEW YORK TIMES

'One of the books of the decade' TIME

China Men £2.95

This book, the companion to *The Woman Warrior*, reconstructs out of memories and imagination the saga of magic and history of the author's patriarchal forebears, as succeeding generations journey from their homelands to the Gold Mountain.

'A triumph of the highest order, of imagination, of language, of moral perception' NEW YORK TIMES BOOK REVIEW

'Tells of emigration, persecution, work, endurance, ritual, change, loss and the eternal invention of the new – stories sprouting like mushrooms after rain' NEWSWEEK

'A history at once savage and beautiful, a combination of bone-grinding reality and lumious fantasy' NEW REPUBLIC

Annie Dillard
Teaching a Stone to Talk £2.50

expeditions and encounters

Personal narratives which have all the warmth, vitality and power of Annie Dillard's Pulitzer prizewinning *Pilgrim at Tinker Creek*. From eastern woods, to the Pacific coast, to tropical islands and rivers, this book explores the world of natural facts and meanings.

'In the fourteen *pensées* that make up this book she bears witness, reflects on her observations . . . it is a tonic to share in her findings' NEW YORKER

'Not many people care to look a weasel in the eye. Or to sit in an Ecuadorean jungle on the banks of the Napo River studying a giant tarantula the size of one's hand. Or to stroke a giant tortoise's neck in the Galapagos islands . . . Annie Dillard is a fine wayfarer'
NEW YORK TIMES BOOK REVIEW

Pilgrim at Tinker Creek £1.95

A rich and colourful chronicle of the changing seasons at Tinker Creek, a valley in the Blue Ridge Mountains of Virginia. Annie Dillard has used her sensitivity to the beauties and cruelties of nature to assemble a 'meteorological journal of the mind'. The result is a moving statement of beliefs.

'The central metaphor for the book . . . is the vision, the spiritual conception, that Annie Dillard will spend her days tramping the Roanoke Creek banks and the Blue Ridge Mountains in search of herself . . .'
NEW YORK TIMES

Robert Byron
The Road to Oxiana £2.95

In 1933 Robert Byron went to Persia and Afghanistan, and the result was this vivid record of his journeys with its exact observation of people and places and very funny dialogue. With an introduction by Bruce Chatwin.

'An improviser of genius, a natural player-by-ear. Into *Oxiana* went scholarly essays, aphorisms, farcical playlets, wonderfully exact notations of moments of time . . . along with documents like visa forms and newspaper cuttings . . . a portrait of an accidental man adrift between frontiers' NEW YORK TIMES BOOK REVIEW

'What *Ulysses* is to the novel between the wars and what *The Waste Land* is to poetry, *The Road to Oxiana* is to the travel book' PAUL FUSSELL

Christina Dodwell
In Papua New Guinea £3.50

Papua New Guinea is 'the last unknown', one of the least explored places on earth, its jungle more treacherous and impenetrable than any to be found in Africa or the Amazon. This is the story of Christina Dodwell a woman whose 'restless and sometimes reckless nature' compelled her to set off on a lone journey through the jungles and highlands of Papua New Guinea. She trekked 1000 miles on horseback and spent four months paddling a dugout canoe down the Sepik river. She became a legend to the people and learned their customs and took part in their rituals and celebrations. Her journeys remain a part of their history.

Dee Brown
Bury My Heart at Wounded Knee £4.50

'The white man made us many promises, more than I can remember, but they never kept but one; they promised to take our land, and they took it' *Chief Red Cloud of the Oglala Sioux*

'Damn any man who sympathizes with Indians. I have come to kill Indians, and I believe it is right and honourable to use any means under God's heaven to kill Indians' *Col John M. Chivington*

This Indian History of the American West tells the red man's side of the story. We see their faces, hear their voices as they strive to prevent the encroachment of miners, ranchers, saloon-keepers and soldiers upon their land, their heritage and, finally, their liberty.

Isak Dinesen
Letters from Africa 1914–1931 £3.95

These letters were the raw material Isak Dinesen was to translate into her later works, introducing us to someone who is never mentioned in her memoirs – the young, vulnerable Karen Blixen: the miseries of a failed marriage, her illness, the financial collapse of her coffee plantation, the death of her lover, and her irrepressible spirit.

'Deserves to rank beside other great collections of letters, like those of Virginia Woolf, or her much admired Byron' THE TIMES

'Above all else, this collection illuminates Karen Blixen's skill as a writer, but unlike her earlier published work, the letters enable you to see her as herself' LONDON REVIEW OF BOOKS

'A major voice of the century' OBSERVER

Picador

☐	**Burning Leaves**	Don Bannister	£2.50p
☐	**Making Love: The Picador Book of Erotic Verse**	edited by Alan Bold	£1.95p
☐	**Bury My Heart at Wounded Knee**	Dee Brown	£4.50p
☐	**Cities of the Red Night**	William Burroughs	£2.50p
☐	**The Road to Oxiana**	Robert Byron	£2.95p
☐	**If on a Winter's Night a Traveller**	Italo Calvino	£2.95p
☐	**Auto Da Fé**	Elias Canetti	£3.95p
☐	**Exotic Pleasures**	Peter Carey	£1.95p
☐	**Chandler Collection Vol. 1**	Raymond Chandler	£4.95p
☐	**In Patagonia**	Bruce Chatwin	£2.75p
☐	**Crown Jewel**	Ralph de Boissiere	£2.75p
☐	**Letters from Africa 1914—1931**	Isak Dinesen (Karen Blixen)	£3.95p
☐	**The Book of Daniel**	E. L. Doctorow	£2.95p
☐	**Debts of Honour**	Michael Foot	£2.50p
☐	**One Hundred Years of Solitude**	Gabriel García Márquez	£3.50p
☐	**Nothing, Doting, Blindness**	Henry Green	£2.95p
☐	**The Obstacle Race**	Germaine Greer	£6.95p
☐	**Roots**	Alex Haley	£4.95p
☐	**The Four Great Novels**	Dashiel Hammett	£5.95p
☐	**When the Tree Sings**	Stratis Haviaras	£1.95p
☐	**Dispatches**	Michael Herr	£2.75p
☐	**Riddley Walker**	Russell Hoban	£2.75p
☐	**Three Trapped Tigers**	C. Cabrera Infante	£2.95p
☐	**Unreliable Memoirs**	Clive James	£2.50p
☐	**Man and His Symbols**	Carl Jung	£3.95p
☐	**China Men**	Maxine Hong Kingston	£2.95p
☐	**Janus: A Summing Up**	Arthur Koestler	£3.50p
☐	**Memoirs of a Survivor**	Doris Lessing	£2.95p
☐	**Albert Camus**	Herbert Lottman	£3.95p
☐	**Zany Afternoons**	Bruce McCall	£4.95p
☐	**The Cement Garden**	Ian McEwan	£2.50p
☐	**The Serial**	Cyra McFadden	£1.75p
☐	**McCarthy's List**	Mary Mackey	£1.95p
☐	**Daddyji/Mamaji**	Ved Mehta	£3.50p
☐	**Slowly Down the Ganges**	Eric Newby	£2.95p
☐	**The Snow Leopard**	Peter Matthiessen	£3.50p

☐	**Lectures on Literature**	Vladimir Nabokov	£3.95p
☐	**The Best of Myles**	Flann O' Brien	£3.50p
☐	**Autobiography**	John Cowper Powys	£3.50p
☐	**Hadrian the Seventh**	Fr. Rolfe (Baron Corvo)	£1.25p
☐	**On Broadway**	Damon Runyon	£3.95p
☐	**Midnight's Children**	Salman Rushdie	£3.95p
☐	**Awakenings**	Oliver Sacks	£3.95p
☐	**The Fate of the Earth**	Jonathan Schell	£2.50p
☐	**Street of Crocodiles**	Bruno Schultz	£1.25p
☐	**Poets in their Youth**	Eileen Simpson	£2.95p
☐	**Miss Silver's Past**	Josef Skvorecky	£2.50p
☐	**A Flag for Sunrise**	Robert Stone	£2.50p
☐	**Visitants**	Randolph Stow	£2.50p
☐	**Alice Fell**	Emma Tennant	£1.95p
☐	**The Flute-Player**	D. M. Thomas	£2.50p
☐	**The Great Shark Hunt**	Hunter S. Thompson	£4.95p
☐	**The Longest War**	Jacob Timerman	£2.50p
☐	**Aunt Julia and the Scriptwriter**	Mario Vargas Llosa	£2.95p
☐	**Female Friends**	Fay Weldon	£2.95p
☐	**No Particular Place To Go**	Hugo Williams	£1.95p
☐	**The Outsider**	Colin Wilson	£3.50p
☐	**Mars**	Fritz Zorn	£1.95p

All these books are available at your local bookshop or newsagent, or can be ordered direct from the publisher. Indicate the number of copies required and fill in the form below   12

Name_____
(Block letters please)

Address_____

_____

Send to CS Department, Pan Books Ltd, PO Box 40, Basingstoke, Hants
Please enclose remittance to the value of the cover price plus:
35p for the first book plus 15p per copy for each additional book ordered
to a maximum charge of £1.25 to cover postage and packing
Applicable only in the UK

While every effort is made to keep prices low, it is sometimes
necessary to increase prices at short notice. Pan Books reserve
the right to show on covers and charge new retail prices which
may differ from those advertised in the text or elsewhere